Booked on the Morning Train

Algonquin Books

of Chapel Hill

1991

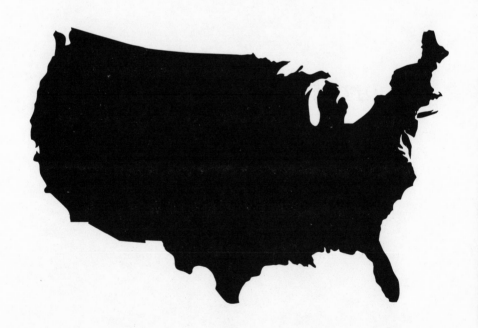

Booked on the Morning Train

A Journey Through America

George F. Scheer III

Published by

Algonquin Books of Chapel Hill

Post Office Box 2225

Chapel Hill, North Carolina 27515-2225

a division of

Workman Publishing Company, Inc.

708 Broadway

New York, New York 10003

Printed in the United States of America.

Design by Molly Renda.

Grateful acknowledgment is made to the following for permission to reprint
previously published material: Doubleday, a division of Bantam, Doubleday,
Dell Publishing Group, Inc., for material from Duke Ellington, *Music Is My
Mistress*, © 1973, Duke Ellington. Harper Collins Publishers and the estate of
E. B. White for material from the E. B. White essays "Progress and Change"
and "Sanitation," collected in *One Man's Meat*, © 1938–44, E. B. White.
Harper Collins Publishers and the estate of E. B. White for material from
E. B. White, *Letters*, © 1976.

Library of Congress Cataloging-in-Publication Data

Scheer, George F., III, 1952–

   Booked on the morning train : a journey through America / by George F.
Scheer III.

     p. cm.

   ISBN 0-945575-40-8 : 21.95

   1. United States—Description and travel—1981– 2. United States—
Social life and customs—1971– 3. Railroad travel—United States.
4. Scheer, George F., III, 1952– —Journeys—United States. I. Title.

E169.04.S34 1991

917.304'9—dc20   90-23404

                 CIP

10 9 8 7 6 5 4 3 2 1

First Printing

For my parents, who taught me that it was worth the trouble to find the right words

That old soul, you know, went down to the Union Station,
    you know,
she asked the depot man what time it was,
she heard eight-thirty freight blowing,
but she was gonna catch that fast Panama Limited, you know,
it kind of blow a little different, you know.
And after she heard this freight, you know,
she ask the man again what time it was,
he told her to go and lay her head on the railroad line,
and if she heard the rail popping,
the train time wasn't long,
old soul stooped down, and she heard the rail popping, you know,
she got up and sang, you know.

I'm a mother-less child,
I'm a long ways from my home
Mmmmmmmmmmmmmmmmmmmmmmmmmmmmmmmmm
Mmmmmmmmm mmmmmmmmm mmmmmmmm mmmm

    —Booker White, "The Panama Limited"

Contents

Booked on the Morning Train

 **Mistaken for Destiny**

I was about four years old, as best I can remember. I was standing, in full pout, in the corner of a Cincinnati hotel room. I wasn't crying. I was much too big a boy for that, but I was not too big to blame my poor mother for the missed connection that had cheated me of a thrill I had long anticipated, an overnight trip in a "bed-train." Our train from Lynchburg had run late: there was nothing she could have done about it, but I didn't care. I was still at an age when everything in the world—flood and famine, certainly train connections—seemed within the power of my parents to control. Not yet had I come to understand, with all its frightening consequences, that there are forces at work in the world that would yield no more to their power than to mine. I understood only that a departing train is a lost opportunity.

In a September 1940 essay, E. B. White described his father's horror of being left in the station: "My father taught me, by example, that the greatest defeat in life was to miss a train. Only after many years did I learn that an escaping train carries away with it nothing vital to my health. Railroad trains are such magnificent objects we commonly mistake them for Destiny."

Our destiny had stranded us in Cincinnati for the night, in a hotel room I remember as plain, even by the standards of an artless child. I can imagine how gladly my mother would have hurried our tardy train from Lynchburg, had she been able. And, looking back, I realize now what I could not have known then: that by accident of birth I was living in the twilight of American rail travel.

I grew up in the era of the automobile, the airplane, and the motel. My travels were by highway; my stopovers by the roadside. To traverse long distances I resorted to flight. I knew trains mostly as nostalgia, part of our social history, a colorful motif in our American mythology, celebrated in story and song: Tom Thumb, The Iron Horse, John Henry, The Panama Limited, "private varnish," The Super Chief, Casey Jones, The Southern Crescent, The Age of Steam, the Brotherhood of Sleeping Car Porters, The Zephyr, "The Orange Blossom Special," "The Wabash Cannonball," "The Wreck of the Old 97," "Honky Tonk Train," "Daybreak Express," "The Happy Go Lucky Local," "Pacific 231," "Blood on the Tracks."

In the year 1916 one could buy a ticket and board a train at any one of 85,000 railroad depots in the United States. Most of them probably handled more freight than passengers, but if you wanted to catch a train you could do it almost anywhere, and you could ride it to just about anywhere else. By 1942 service was more circumscribed, but 50,000 railroad terminals still served passengers. As of September 1984, when I began to think again of trains, Amtrak stopped at only 506 places. Add to that the points served by commuter lines, intracity lines, subways, and such modern-era hybrids as San Francisco's Bay Area Rapid Transit, and even throw in every surviving seasonal narrow-gauge line that stokes up a rusty steam engine to haul tourists and shutterbugs into the mountains on a sentimental tour of the autumn woodlands, and the possibilities for rail travel have still diminished by several orders of magnitude.

Early in this century, with track in place and restiveness stirring in the population, railroads were our primary transportation from city to city. In 1929, twenty thousand passenger trains were on the move every day, and three of every four long-distance travelers rode trains. The railroads competed for those travelers. The major lines invested their prestige in crack overland trains with charismatic names. They strove mightily to outdo one another with lavish service. They furnished their coaches with style. They pampered their passengers. They offered amenities to make life on board alluring. Smoking cars, observation cars, lounges, and dining cars, even libraries and baths, appeared on the flagship trains. The best trains carried barbers to cut your hair, stenographers to take your letters, porters to plump your pillows. The crack expresses of the Santa Fe, Burlington, Baltimore and Ohio, Great Northern, Pennsylvania, and New York Central were rivaled in prestige only by the grand ocean liners.

Duke Ellington, in his autobiography, *Music Is My Mistress,* recalled traveling from Washington, D.C., his hometown, to his first engagement in New York City: "Because I had a gig waiting for me, I felt entitled to travel in style. I hopped a train, took a parlor car, ate a big, expensive dinner in the diner, and got a cab at Pennsylvania Station to take me uptown." In the Swing Era, when the Ellington orchestra toured the South, it circumvented the Jim Crow laws by traveling in "private varnish," private railroad coaches where the Ellingtonians ate, slept, and partied, living a better life that was their own revenge. "We used to charter two Pullman sleeping cars and a seventy-foot baggage car," he recalled. "Everywhere we went in the South, we lived in them. On arrival in a city, the cars were parked on a convenient track, and connections made for water, steam, sanitation, and ice. This was our home away from home. Many observers would say, 'Why, that's the way the President travels!'"

As diesel-electric locomotives replaced steam locomotives beginning in the late thirties, trains became faster. No more did locomotives require frequent stops for water and coal; transcontinental trains roared past the tank towns. Prospects were of still faster trains and more sumptuous service.

But forces were at work, had been at work since the turn of the century, that finally overtook the passenger trains. The automobile, at first dismissed by railroaders as nothing more than a passing fad, quickly captured the imagination of Americans. And when Henry Ford's assembly line began cranking out new Model T automobiles in 1914, they soon became affordable: within three years $400 would buy a new Ford. At the turn of the century only eight thousand automobiles were registered to private owners. By 1951 there were nearly forty-three million. As roads improved, the automobile replaced the railroad as a means of transport. In the 1870s the first roads were laid with asphalt in New York City. By 1945 more than a million and a half miles of roadway were paved.

Railroad passenger travel began to decline as early as the 1920s, even while the U.S. population increased. The first to suffer were the interurban electric railways, while profit margins on even main-line passenger service grew slimmer. The highways, built with public money, not only induced drivers to set out in their automobiles, they also supported the intercity bus carriers, who competed with the railroads. In the late 1940s, about 425 million travelers were riding those buses each year.

And they began to fly. The first scheduled passenger air service, between Boston and New York City, began in 1927. The 1926 Air Commerce Act committed the government to support civil air transport. Taxes not only built highways; now they were putting planes in the air by building airports, paying air traffic controllers, and providing the sophisticated weather forecasting and navigational services without which flying would be a seat-of-the-pants adventure. Railroads, which had gorged on federal land grants in the nineteenth century, now faced subsidized competition from this new mode of travel. With government support, air transport developed rapidly. Airlines carried 5,782 passengers in 1926, 1,365,706 in 1938, and 12,890,208 in 1947.

For a time, the railroads competed for those travelers out of pride. They streamlined their locomotives, air-conditioned their coaches. The advent of the diesel streamliner in 1934 inaugurated a new era of faster and more attractive railroad passenger service. But the great distances between American cities made reductions in railroad travel times seem trivial when compared to flight, and the amenities that railroads hoped would woo travelers away from the airlines —luxurious new coaches, elegant dining cars, attentive service —proved ruinously expensive. Moreover, passengers were demanding. They complained if the track was bumpy. They complained if the train was slow. They complained if the coaches were too hot or too cold. They demanded comfortable stations and helpful ticket agents. They wanted porters and redcaps, dining car waiters and stewards. Freight, on the other hand, never complained.

Did railroads lose interest in passengers first? Or did the passengers abandon the railways? Partisans still debate whether the railroads orchestrated a self-fulfilling prophecy by degrading the service and driving passengers away. (The railroads were often compelled by federal regulation to maintain passenger service unless they could demonstrate a clear lack of demand. With a few glowing exceptions, railroads operated passenger trains only grudgingly in the ten or fifteen years before Amtrak.) It is hard to say. But, indisputably, travelers began to ride buses, to drive their own cars, and to fly, and the passenger trains disappeared.

Like most Americans, I hardly noticed. The automobile was too convenient, the airplane too fast. I owned my first four cars without a thought of gasoline mileage. By the time I awoke to the limits of resources, passenger train travel had atrophied into decrepitude. In 1967, the year we bought an Oldsmobile with a four-barrel carburetor that ladled a gallon of gasoline through its voracious 350 cubic-inch V-8 every eight miles, the storied Twentieth Century Limited made its last run from New York City to Chicago—and stumbled home ten hours behind schedule.

After my childhood travels, I turned my back on the railroads. My life was touched in ways I never contemplated by the freight they hauled, but as a traveler I chose other means. So did most Americans, and, by and large, the railroads were just as happy not to have to bother with us. By 1970 passenger service was almost extinct. Some railroads still ran their flagship express trains, and the Santa Fe, the Seaboard Coast Line, the Union Pacific, and a few other railroads still took pride in their passenger trains, even as patronage waned. Other railroads, compelled by regulation to continue service, did so grudgingly, damaging both their own balance sheets and the reputation of rail travel.

With the Rail Passenger Service Act of 1970, Congress created a national quasi-public corporation to provide railroad passenger service, and on May 1, 1971, Amtrak began operation. It was not properly a railroad, but a passenger service to operate in cooperation with the private railroads. It would provide locomotives and cars, service personnel, and marketing, scheduling, and ticketing services, and the private railroads would provide the train crews and the track. Attitudes within the Nixon administration ranged from unenthusiastic to openly hostile. No one was certain whether Amtrak would give birth to a new era of successful rail service or preside over its demise.

The first few years were traumatic. Overnight the system of passenger railroads was cut from 43,000 to only 16,000 miles. Most of the rolling stock inherited by Amtrak was nearly worn out, and what equipment still had useful life was mismatched. The first timetable went to press before final arrangements could be made with all the railroads, and a few chose not to participate. The two best known holdouts were the Rio Grande, which operated its own Rio Grande

Zephyr, and the Southern, which continued to operate its own Southern Crescent. (Both later joined Amtrak.) Succeeding years brought successes and failures for the Amtrak system. Ridership fluctuated, increasing dramatically during the oil shortages of the mid- and late seventies and occasionally declining over the short term. Subject to political whim, Amtrak has been regularly threatened with crippling, even fatal, budget cuts. Yet railroad travel survives.

But what remains of the grand old tradition? The trains still run, but what is it like to ride them? Has the excitement of traveling by train vanished beneath the uniform red, white, and blue livery of Amtrak? Or is there something intrinsic about travel by rail that endures?

Trains were woven into the lives of several generations of Americans. Men and women left home by train, took their honeymoon by train, changed jobs and towns and sought their fortune by train, went off to war and returned by train, and came home again by train to bury their parents. Today, when airplanes and automobiles have allowed us to travel in ways our parents never could, this country doesn't seem as exotic, from end to end, as it once did. I wondered: is it different seen by train? So I set out to see.

Part One

The

Southern

Way

I   Aboard the Crescent

In a Pullman berth, a man can truly be alone with himself. (The nearest approach to this condition is to be found in a hotel bedroom, but a hotel room can be mighty depressing sometimes, it stands so still.)

—E. B. White, "Progress and Change," December 1938
(collected in *One Man's Meat*)

The bags—the big red pullman, the square brown bookbag, the squat gray camera bag—sat by the door, neatly packed. The thick bundle of tickets lay under the lamplight on the desk. I was due to catch the Amtrak Crescent at Greensboro, North Carolina, at 12:30 in the morning as it passed through on its way to New Orleans.

My plan was to ride as many of the overland routes as I could, keeping in mind the heritage of American train travel but not letting myself be tyrannized by it. The glimmering days and nights of rail travel, when the dining tables were clothed with linen, the sleeping rooms were paneled with exotic woods, and train crews included hairstylists, barbers, and wine stewards, are gone and will never return. We may take pleasure in recounting them, in reminding ourselves that progress is not always a straight line, but I see no point in pining for their return. No woeful lamentations for a gentility gone forever and founded in part, if we look around to the back door, on some social conventions we have done well to leave behind. No paeans to the golden days. I would take my journey on its own terms.

The last day had become an endless quickstep of cross-continent telephone calls, quick recalculations of the itinerary, and quickening misgivings as the pieces got harder and harder to fit together and the threads threatened to unravel.

On my last evening, I sat on the sofa and looked around. The house was still in dishabille from the exterminator's visit. The contents of kitchen drawers were piled in cardboard boxes on the living room floor. Clean clothes and dirty laundry were heaped together on the bed. Books and letters and papers from two works in progress were piled haphazardly on my desk, with more filed stack by stack on the study floor. Somewhere among them all must have been the previous month's unpaid electric bill: the power company was threatening to pull the plug. In my last several frantic days of preparation I had reduced my surroundings to such confusion that my only hope lay in escape, pure dishonorable retreat.

I was tired, grumpy, frustrated, and nervous. I longed to be on the road and leave my troubles behind. And still I was troubled by the prospect. Travel cuts us loose from our moorings. It's why we want to go, but at the last minute it seems so snug in the harbor. Travel takes practice. I was rusty.

Boarding passengers were already waiting on the platform in Greensboro when we pulled into the small parking lot ten minutes before train time. The station itself was one of a number of nondescript cracker boxes erected by Amtrak to replace city stations that have been razed or are no longer feasible to maintain. It was too late to check any of my bags. I carried them through the gap in the chain link fence straight to the platform, and just as I set them on the concrete the locomotive's headlight appeared down the tracks. When the Crescent rolled up to the platform, air brakes hissing, the ground shook, and I had to steel myself not to jump back. It is easy to forget what an awesome kinetic force rides with a railroad train. It's like a toppling building, something so heavy moving so fast. Remember how the locomotive of your childhood electric train was so heavy, so dense, such a surprising mass in your small hand and how it made the floor rumble when it pounded around the track? A big train has the force of a river.

Boarding at Greensboro I experienced the sudden, giddy freedom of the traveler, who by the simple expedient of climbing aboard leaves at once his workaday cares behind. It seemed so simple now: farewell to friends, just two steps up, all the way to your left, stow your luggage, find your seat, and for six weeks, everything would follow from there.

I stored my suitcase and bookbag in the luggage rack at the head of the coach and walked softly through the aisle, past huddled passengers all trying to ignore the intrusion on their sleep. I found an empty seat, slid my camera bag in front of it, and sat down. This was the moment I had been looking forward to for months, the cusp where anticipation became experience. It went uncelebrated. I sat in the dark and longed for some human contact, even a conversation about the weather. The passengers on the Amtrak Crescent that night were not interested in my story. They wanted only to pass the night in peace.

Later I would realize that there is a continuity to train travel that distinguishes it from, for instance, air travel and helps define the experience. Planes go from here directly to there. Fellow passengers share a common experience, a common schedule, common expectations. An overland train is something different. On it ride passengers who may have boarded at any one of dozens of points and may be headed to any of a dozen more. Stops come regularly, all through the day and night, and no one stop is an event. Travelers finishing their journey get off, travelers beginning their journey get aboard, and most just keep on. I got on at Greensboro. All around me my fellow travelers just kept on.

I waited apprehensively in the dark car for the conductor to come and collect my ticket. My arrangement with Amtrak was unorthodox and I was uncertain of its reception from the railroad conductors, who were then officials of the independent railroads, not Amtrak employees, and who are a law unto themselves on the trains. But the conductor accepted my thick book of tickets without comment, as most would do throughout the journey, and I was soon alone again.

The Amtrak car attendant followed closely behind, marking and posting seat checks, and he changed my seat to afford me two unoccupied seats side by side so I could stretch out a bit. I thanked him for the courtesy, and he asked me, "Is this your first time on a train?" The first in many years, I told him. He commented on my bulky camera bag, and we spoke for a few minutes about my plans and his work, the first of many impromptu conversations I would have with Amtrak people in the wee hours of the weeks to come.

As I looked around, the night coach seemed like steerage in an ocean-going vessel, with determined emigrants huddled amidst their belongings. Some held children, others cuddled together, limbs entwined. A few stretched out, legs scattered, breathing or snoring through a slack mouth. The darkness afforded us all an illusion of privacy.

By dumb luck I stumbled that first night on the secret of survival in coach by realizing that I was free to move about and seek my own company. I tucked my camera bag like a precious bindle into the aisle seat and made my way to the rear, out for a stroll. I passed the Amtrak attendants in their seats at the rear of the coach, stepped through the clamorous vestibule, walked with a wobbling gait, still unaccustomed to the swaying train (I decided many weeks later that one never grows accustomed to it, because even the train crews who spent their working lives aboard stumbled about like rank cabin boys), through several more coaches of slumbering passengers, and finally found life in the lounge car.

What I found was the dregs of a cocktail party. Most nights, on most long runs, the lounge car of a passenger train is the neighborhood tavern for a neighborhood that exists for one night only astraddle the rails. An evening drama in a lounge car progresses through the same scenes staged every night in the local around the corner: a few determined souls start the evening with the sun barely over the yardarm; the cocktail crowd stops by for a pick-me-up on the way to dinner; the brandy and cigar crowd relaxes after dinner (allowing for the fact that Amtrak prohibits the smoking of both pipes and cigars in the lounge cars, a rule that is occasionally broken but seldom abused); a little later celebrants looking for a night on the town congregate in noisy conclaves; and as the night wears down, the lounge thins out, leaving by the wee hours the usual assemblage of overindulgers, truly gregarious creatures, insomniacs, and those who have nowhere else to go.

It was after one in the morning, well past last call. Toward the end of the coach, a young man on leave from the navy sat alone at his table, a meaningless grin on his face and an evening's worth of bar litter—empty cellophane pretzel bags, a couple of overflowing metallic paper ashtrays with crimped edges, scattered poptops, and three or four empty beer cans—on the table around his elbows. Neatly arrayed along the edge of his table were three more unopened cans laid in at last call.

The conversation at the center of the coach was about railroads. A young Southern Railway trainman, deadheading home to Salisbury, was discussing the advantages of concrete ties with a beefy German, who, with elaborate ceremony, filled, tamped, and smoked a large Scandinavian freehand briar. I never learned the German's trade, but he had traveled extensively over the American rails, which suggested that his work afforded him time and opportunity, and he was obviously sensitive to mechanical matters. There were two other passengers in the lounge car: a quiet and apparently sober man sitting to my left and an overbearing drunk across the aisle, who desperately wanted someone to listen to tales of his days in military intelligence and to his analysis of American defense policy, an analysis that benefited from some mysterious insight he constantly hinted at but could never explain. Eventually he found in the young sailor an appreciative audience for his tales of whoring in old New Orleans. Together they hatched elaborate and boastful plans for a night on the town in that wicked city.

As we passed Spencer, North Carolina, the young trainman pointed out the former site of the old Spencer shops, the largest railroad repair shops ever built in the South. From the turn of the century onward, the steam behemoths that were the motive power for the Southern Railway were repaired, rebuilt, and kept in their distinctive green and gold trim here in a shop that included a roundhouse with more than thirty stalls. Spencer was named for the Southern Railway's president, Samuel Spencer, who died in the wreck of Southern No. 37 at Lawyers, Virginia, south of Lynchburg, in 1906. Three years prior, another Southern train, the Southern Fast Mail from Washington, D.C., to New Orleans, left the tracks on that same run and derailed straight into folklore:

> *Oh, they handed him his orders at Monroe, Virginia,*
> *Saying, "Steve, you're away behind time.*
> *This is not 38, but it's old 97*
> *You must put 'er in Spencer on time."*

The trainman left at Salisbury, headed home to a new wife. He had told me that he had a boy from a previous marriage and wanted desperately to father a girl. Salisbury was just past 1:30 in the morning, and the German, the sailor, the traveling salesman, and the quiet man to my left were all traveling through to New Orleans, so they spoke their parting words, promising to meet for breakfast, although I doubted any would make the first call, and made their way to their respective nights' rest—the German and the salesman, traveling on his expense account and proud of it, to their sleepers in the rear of the train, the sailor forward to snore away the remaining night hours in a coach. The quiet, informally dressed man at my left, who might have been a high school football coach, or even a biology teacher, turned out to be an engineer from upstate New York working for a company that manufactures and installs oil drilling equipment. He commuted every month to Slidell, Louisiana, outside New Orleans, to be near the Gulf.

"Do you usually take the train?" I asked him.

"Never done it before. One of our representatives takes the train to conferences now and then and he persuaded me to try it. Said it had improved. And I'm tired of flying. If I hurry down there, I'll just be on a chopper for the Gulf in the morning, so I thought I'd take my time."

We were alone in the lounge car at ten past two when my car attendant, a young, redheaded woman working one of her first runs, came to fetch me. "Charlotte in ten minutes."

The once-a-day schedules of most Amtrak long-haul trains dictate awkward arrival times for many intermediate destinations. A train that runs only once a day cannot arrive everywhere on its route at five in the afternoon. Fortunately, I have a very good friend in Charlotte, one willing to meet my train at two-twenty in the morning.

I spent twenty-four hours in Charlotte while the Crescent rolled on to New Orleans without me. At 3:00 A.M., by the time Celia and I had gotten my bags out of her Karmann Ghia and into her apartment, the Crescent was leaving Gastonia, North Carolina, its next stop. At 4:00 A.M., while Celia and I were sitting in her tiny kitchen drinking a beer and talking, the Crescent was changing crews at Spartanburg, South Carolina, its next division point. As we slept, the Crescent traveled on, reaching Tuscaloosa, Alabama, about the time we arose at noon.

I spent the afternoon calling ahead to confirm arrangements, repacking my bags, reconsidering my provisions. After lugging my suitcase down just two station platforms, I was tempted to jettison everything except a pipe, a necktie, and a change of underwear. At about six-thirty in the evening, while Celia and I were still waiting for a table in a Mexican restaurant, the Crescent was arriving in New Orleans without me. But that afternoon, another train, another Crescent, had left New York's Pennsylvania Station at two-thirty, and when it arrived in Charlotte twelve hours later, at two-twenty on Thursday morning, I would be there to board it.

Celia ran four stoplights in downtown Charlotte, which was deserted at 2:00 A.M., to get me back to the station by train time. I knew that somewhere down the line I would miss a train, but this was not to be it.

"Look," she told me, "if you want to miss one next week, that's your business, but you're not doing it on my shift!"

We dashed through the station and up the steps just as the Crescent rolled up. On the platform, Celia handed me a going-away present, a blue toothbrush with the name "RICK" on the handle in white letters.

"Don't you think it's funny?" she said.

I climbed aboard the sleeper car for my first encounter with a roomette.

The Amtrak attendant, a black man in his late fifties, gave me a ritual demonstration of the roomette's features. He showed me how to work the lights—there were four of them in my little warren, with one doubling as a night light, emitting a pale blue light that was at first eerie but soon became soothing.

On its long-distance routes east of the Mississippi, Amtrak employs what it calls its Heritage Fleet, refitted and completely reequipped cars inherited from the private railroads. This car I was riding to New Orleans might once have seen service on the Santa Fe line, or the Union Pacific, or in the Chessie system.

In a space no larger than a closet, I found a seat, a toilet, a table or hassock, a coat closet, a sink with hot and cold water taps, a water fountain issuing potable water and stocked with a supply of paper cups, a shoe locker, four lights positioned variously about, a folding bed, a window, and a mirror large enough to reflect it all. The sink was particularly clever—an oval stainless steel bowl with no drain but instead an opening along and just below its back rim. When the sink folded upward into the wall, the water held in its bowl escaped through that opening down a pipeway that also drained the water fountain immediately above. The shoe locker higher up was a reminder that these cars were designed for an earlier and more formal day, and that train travel once offered grace notes of service found today only in luxury hotels. There were no rough edges or sloppy fittings, and the overall impression was of impenetrable construction. In its solidity the Heritage sleeper reminded me of my '55 Chevy. Dated though it was, my little cubbyhole seemed to be the product of a superior design tool: common sense. It fit a human being just about right. At least I thought so until the first time I needed to use the toilet in the middle of the night and discovered that, to raise the bed and get to the toilet beneath it, I had to poke my own caboose into the hall.

I slid the heavy steel door closed, dropped the latch, propped myself up in bed, unpacked my typewriter and papers, and spent the hours writing notes and letters, pausing for minutes, hours it seemed, to watch the hypnotic lights of the night. Frequently I would douse my own dim light to allow my eyes to penetrate farther into the shadowy world passing my window. Night in a railroad sleeper, particularly a single berth, is too glorious a glimpse of solitude to waste entirely in sleep; I relished it as we rocked on through the darkness, past the farm villages, small towns, and little cities of North Carolina —Juneau, Belmont, Lowell, Gastonia, Bessemer City, Kings Mountain, and Grover—and of South Carolina—Blacksburg, Gaffney, Thickety, Cowpens, Clifton, Converse, and Zion Hill.

Between Charlotte and Atlanta, the Crescent stops roughly once each hour. The stations seemed old and shopworn at night, with baggage carts that would have looked at home trailing behind a mule, simple wooden beds riding on spoked wheels with strap-iron rims. Sometime in the dark morning hours, somewhere in South Carolina, I stood in the open doorway of the vestibule savoring the night air, looking at a long row of these venerable carts lined up beneath the overhang of a station's shed roof, and wondering how a station could have changed so little in so many years.

On the way back to the lounge car, I passed through the empty dining car where a trainman sat quietly by himself reading his Bible. He seemed willing to put it aside for a moment and talk. I noticed he was somewhere in John. He suggested that I could find something to drink at the Greenville stop, coming up soon. "If you walk ahead about three cars, there will be a door open, and you can get off and find yourself a soft drink in the station. Don't worry, we don't leave Greenville until 5:00 A.M., and we're running plenty ahead right now. We'll probably get in there sometime around four-forty. They spend some time on the train at Greenville, checking it out, putting on water, changing engineers, looking under the cars for problems."

We drifted into a conversation about the way Amtrak had changed things. "I went to work for Southern in 1968, and it was a different company then, a different atmosphere," he said. "Nobody at the company cared about drinking. I would see men come to work so drunk they couldn't do their job at all. Somebody would put them on the train and then just look out for them until the day was over. The company people knew what was happening but they were interested in the bottom line, and as long as the jobs got done they didn't care who did them or how they got done. It's true, they showed some heart. A lot of the worst were nearing retirement and the company just carried them along until their time was up. But it's not like that anymore. The company changed completely in about five years, which might seem slow to you, but for a man who has been with the company a lifetime, his whole career, it seemed like overnight. And now the company doesn't care that you get the job done, as much as they care that you don't break any of the rules."

He voiced an opinion I would hear again from other trainmen on other roads. "You know, Amtrak is always trying to get control of the trains. They want us to work for them, just like the dining car waiters and the porters. But I don't think the Southern will ever let that happen. If we worked for Amtrak, they'd never be able to hold us to the same standards that Southern can, even with the unions." Amtrak, naturally, has argued just the opposite and has since acquired control of the crews on many of the trains.

We made Greenville ahead of schedule a few minutes before five in the morning. My first night in a sleeping compartment was nearly over. So, while it was still dark, somewhere south of Greenville, I clambered again onto my bed, reached back and slid the door closed, dropped the latch, undressed, and slipped between the sheets. I lay half-upright, drifting between sleep and wakefulness, as we crossed from South Carolina into Georgia. A few minutes past seven I began to notice the sun, not yet over the horizon, beginning to color the morning sky. In a field, I could just make out the dark forms of cows lying scattered about, their forelegs tucked up tightly like snoozing house cats.

By quarter of eight, we were moving slowly through the outskirts of Atlanta, past lumberyards and building supply lots, past an abandoned railroad trestle now leading nowhere, covered with kudzu. We stopped, started, and then stopped again, and in a moment a Southern locomotive tandem passed with a freight behind, flatcars of building materials: Weldwood, Westar, plywood. Road crews were building a freeway overpass. The work day had begun. The sun already glared. It promised to be hot long before noon.

The grim energy of Atlanta in the early autumn heat and the new passengers crowding onto the train seemed oppressive after the lonely overnight run through the Carolinas. As lagniappe for travelers in sleeping cars, Amtrak offers morning coffee, tea, or juice, and often a local morning newspaper. I cracked my door just long enough to take the coffee and the paper, latched it shut again, drank a few sips, checked the headlines for catastrophes, pulled the shade down tight, and fell sound asleep before we left Atlanta.

When I lifted the shade, the late afternoon Mississippi sun flashed through the trees, stuttering through the gaps and hitting my window like a strobe. The dazzling light flickered across my retinas and ricocheted around in my eyeballs and made me queasy. I was on the right-hand side of the Crescent, the western shoulder of the consist.

I slowly came awake and after a while I began my housekeeping. I sifted through the notes I had taken the night before and set aside a letter to be mailed from New Orleans. I crawled to the foot of the bed and, kneeling there, brushed my teeth and splashed cold water on my face. I took my pants and shirt from their hook on the wall of the compartment between the window and the mirror at the foot of the bed, lay back down, and wriggled into them. Dressing from the supine position is a humbling experience, shared by railroad travelers and campers in mountain tents. I pulled myself back to my knees and rummaged blindly under the foot of the bed for my shoes. During the night, they had walked too far back beneath the bed to be reached from above, so I gave up and opened the door. I stepped out in the aisle in my stocking feet, my shirttail hanging loose and my belt unfastened. As I fell to my knees to grope for my shoes, I heard my porter say, "Well, cowboy, I see you're gonna get up today."

By the time I had collected myself and rearranged my compartment from night to day configuration, from bedroom to sitting room, the sun was getting low and red. A few minutes after I settled into my chair the trees fell away and we rolled slowly out over Lake Pontchartrain, 630 square miles of brackish water. The Crescent crosses this wide lake on a rickety causeway, built a century ago, that is five and three-quarters miles long, still one of the longest railroad bridges in the world. The trestle is so low and so narrow that nothing of it can be seen from the coaches. Look out and you see only water. The sun hung swollen in the thick atmosphere just over the lake. Its rays skipped off the light, even chop, ticking each crest.

The open water became a cove and then a marsh and then sandy soil, and I heard the announcement for New Orleans. The Crescent approaches the city through its northeastern suburbs, skirting the south shore of Lake Pontchartrain, crossing the Inner Harbor Navigation Canal, and then turning south to cut through City Park. When I saw the bright white masonry burial vaults of Metairie Cemetery, built above ground because the terrain is so low and wet, I knew we were in New Orleans. When I stepped down to the platform in Union Station, the first thing I noticed was the ballast between the rails: pearly white oyster shells.

My watch said almost seven-thirty. I thought we were more than an hour late. In towns all up the line—Choccolocco, Eastaboga, Cook Springs, Weems, Burstall, McCalla, Coaling, Cottondale, Moundville, Boligee, Cuba, Toomsuba, Enterprise, Pachuta, Moselle, Okahola, Talowah, and Pearl River—men and women were just coming home from their work, stowing away the tools of their trade, briefcase or pipe wrench, sitting down to dinner, and contemplating

the end of their day. It was early evening and my day was just beginning. In New Orleans, chefs and bartenders and musicians and pick-
pockets were beginning theirs, too.

Not only is New Orleans the end of the line for the Crescent
from the East Coast, but for the City of New Orleans from
Chicago and the Sunset Limited from Los Angeles as well.
New Orleans is also the end of the line for conformity. Puri-
tan values and the Protestant ethic get off somewhere north of Lake
Pontchartrain. The dollar is legal tender in New Orleans and people
there work, many of them no doubt work hard, but the city as a
culture doesn't celebrate work as a virtue. Necessary maybe, sometimes even enjoyable, but not necessarily good for the soul or con-
structive of character. New Orleans is not about saving souls or building character.

From a pay phone in Union Station on Loyola Avenue, I phoned an
old friend who had been living in New Orleans for a few years. Jim is
a traveler and a wanderer. I've known him for nearly twenty years
and he is well into his third page of my address book by now, with
mailing addresses ranging from New Jersey to Minnesota, San Francisco, Hawaii, and Fiji. Unlike many wanderers who glance across
the surface of the earth, Jim sets root everywhere he stops, immers-
ing himself in his surroundings with a ravenous curiosity. I have come
to expect that Jim will know more about a city or a country, having
lived there six months, than all but a few natives.

"George, you made it," he said from work, where I reached him. "I
can't talk now. I've arranged for you to stay in a quintessential New
Orleans house on Governor Nicholls Street in the Treme, near the
French Quarter. This house was built in the 1820s. Marcia, a friend
of mine, grew up there and owns it now. You'll meet her later. Why
don't you walk around in the Quarter this evening. You know your
way around. I'll meet you when I get off at eleven."

"Where shall we meet?"

"On the corner of St. Philip and Chartres" (he pronounced it "Char-
ters" as they do in New Orleans) "there is a coffeehouse called Until
Waiting Fills. That's F-I-L-L-S. Don't ask. This is New Orleans. The
people will look very strange to you, but don't worry. You'll look just

as strange to them. If you're hungry when you get there, you can get some good Brazilian food in the back. I'll get there as soon as I can."

Instead of plunging immediately into the Quarter, I turned right onto Canal Street and walked toward the river. A boisterous group of black kids surged along the street, each carrying a brass instrument. For the tourists, the New Orleans brass band is frozen in time, preserved as it was generations ago, playing familiar melodies in familiar ways. What passes for jazz in the New Orleans nightclubs where the drinks come in fancy glasses is often a derivative of Dixieland (itself derivative of early black jazz). In the streets of the French Quarter, any charlatan who can crank out a chorus of "When the Saints Go Marchin' In" on a kazoo is out plying the tourists for change.

But the genuine musical spirit coursing through New Orleans has nothing to do with that. You can see it in the young boys walking the streets with cornets and trumpets and trombones under their arms. You hear it in the blues and zydeco and bizarre amalgams of European and American music—even Caribbean and Latin American music—that find an audience in a city that isn't interested in category. New Orleans has preserved its musical tradition by allowing it to grow and adapt. Today the brass bands meld traditional instrumentation and sound with contemporary, even avant-garde, musical impulses. A young New Orleans band today is likely to play a Thelonious Monk composition or a Stevie Wonder song, but the timbre, the arrangement, the rhythms will be distinctly New Orleans. So are the band names: Rebirth Brass Band, Avenue Steppers, Onward Brass Band, Kid Sheik and His Storyville Ramblers, Sammy Berfect and the Dimensions of Faith Community Choir, Rising Star Drum and Fife Corps, Chosen Few Brass Band, Sady Courville and the Mamou Hour Cajun Band, Kid Thomas and His Algiers Stompers, Young Tuxedo Brass Band, Dirty Dozen Brass Band, Percy Humphrey and His Crescent City Joymakers, Olympia Brass Band, Albert Lange and The Dixie Stompers.

At a cross street, a middle-aged man in plain clothes stopped me. "Excuse me, sir. Can you read me this phone number?" In his hand he held a pink business card from The House of Beauty. As I read out loud the phone number printed under a woman's name in a bottom corner, he repeated it after me. When I looked up, he was mouthing the number through again and again, like a reader moving his lips, his face lost in concentration as he struggled to imprint the number in his memory.

The air on the street, even at nine in the evening, was hot and steamy, and my drip-dry shirt clung to my back, matted with sweat. I walked down Canal Street as far as Decatur, crossed over to the French Quarter side of the street, and walked back away from the river, past cut-rate electronics emporiums and urban-hip clothing stores.

The lower streets into the Quarter were quieter, less crowded. Well-dressed window shoppers strolled along Royal Street peering into the display windows of posh antique shops. But I kept walking on to Bourbon Street, the most shameless parody of sin the city has to offer, jammed with tourists gutter-to-gutter. Just ahead the pedestrian traffic was bottlenecked. A ragged line of gawkers, mostly middle-aged and tickled pink, had formed in the street, all jockeying for a glimpse into the open door of a strip joint. I peered in as I passed and saw a naked girl writhing on the bartop, with mirrors strategically hung above and around to reflect her gyrations. The effect was clinical.

I turned back to the quieter streets of the Quarter, walking toward the river on St. Peter Street, along the edge of Jackson Square past the Pontalba Building. At night, life migrates away from the square and the river to the restaurants, bars, and clubs of the Quarter. I walked past the deserted square, across St. Ann Street, past the Café du Monde coffeehouse in the old meat market of the French Market, and turned up St. Philip Street away from the river. Past a dark and gloomy block above Decatur Street, I came to the corner of Chartres and heard, as I rounded the corner, not the stylized quaintness of Dixieland, but the furious minor-keyed rip of hard bop.

Until Waiting Fills opened onto Chartres Street. Two tall, battered solid wood French doors, a pair of glass folding doors papered with old handbills and flyers, and one rolling steel garage door were open to the sidewalk, leaving only a few pillars to interrupt the warm air as it flowed in off Chartres Street. Scarred wooden tables, no two alike but some that would have passed for antiques in a city without so ready a past, were scattered out toward the sidewalk. An intense young black man and a lightly whiskered white man of twenty or so sat at a table illumed more by the street lamp on the corner of St.

Philip than by the dim light inside. Their attention was focused entirely on a cheap paper chessboard and its plastic men.

The familiar tones of Miles Davis and John Coltrane, circa 1958, rang from a ghetto blaster on the bar. At the back of the house two Brazilian men were cooking calamari. On the wall behind the bar was a bill of fare: coffee & chicory, 50 cents; espresso, $1.00; cappuccino, $1.25; café au lait, mochaccino, $1.25. I ordered some hummus and pita, asked for coffee and chicory, and watched as the boy behind the bar, in well-worn jeans with a heavy silver belt buckle and a tight white tee shirt, preened as he drew the coffee from a silver urn the size of an oil drum.

No one paid attention to me as I sat and sipped my coffee, as good as I had remembered New Orleans coffee to be. My hummus came, cool and spicy, and I scraped away at it for half an hour with scraps of pita. Four industrial-grade ceiling fans hung from the bare joists, and although they imparted no perceptible motion to the air, it was cooler off the street and seemed less fetid. Patrons left and returned, sometimes with friends and lovers, sometimes alone. A young, lank-haired man, in floppy canvas basketball shoes on bare ankles and a loose-hanging Hawaiian shirt, rode around the corner and stopped his bicycle on the sidewalk in the yellow puddle of the street lamp. He left it leaning against the lamppost, not bothering to lock it, and came in, greeting his friends along and behind the bar. A few minutes later he produced a hammer dulcimer, resting it flat on the top of a table near the street, and began to play it with mallets, wringing from it a high, sweet, modal music that drifted back over the bar and out into the street. After a few minutes he began to sing in a lilting voice that rose and fell in tune with his cycling changes, producing a chant, an incantation. Across the street, a cook stepped from the side door of a restaurant and bar, the only light on that part of the street, and stood on the sidewalk listening. He wiped his hands on a dirty apron and the sweat glistened on his broad, black face. Sitting at the player's elbow, listening intently, her face proud, was a black woman in a frilly white plantation dress, its low bodice showered with ruffles and pleats. Her shoulders were bony and her breastbone gleamed. Her face was sharp, cut in clean planes, and her hair was etched in tight corn rows. He finished his song and we all applauded, spontaneously, as he looked around sheepishly. When he left, the black woman who had been listening and watching left with him. When she stood up to go, she was too tall.

When Jim drove up in a borrowed Plymouth Horizon, my watch read one-thirty. I had forgotten the time change: New Orleans was on Central time and I was still on Eastern. Schlemiel goes to Warsaw. The rube leaves home. It was still early, only a bit after midnight —the train had not been late, after all.

So we took a drive. After retrieving my bags from Union Station, we skirted the Quarter, turned away from the river on Bayou Road and followed it past the fairgrounds. Through back streets we made our way over to Bayou St. John, a long and placid tendril of water that flows through the city into Lake Pontchartrain. Jim pointed out to me the Caribbean cottages that were the first plantation houses along the Bayou. With the car windows down, the sweet night air flowed through the car. After the heat of the bright afternoon and the still humidity of the Quarter, it felt good to lean back and let it wash over me.

Afterward, we drove back toward the Quarter and parked at the corner of Governor Nicholls Street. "This is it," Jim said, indicating with a glance the high brick wall on our side of the street. Tangled vines scaled the chipped and crumbling masonry. A wooden gate, midway along the wall, was the only breach. Inside I saw what might have been a movie set for Poe's "Fall of the House of Usher." A brick walk, narrow and uneven, led from the gate to the front steps of an antebellum mansion in decay. On either side of the walk were fallow garden plots edged with soldier rows of crumbling bricks. Against the inner wall vines grew uncultivated and unkempt. The entire scene was lit with a soft, pale glow that might have been moonlight.

More than the faded paint, more than the dark windows, something made that house a forbidding presence. There is about much of New Orleans an air of decay. Paint peels so quickly it hardly seems worth the bother. Vegetation threatens to reclaim the city, vines tugging at every wall and crumbling the sidewalks. Lizards and cockroaches are the living things best adapted to the climate. It's a climate that breeds mosquitoes. And it breeds indolence and madness.

I followed Jim along a narrow brick passageway squeezed between the house and the banana plants along the wall. At the rear, we crossed a brick patio under a broad magnolia tree to a two-story frame outbuilding with a balcony drooping off the upper story.

"I think she's going to put you in the slave quarters." Jim opened the door and we stepped into a rustic kitchen. He found a note, meant for us, on the spindly, painted wood table near the hearth. "She wants you to take her bedroom in the main house. I guess she's staying here in the slave quarters. Follow me."

Back out and through the yard we went, as quietly as possible. We climbed the back stairs and came into a long hall that ran straight through the first floor of the house, from the rear door to the front. To the left a sweeping staircase climbed up one wall, turned and continued up the side wall, and turned again and climbed out of sight to the second floor. The ceiling was too high to take its measure.

"I think this is her room." Jim tentatively pushed open one of a pair of French doors, looked in, then opened it wide, beckoning me to follow. Inside was a once-handsome room, now nearly bare. A mattress and springs, made with serviceable linen and a quilt, a massive, scarred wooden desk, an armoire, a sewing table, and an ironing board were the only furnishings. A battered box fan stood on the floor in the corner. Hanging over the mantle were two masks, grotesque exaggerations of the human visage, waiting there like a coat or scarf that the owner could grab on his way out the door.

"I met Marcia through a friend who works at the coffeehouse," Jim said. "She came to New Orleans as a girl when her father was named director of the New Orleans Museum of Art, and she grew up here in this house. The neighborhood was genteel then. Now she lives in California most of the year, but she keeps coming back to try to restore the house."

Jim and I made plans to meet the next afternoon at the restaurant where he worked. "The weather should be good. I'll borrow a bike for you and we'll take a ground-level tour of the city."

Jim left and I was alone. I turned out the lights and then turned one back on, a floor lamp next to the bed. I wasn't ready to sleep in that house in the dark. I looked for something to read and found a paperback copy of Janet Flanner's memoirs from Paris. A shiny black roach crawled over my leg and continued across the bedspread. I gently flicked it across the room. My dreams turn violent if I sleep in a warm room, so I switched on the fan and aimed it toward the bed.

It began to turn, slowly at first, and then picked up speed, roaring in the empty house, the rattle of its bearings drumming the resonant wood floor and echoing off the ceiling. I regretted the noise. I had no wish to be noticed until morning. But I was gummy with sweat from the long train ride and my long evening's ramble through the Quarter, and the air in the tall room was still and thick.

I dreamed of ghostly figures drifting in ones and twos through the hall and peering in at me while I slept. I dreamed of a succubus in a hideous mask. The heat, perhaps.

2 New Orleans: A Spin along the Levee

There's only three men
    that can flag this train of mine
There's only three men
    that can flag this train of mine
There's the working man and the gambler
    and the one that loves me all the time.

—Alice Moore, "Three Men"

I awoke early, after only a few hours of uneasy sleep, eager to see my surroundings in daylight and to meet my hostess. Through the tall French doors of the bedroom, I walked into the vacant hall, where daylight flooded through from the panes on either side of the front door and washed down the passage to the open rear doors. In the night, a few hours before, I had imagined hideous spirits in that hall. The cleansing early light was as encouraging as morning coffee. Through the open doorway I could see the green of tropical plants in the backyard. It was sunny when I wandered out the back door into the yard and still cool enough so that the sun felt good. Across the yard the door to the slave quarters stood open. A slight woman with graying hair sat at a table beneath a window, writing in longhand in the light from the window.

"Good morning, you must be Jim's friend," she said. "I'm Marcia. Come in and have some coffee. Do you mind coffee and chicory?" She was wearing baggy, black cotton trousers, soft black shoes, and a mannish white shirt, rolled up at the sleeves.

"I would love coffee and chicory," I said, standing awkwardly near the door. "On my very first visit to New Orleans, my father took me to a little steak house where I discovered New Orleans coffee. I drank about eight cups, black, and it took him two days to get me detoxed."

"It's a small pot, but we can make another." She laughed, and a few wisps of her hair, which was pulled back severely behind her head, came loose and fell across her face and she brushed them back with a girlish gesture.

The process of making coffee gave us both something to do for a couple of minutes. When it was ready we each took a mug. I sat down on the hearth where the bricks were still cool from the night air; she returned to her desk. She asked about my trip and, since she seemed genuinely curious, I told her my plans and we talked about the possibilities. She had an enthusiasm that we unfairly think of as youthful. The conversation turned gradually to other things: New Orleans, of course, the house, and her childhood there. We made a second pot of coffee, and then another.

She was restoring the old house, fighting that hopeless war on several fronts, excavating the basement and plastering the kitchen and trying just to battle time to a standstill everywhere else. Her background in art constrained her to restore the crumbling house as one would a fine painting, destroying nothing that could be saved, no matter what pains were required, and adding nothing inauthentic. She was no dilettante: on my way back through the kitchen I saw the scaffolding she had erected and the arduous job she had begun of restoring the lathing and replastering the ceiling.

Soon the sun that had been slanting into the doorway was overhead and the heat of day drifted in through the doors and windows. We departed in our respective directions: she, on her moped, to fetch supplies from the hardware store; I, on foot, for the Quarter. I closed the front gate carefully behind me, turned right, and stepped out lively down Governor Nicholls Street toward the river. As I crossed Rampart Street, I passed a delicately dressed man strolling with his well-bred dog on a leash. Like most residents of the Quarter he had mastered the ability to ignore tourists as beneath notice, scarcely sufferable annoyances, like cockroaches, the price to be paid for living where others can only visit.

I walked through the busy side of the Quarter and crossed Canal Street to wait for the St. Charles Avenue trolley. I had only Jim's hastily drawn street map, but with it I found the right cross street and stepped down from the trolley onto the soft green sod of the "neutral ground," as they called it here. I crossed the trolley tracks and walked toward the river, into the Garden District.

I was early, so I walked a half-block past Commander's Palace and turned into Lafayette Cemetery No. 1. In the 1830s, when the cemetery was first built, this part of New Orleans was the city of Lafayette, a collection of settlements upriver of the main Anglo neighborhood, Faubourg St. Mary. In the nineteenth century periodic epidemics of yellow fever devastated New Orleans, and by the time of the Civil War its victims had nearly filled this cemetery. They called it Bronze John, Yellow Jack, or "the miasma," and no one knew its cause. Some attributed it to a "terrene poison" emanating from the swamp; one physician proposed that it was inflicted by a "wingless animalcula" of summer. At the peak of the horrendous epidemic of 1853, a dozen New Orleanians died every hour, 269 on a single day in August. The *Aedes aegypti* mosquito, the carrier of yellow fever, bred in the backyard cisterns built so that New Orleanians wouldn't have to drink water from the river.

Two macadam drives quartered the cemetery, which occupied a city block, and the tombs broke the remaining ground into a disjointed maze of crooked pathways. The midday sun glared off the whitewashed brick vaults. Burial below ground is impracticable in New Orleans, where drainage is always a problem, but space in the tombs above ground is too precious to grant for eternity. Family tombs usually have two vaults, an upper vault for the newly deceased, and a lower vault where his bones will join those of his ancestors after a year and a day. The cemeteries of New Orleans are called Cities of the Dead. As in cities of the living, the prosperous purchase, the poor rent. They rent vaults, called oven vaults, in the thick outer walls of the cemetery for a couple of years, after which they must vacate to make way for a new occupant. Mark Twain once said, "New Orleans has no real architecture except that which is found in its cemeteries."

For an hour I strolled through the Garden District, where every home is a showplace. These were the homes that the Creoles, considering their owners nouveaux riches, derisively called Prairie Palaces. Along Magazine Street, on the edge of the Irish Channel, the opulence of the Garden District began to fray at the edges. The iron fences were bare of decorative hedges, and finally they gave way entirely to chain link—practical, ugly, and unthinkable in the Garden District.

As I walked along Magazine Street, I saw a choice example of New Orleans' most significant contribution to residential architecture. The Garden District offers well-kept examples of a smorgasbord of architectural styles: Italianate, Queen Anne, Greek Revival, and others. The French Quarter is a heady, unpolluted concentration of ornate Old World architecture. But the salient creation of New Orleans is the shotgun, that frame-and-board archetype of the mobile home: rooms lined up one behind the other in a soldier course, from the front of the lot to the rear, with no hallway, only a series of doors from each room into the one behind. Along Magazine Street I saw a classic of the genre, a dilapidated double shotgun in a bald gritty yard separated from the street by a chain link fence on which climbed only a few hardy weeds. From every window along each side of the house a window air conditioner drooped, and two electric meters were tacked to the outside wall halfway to the rear.

Jim and I took the trolley out St. Charles Avenue, through Audubon Park. Schoolchildren crowded the trolley, teasing one another and celebrating their afternoon emancipation. The air was balmy. We rode all the way out to Carrolton and on to the end of the line at Claiborne Avenue. From there, we walked a dozen or so blocks back downtown to the house on State Street Road where Jim had arranged to borrow a bicycle for me. We packed a couple of city maps and a water bottle in the panniers of Jim's bike and set out. For the rest of that day, from midafternoon until after midnight, we toured New Orleans by bicycle, glorying in the weather.

For the first few miles, as we traversed the town, headed downtown toward Canal Street, we could pedal abreast and talk.

"Help me get oriented, Jim. Are we going east?"

"Forget east. No one uses compass directions in New Orleans. Directions are lakeside, riverside, uptown, and downtown."

"I'm confused."

"Well, lakeside and riverside are obvious: anywhere in the city the Mississippi River is in one direction and Lake Pontchartrain is in the other. Uptown and downtown correspond to the flow of the river. Originally downtown was Creole and uptown was Anglo. That broke down a hundred years ago, but the distinction remains and Canal Street is still the boundary. That's where the expression 'neutral ground' comes from."

We pedaled through Broadmoor and on through Gert Town, and the neighborhoods became progressively poorer as we crossed Martin Luther King, Jr., Street, Erato Street, and the Calliope Projects along Earhart Boulevard. We crossed the freeway, Interstate 10, on Jeff Davis Parkway, and traveled through MidCity, a middle and working class neighborhood that is racially mixed to a degree more common in New Orleans than in most American cities. From one end of a block to the other the color of the children in the street and the men on the stoops would change, and nowhere did I sense that I was completely out of place.

We went as far as the southern tip of Bayou St. John and then cruised through the Seventh Ward, the traditional Creole quarter, first on Esplanade headed toward the river and then back along Bayou Road and Gentilly Boulevard, past the fairgrounds.

We stopped for a drink along the way at a market across the street from a small park where a stand of palm trees was struggling to recover from a hard freeze the previous winter. Their fronds had frozen and fallen and, in the single summer since, the trees had sprouted small tufts, pitiful cowlicks of new growth. As we leaned on the front wall of the market we exchanged pleasantries with a burly black man whose speech was a combination of Deep South syntax and a lilt that reminded me of Jamaican speech rhythms. New Orleans will confound anyone listening for a simple Southern accent.

North of the fairgrounds we passed the St. Bernard Project and then, just a few blocks farther north, we crossed over to City Park Island, the affluent island in Bayou St. John. After a quick spin around City Park, the only neighborhood in the city where we got suspicious stares, we headed north to Mirabeau Avenue and turned east toward Gentilly.

It was late in the day by then, not dark, but dim. I followed Jim off the street, over the sidewalk, and down a bank onto the grassy shoulder of the London Avenue Canal. In the fading light, the water of the canal was black. The ground sloped steeply away from the canal and trees grew thick and dense at the foot of the bank. Stars emerged as the skylight faded to a deeper blue, and I could hear woodland sounds around me as I geared down and bumped slowly along the worn dirt path, pedaling just fast enough to keep my balance. I wanted to prolong this quiet interlude and I let Jim draw ahead, almost out of sight in the dusk. Near Dillard University, we coasted down from the embankment onto the circle at the end of a dead-end street and the streetlights blotted out the stars.

We continued on toward the river and wandered, a bit disoriented, into the Eighth Ward, where we took refuge for a few minutes in St. Roch Cemetery, then continued on through the Faubourg Marigny to the river.

"Faubourg originally meant suburb and it is coming back into vogue," Jim said. "Many areas of the city are starting to refer to themselves as Faubourg such and such, but the Faubourg Marigny has always been called that."

We turned downtown on Chartres Street and rode along the river through the Bywater, past the banana wharves. We crossed the Inner Harbor Navigation Canal on the St. Claude Avenue drawbridge. It was a familiar route for Jim. "I used to ride home this way every night, in the wee small hours after work. In just a minute, you'll see one of my favorite views of New Orleans, one that very few people ever see."

I followed Jim onto the canal levee and we rode toward the river in the moonlight. The levee, a wide earthen dam, was flattened along its crest and we rode down a narrow dirt path through the grass. The river and canal were low that night and far below on our right rocks were strewn along the water line. On our left the quiet, dimly lit streets of the Lower Ninth Ward seemed far away, and as we approached the river the view across the point opened up and we could see the lights of the Quarter and the taller buildings of the business district far upriver. The river itself, wide and black as oil, curved around Algiers Point out of sight. At the mouth of the canal, where the levee turned to follow the river downstream, we sat on the bank and watched an excursion boat, modeled after a steamboat, make its way past in midriver. Lights were strung all along its decks and the river mirrored them as it moved; it was so quiet we could hear talk and laughter across the water.

"I've seen the river almost up to here, where we're sitting," Jim said. We sat silently for four or five minutes. The excursion boat passed around the point. It was still warm, and the air off the river had a moist, used feeling as I breathed it, like the exhalation from the nostrils of a great, sleeping, warm-blooded beast. Behind us, the Lower Ninth Ward seemed like a small coastal town, with tree-lined streets, no sidewalks, and small frame houses set in fenced grassy yards.

Jim pointed down into the ward at an elevated shotgun house on a wide grassy lot. "That's the house I lived in two years ago. It's criminal what they've done to that house. See along the side, what used to be a beautiful side gallery, they've closed in, and they've cut down the trees in the yard. We used to sit out on the gallery at night and look into the treetops, listening to the tree frogs and the crickets in the grass."

We rode on downriver on the crest of the levee. After about a quarter of a mile, I discovered that my tire was completely flat—victim of a long day bashing through potholes and bumping along levees. Suddenly, the exhilaration of the day began to ebb. It was nearly eleven, we were both exhausted, and we were now on foot. The neighborhood that had seemed so friendly now seemed a bit menacing and I could detect an edge to Jim's voice.

"Let's keep moving. We'll have to find a phone and call a cab. It'll be hard to persuade a cab to come down here at this hour, but I don't see another way. We'd better just get out of here."

We walked quickly two or three blocks through the streets back toward the canal. Lights were on in only a few houses and the streets were dark and deserted. I noticed a group of four or five teenage boys following us, walking slowly a block behind, and I knew Jim also saw them. He has been mugged three times in the city, twice by bands of schoolkids.

"Jim, I'll argue and I'll hassle, but don't expect me to put up much of a fight for your bicycles. You can ride away if you like, though. I won't take it personally." He just laughed, but it was a grim laugh.

Down a side street, a cab turned at the end of the block and started toward us. Halfway down the block it pulled off into a yard and the door opened. We stopped and watched and after a long time, it seemed, a man with a pint bottle pulled himself unsteadily out of the back seat and to his feet. He was talking loudly at this point, on his way to a party, and a woman came out of the house to help him find his way inside. The cab continued slowly up the street toward us and we stepped out into the street and flagged it down.

"How about a ride uptown?"

The driver rolled his window down a few inches, "What about the bikes?"

"We can fit them in the trunk, if it's empty. That OK?"

He pulled to the side of the street. There was no curb, only a shallow, weedy ditch. The trunk popped open a few inches. We were already pulling the front wheels off the bicycle frames, breaking them down. With some fumbling we made almost everything fit. Jim fell into the back seat, with the wheel of his bike under his arm. I sat in the front seat. The driver started the meter.

"Do you gents mind the radio?" The driver flicked his eyes at Jim in the mirror and nodded toward me. He looked a lot like Count Basie, even to the yachting cap that Basie favored in his later years. Zydeco music filled the cab. I relaxed in a few minutes and noticed that we were already over the canal and headed back through the Bywater.

We ended our night at the Napoleon House on Chartres Street. We shared a muffuletta and I had a Guinness and we didn't talk much. Our energy was flagging and we were both thinking ahead to the following day. It was Friday night and drinkers crowded the bar, but the weekend had no meaning for either of us. Jim was due at work early and I was booked on the afternoon train, headed north. I wouldn't see him again.

I slept until midmorning. I found Marcia on scaffolding in the kitchen, wearing spattered pants and shirt and pulling chunks of plaster from the lathing in the ceiling. It came off in her hands in flakes and clumps, exposing the strips of wood beneath, like white-cooked flesh from the rib cage of a fish.

She looked down at me and wiped her hands on her trousers. "I left some coffee on for you this morning," she said. "It's probably soot and ash by now. Make some more if you like. I'm going to keep at this for a little while. When's your train?"

"Between four and five this afternoon. I'll have to check the time."

"Why don't you sit out in the garden? I'll join you when I'm through here. Or when I can't stand it any longer. I'll never be through."

I found the coffee, simmered to sludge, still on the stove, poured an immediate dose, then started a fresh pot. I dragged an old wooden chair with a cane seat, pieces of the cane snapped and curled like busted banjo strings, a few feet into a patch of sunlight. The cat of the house, an old tom named Percy, lay about with me, moving from one sun-warmed patch of brick to another. He dozed with one eye propped open to a slit, occasionally switching his tail in warning to a young male kitten recently brought to the house by one of the renters. The kitten was uncertain of himself, and Percy encouraged the little usurper to believe that his life hung by a thread.

Marcia came out of the house, disappeared into the kitchen of the slave quarters, and returned with a few sliced tomatoes, some leftovers, and a couple of bottles of beer. We ate lunch at the table under the magnolia tree in the back garden. I could feel my ambition for the afternoon slipping away.

She brushed a few flecks of plaster off her shirt. "Ah, yes, we preserve things down here, it's all we do." She was looking over my shoulder at the house and she was smiling, but there was resignation and a touch of despair in her voice. "I don't want to run a museum. That's what my parents did. I found an old letter from my mother, 'Well,' she said, 'you just have to keep the place up. It's like an old pet.' She was right. You can't restore its youth and vigor, you just have to make it comfortable in its infirmity."

"Jim calls it 'the virtue of decay.'"

"Is it virtue? It all returns to the earth. I know this to be true. I think the house will outdo me, though." She sounded wistful.

We had finished the beers and the small bottle of wine I had saved from my complimentary basket on the run down to New Orleans. The house that had seemed so gloomy, so indifferent, that first night now seemed warm and comfortable. The peeling paint and crumbling plaster, the overgrown wall, the neglected garden full of big banana trees and tiny green lizards all now seemed in order, in keeping with the city. Behind the garden wall, those "convent walls," as Marcia called them, I felt the same security that she felt. I was coming under the same spell. I was beginning to understand why, in the face of all reason, in the face of hostility surrounding her, in the face of upkeep beyond reason and taxing to exhaustion, she soldiered on, returning every year to patch the old place together.

Marcia smiled. "It's hard to leave, isn't it? New Orleans gives you a million excuses, excuses for not working, excuses for not leaving."

"I've got a four forty-five train. I'd better go call a cab."

"Yes, you'd better."

I went into the house and called the taxi company she had suggested and we carried my bags to the front garden. On the porch, next to the door frame, was a plaque. I had noticed it the day before.

The Meilleur-Goldthwaite House, erected 1828–1829. The residence of William F. Goldthwaite, antiquarian, 1859–1889. The site was once part of the plantation of Claude Treme, where the first brickyard in New Orleans had been established in 1725 by the Company of the Indies.

We stood and waited just inside the gate. "The taxi drivers won't wait for you if you're not ready to go. They don't like to hang around in this neighborhood. Danger is a part of life in New Orleans. So much violence. Black and white people live side by side all over New Orleans, but whites still fear blacks and blacks are still angry over four hundred years of mistreatment. In little ways . . . they throw their trash in front of my gate, as if to say, 'Here, you pick up after me now.' And every day, I go and pick it up. It's my lesson in humility."

On the way to Union Station the taxi driver said, "Summers are very hard on us here." It was a short ride, but it broke the spell.

3 Aboard the City of New Orleans

When we'd cross the country on the train in the early forties with Louis
Armstrong's big band, Sid [drummer Sidney Catlett] and I would go back
to that little platform outside the observation car. We'd sit there and get
all smutty, get soot in our noses and mouths, and we'd listen to the
humming of the wheels on the tracks, to the different rhythms the train
made when it went over a crossing, to the changes in the rhythms when
the train slowed or speeded up. Sidney would tap out the rhythms with
his hands on the railing around the platform, and later I'd hear those
rhythms in one of his solos.

—bassist Johnny Williams, quoted in Whitney Balliett,
American Musicians: Portraits in Jazz

This was to be my first overnight in a coach seat. The cost of
sleeping accommodations can quickly bid an Amtrak ticket
into the luxury class and, anyway, I wanted to sample American train travel in all its variety. I had no intention of spending six weeks sleeping on my tailbone, but I wanted to make
my share of night trips in coach.

The City of New Orleans travels from New Orleans to Chicago, 925 miles, on the tracks of the Illinois Central Gulf Railroad.
The City of New Orleans was the Illinois Central's day train on this
route; overnight travel was provided by the luxury Panama Limited.
When Amtrak took over in 1971, it discontinued the Panama Limited
and eventually converted the City of New Orleans to an overnight
schedule.

I found an empty aisle seat and stowed my bags. My coach was
fitted with eleven rows of seats, two on either side of the center aisle,
forty-four in all, and was about as spacious and comfortable as any
of the Heritage coaches. I settled in and found that I could stretch
my legs full out in front of me. A footrest pulled down from the seat

in front and a leg rest folded up from beneath my own seat. The position was not uncomfortable and I anticipated getting at least some sleep.

We made our way out of New Orleans in the low-angled light of late afternoon, through a warehouse district and the industrial flats. By 5:00 P.M. we were in the suburbs: no more shotguns, only red brick ranch houses. A few minutes later, mobile homes, lumberyards, and a high school ball field flashed by as we moved through Kenner. At 5:08 we passed beneath the interstate and emerged amid tract homes, weathered, unpainted houses, and warehouses. New buildings were interspersed with old, prosperous with pitiful.

And then the landscape changed abruptly to marsh: thick sedge in boggy earth, with cedar and cypress trees thinly scattered, hung with Spanish moss. The tracks crossed the isthmus between Lake Pontchartrain on the east and Lake Maurepas on the west. On both sides of the train, marshes alternated with pockets of open water where herons foraged in the shallows. At 5:30 we passed wharves, docks, lakeside shacks, and fishhouses on a stretch of open shore. The sun was setting, almost into the water to the west. An open savanna stretched away to the east. The light glanced over the bayou so obliquely that every tree or shrub taller than the marsh grass cast a shadow through the windows, and as we moved along, the flickering light and shadow rippled down the coach, strumming across seats and faces.

Our speed had been varying and seemed oddly cautious at times. At 5:39 we stopped in the pine woods and I could hear the brakeman's voice crackling over the conductor's radio in the front of my coach. The problem seemed to be a coupling on one of the coaches ahead, but I could only surmise. The halt was brief and by 5:43 we passed the bright red station at Ponchatoula.

Between Ponchatoula and Hammond I noticed a sawmill, where rows and rows of logs were stacked waiting to be sawed. A car wash was overgrown with weeds. A temporary storage building, rows of cubicles with steel doors, seemed a sad compound. Once we had tall houses with attics; then we moved to the suburbs and stowed our old furniture in garages; now we lock it in these concrete bunkers and keep moving.

At Hammond I wanted to photograph the old station, but the light was fading and there was no time. Most stops on the long-distance runs are as brief as possible. Only if a train arrives ahead of schedule will there be a wait; otherwise, it stops only long enough to board passengers. The City of New Orleans makes only two scheduled pauses between New Orleans and Chicago—seven minutes at Memphis and fifteen minutes at Carbondale—and if it is running late even those may be cut short to make up time. At Hammond only one passenger boarded my coach, a toothless, big-cheeked farmer in dungarees, wearing a red baseball cap with an embroidered patch of the Confederate battle flag.

In 1850 the Illinois Central Railroad received the first federal land grant issued by Congress to a railroad, and by 1856, with seven hundred miles of track, had become the longest railroad in the world. During the Civil War, it carried soldiers to the war, hauled matériel to their support, and carted home the wounded. It was one of many railroads built in the 1850s that contributed to the Union cause by bringing the resources of the upper Mississippi and Ohio valleys to bear on the war effort.

When the last light finally faded, I took a notebook and wandered back to the lounge car. I found a table where I could write and nursed a beer for a while. The peak of the cocktail hour had passed: empty snack trays and cigarette butts littered the tables. But the remaining patrons were in a convivial frame of mind, most of them reluctant to let go of their celebratory New Orleans mood.

A young man in his early twenties sat with his foot in a heavy cast propped on an adjacent chair. He was in no pain as he told his story to an older couple across the aisle, gesturing as if for the hearing-impaired and spinning out the tale with obvious relish. "I was sitting in Jackson Square, just enjoying the afternoon, sitting on a sidewalk bench, watching the people, and a moped zooms by. Ran over both of my feet. I couldn't believe it. He didn't even stop. I jumped up to yell. I couldn't stand up. So I collapse back to my seat in a heap and wonder what to do next. I finally had to get a street clown to call a friend. Turns out bones in both of my feet were broken. But I needed a vacation anyway, so I'm taking advantage of my misfortune to go home to Champaign to visit my folks. I don't get home very often. It's hard to get enough time off."

"What do you do?" asked the woman across the aisle.

"I'm a waiter at Brennan's, the restaurant on Royal Street."

"We know Brennan's. We had breakfast there one day. We'll remember it. We couldn't believe breakfast could be so expensive. It's a nice place, though."

"I think the house was once owned by a chess master. I've heard that the floor of one of the rooms is laid in the pattern of a chessboard. There's a carpet over it now, so I can't say if it's true."

Paul Morphy, a precocious genius who was acclaimed chess champion of the world at twenty-one, was born in 1837 at 417 Royal Street, later the site of Brennan's. When Morphy defeated the German master and world champion Adolf Anderson, Oliver Wendell Holmes crowed that there was now an American who could "checkmate all of Creation." Anderson, who managed only two wins and two draws to Morphy's seven wins, conceded, "It is no use struggling against Morphy. He is like a piece of machinery." He proved, however, all too human. His mind, which had dazzled the world, spun off its axis, plunging him into illusion and paranoia. He died at forty-seven in the bathroom of his home at 417 Royal Street.

The young waiter ordered another Scotch and asked the elderly couple, "What did you like about New Orleans?"

"We loved the bar on Bourbon Street with the female impersonators. We went back three nights."

The old lounge car had only a few small windows and they showed little but darkness as we traveled northward, through the little towns along the Illinois Central line: Natalbany, Tickfaw, Independence, Amite, Roseland, Fluker, Tangipahoa, and Kentwood in Louisiana, and then into Mississippi and through Osyka, Chatawa, Magnolia, and Fernwood. We stopped briefly at McComb about 6:30 P.M., traveled quickly through Summit and Bogue Chitto, and made stops at Brookhaven and Hazlehurst. On my timetable, Hazlehurst was marked with a black diamond signifying an experimental stop to be continued only if demand warranted. In a figurative but very real sense, that black diamond marks every American passenger railroad station today.

It was by now approaching eight o'clock and I resolved to have my first dining car meal. I chose the last seating because I hate to rush through a meal, particularly on a train. Few things seem more pointless than hurrying while on board a train.

The steward seated me with a quiet black woman who accepted my presence graciously, but without any obvious pleasure. The illuminated capitol dome of Jackson, Mississippi, shone brilliant white in the night sky. I watched her discreetly as we left the city behind. Although her features were still young, there was in her manner a severity that usually comes with age. She wore a white blouse and over it a dark blue pinstripe suit that was heavy for the lingering summer heat of the Deep South. She had come from Chicago to Jackson for the funeral of her uncle. I asked why she had taken the train.

"I don't fly." That was all she said.

But did she like the train?

She looked up from her plate, looked around as if she was considering the question, and the train, for the first time, smiled faintly, and lifted her fork in a tiny shrug.

We both ate short ribs of beef, served with green beans and noodles with mushrooms and a gravy sauce. I had been away from my seat since before six and by the time I had eaten it was after nine, so I went on to my coach, thinking I would transmute the satisfaction of a full meal into sleep. I found company.

"I was wondering if anyone would come to claim these bags." It was a young woman speaking, slim and dark-haired, who had settled into the seat next to mine while I had been dining. She seemed comfortable in the aisle seat so I lifted my camera bag from the window seat and hoisted it into the overhead luggage rack and then stepped over her to take its place.

The aspiration of every overnight coach passenger is two seats of his own. By cunning, intimidation, and a host of transparent psychological ploys, coach passengers endeavor to keep their adjacent seat empty, particularly at night. Few of us relish the prospect of sharing with a stranger what, rude as it is, will serve as our bed. So every time new passengers board a railroad coach the same series of pathetic little deceptions unfolds: a hat, a coat, an open book left casually on the seat suggest to the boarding passenger searching for a seat that this one is taken; at night, a favorite tactic is to sprawl across both seats and feign a deep sleep. And yet an unwritten code seems to proscribe outright lies. If asked forthrightly "Is this seat taken?" or "May I sit here?" the seated passenger will almost always give up the game. Racial and sexual dynamics further complicate the unwritten rules. Watch an attractive woman enter a coach alone and you will see, up and down the rows, men slyly disassembling the walls they have built, changing their demeanor from aloof to friendly, and you will see the poor woman look first for two empty seats where she can sit alone and then, failing that, another woman to sit with and, failing even that, a man who doesn't look too eager.

We had been spared that dance, the young woman and I. She had chosen her seat and I was its consequence. She wore jeans, canvas sneakers, and a baby blue sweater with tiny half-round pearl buttons. Her long fingernails were painted the deep purple of a ripe plum. She was reading a paperback novel, *A Woman of Substance*, or, rather, she was holding it in her lap, her finger marking the place. "Don't let me keep you from your book," I told her.

"It's not you. I can't read while we're moving. I get faint. I can only read when we stop." I was having my own difficulties writing in my notebook while the train swayed and jounced along. In subsequent days I learned to compensate for the motion of the train with a more fluid style of handwriting, but even now, looking over my notebooks, I can judge the quality of the roadbed by the legibility of my notes. So at each stop that night, when the City of New Orleans came to rest, we both used the few motionless minutes. While she read, I scribbled. Between stations, we talked.

I asked if she had been to New Orleans. "Once." She wrinkled her nose. "We went to Bourbon Street and Pat O'Brien's. It was awful. We came home and I don't care if I never go back." She had seen the sideshow and she didn't approve of the circus. "I got on at Brookhaven [Mississippi], but I live in Alexandria, Louisiana. I'm going home to Missouri for a wedding," she said. I asked her where in Missouri home was. "Sainte Genevieve. You've never heard of it. It's an old settlement, but no one else has even heard of it. It's a nice little town. I liked it there," she said, a bit wistfully. "There just aren't any jobs at home, except factory jobs, so my husband joined the air force."

"And you followed him?"

She nodded. "I work at Sears as a training supervisor."

She asked me where I was going and I told her that I was going to Texas to visit an old friend, that I was taking a roundabout route just because I liked trains. It wasn't the whole truth, but it was true.

Part of the pleasure of train travel is the opportunity in chance encounters to lie about one's past, although I found that as soon as I had any inkling that it mattered I began to feel uneasy.

Just before ten, right on schedule, we stopped briefly at Grenada, Mississippi. The town was dark and quiet. Through the station window I could see the illuminated tableau vivant of the small, brightly lit waiting room. On the wall was a TOUR AMERICA Amtrak poster—a carefully posed Middle American family seated in an Amtrak dining car, looking out their window on the sunlit Rocky Mountains. I doubted that any of the three or four families waiting on the platform in the sallow light were off to tour America. They carried cheap suitcases and parcels wrapped with cord.

In the Memphis station we lost power and the coach lights went out. Amtrak has converted the coaches of its Heritage Fleet to head-end power: instead of relying on a generator of its own, each coach now draws power for heating, cooling, and lighting from the locomotive. Maintenance is simpler and power is much more reliable, but whenever the locomotive powers down or is uncoupled the coaches lose their source of electricity. The dim nighttime lighting faded to black. Most of the passengers were asleep and in the quiet of the coach I heard a child's voice, "Mommy, I need to go."

"Can you go alone?"

"Yes, Mommy, I can go alone." A tiny black girl, her hair in two tight pigtails, walked past our seat toward the front of the coach. A minute later she came back, stepping tentatively and peering into each seat looking for her mother in the dark.

Between Memphis, at midnight, and Carbondale, at 4:30 A.M., the City of New Orleans makes only three stops—at Dyersburg, Tennessee; Fulton, Kentucky; and Cairo, Illinois—each stop about an hour apart. After the new passengers from Memphis settled in and the train hit its stride, the coach became quiet. My seatmate from Sainte Genevieve was drowsy, so I sat quietly and thought. In a few minutes she was asleep, one leg curled beneath her, her book resting in the curve of her thigh.

When the conductor had taken my ticket earlier in the evening, he had told me that I would have to move to a coach that would be disengaged at Centralia and coupled to the River Cities for the run across to St. Louis. I had suggested and he had agreed that I should make the transfer to the other car during the fifteen-minute halt at Carbondale, where I could carry my bags along the platform rather than lug them through the coaches, awakening sleeping passengers with the clatter. We were due into Carbondale at 4:37 in the morning, earlier than I like to break camp, but he had promised to wake me.

I had just closed my eyes, or so it seemed, when the conductor tapped me lightly on the shoulder, "Carbondale in ten minutes." He gestured toward my seatmate, "She's for Carbondale, too, isn't she?"

"I think so," I answered. "I'll wake her up."

When the conductor had moved on to find his other passengers, the young woman said quietly, without opening her eyes, "I'm awake." We each slowly stretched our stiff limbs, like a pair of cats, gathered our belongings, and sat back to wait. As the train slowed and rolled into the station, I could see her parents standing on the platform watching the coaches move past. I followed her off the train and the conductor met me on the platform. "Follow me. I'm going to put you on the last coach so you won't have to change at Centralia." I looked up the platform and saw her hugging her parents.

There is something that makes us construct little worlds around us as an antidote to loneliness. Changing trains, even coaches, means abruptly changing worlds. It was 4:40 in the morning in Carbondale, Illinois, and I was cold. I had been sleeping in my corduroy jacket and the damp air chilled the night-sweat at the back of my neck. My bags were heavy and I was still more asleep than awake as I followed the conductor down the length of the train. Our shoes crunched on the gravel of the yard. Air hissed from the undercarriage of the coaches. The moisture in my breath condensed into damp little clouds of mist. I looked back again and she and her family were gone. The platform was empty.

These are E-9s, about three thousand horsepower the way they're set up. Supplying the cars and heating them will draw maybe seven or eight hundred off each one, but she'll get up and go. I'll tell you that. We'll be making close to the road limit near 'bout 'fore we leave the yard."

The sun was not yet up in Carbondale, Illinois. It was a few minutes after five in the morning. I was almost alone in the upper deck of a dome car at the tail end of the City of New Orleans. At the very front of the dome a small party of rail buffs was talking shop.

"These Budd domes are something. What do you figure, Art? Built in the fifties?"

"I don't know the pedigree on this car. I would guess it was built between 1949 and 1956. That's about when it all ended." The speaker was a bear of a man, powerful and wide with just a bristle of reddish hair.

"The diesel?" One of his companions spoke the word with just a hint of disgust.

"That was it."

The modern locomotive is actually an electric locomotive that carries its own diesel-powered generator on board. Dr. Rudolph Diesel first produced power from his compression-ignition engine in 1895, but critical problems remained before diesel power would be useful for railroads: early diesel engines were too heavy for the power they generated and a way had to be found to transmit that power to driving wheels. Only rarely, and only for special purposes, has diesel power been used to drive locomotive wheels directly. The transmission solution came in 1918 when General Electric built a powered railcar for the Delaware and Hudson that used its gasoline engine (not diesel) to drive a generator, which supplied power to electric traction motors. The first diesel-electric locomotive was installed by the Central Railroad of New Jersey for switching in New York City in 1925 and others followed in the early thirties.

At the 1933 Chicago Century of Progress Exhibition, General Motors's Electro-Motive Division displayed a redesigned diesel engine that produced remarkable power for its size and weight. The Union Pacific and the Burlington railroads, two of the pioneers of diesel power, ordered self-contained train sets using the new engine design and put them into service as express streamliners—Burlington's Pioneer Zephyr and Union Pacific's City of Salina—which broke speed records and introduced train passengers to the era of main-line diesel power.

The E-range locomotives introduced by Electro-Motive in 1937 were the first successful standardized long-haul diesel units. Instead of building a range of locomotives, of various sizes, weights, powers, and running characteristics, Electro-Motive built the one standard E-unit but designed it to be ganged together when double- or triple-heading was required to haul heavy trains or to climb steep grades. This principle, together with the much lower maintenance required for diesel locomotives, meant that railroads could keep more of their locomotives in service and fewer in the shop being serviced or on sidings waiting for a specific task to suit their specialized abilities. The design of the E-series locomotives—a cab set well back, separated by a long bonnet from a rounded pug nose—became the almost universal profile of the long-haul diesel locomotive until the 1950s. Electro-Motive F-40 diesel-electric locomotives hauled most of the long-distance Amtrak trains that I rode.

Our car was a half-dome, not a full-length dome car. The elevated cowl, with less than a dozen rows of seats, was at the front end of the coach, lending it the same rough contour as the camelback shotgun houses I had seen in New Orleans. The dome car is said to have been the inspiration of a General Motors executive who admired the view while riding through the Rockies in the cab of a diesel locomotive. The first dome cars were the Vista-Domes, half-length dome cars built by the Budd Company for the Burlington and put into service in 1945. In the mid-fifties, custom-built dome cars used as coaches, lounges, and diners became the most popular achievement of American coachbuilding, ideally suited to the open spaces traversed by American passenger trains, particularly in the West. Those original dome cars have now largely disappeared from service—this was the only dome car I encountered on my entire trip—but they were the inspiration for the bilevel Superliner coaches and Sightseer lounges that now run on the Amtrak trains west of the Mississippi River.

From the front of the dome you could look ahead along the length of the train, over the roofs of the cars to the locomotives at the head end. It was a crow's nest view of the train, and for rail buffs like those riding with me in the dome that morning it was a rare thrill. As they sensed that we were about to depart, they all grew restless, watching the preparations while they talked, eager for the moment we would begin to roll.

"Here it comes. We're rolling!" They followed the pull of the locomotives as it traveled down the train, snugging the slack from the couplings. "Get ready!" The first coaches were already gaining speed when the wave of movement reached our coach and snatched us into motion. As we rolled out of the yard, we did indeed pick up speed quickly. "You know the engines are working. Look at that exhaust!"

At Centralia we faced a dilemma. An Illinois Central Gulf freight had derailed on the track ahead, somewhere between Centralia and Chicago. It would not interfere with my route west to St. Louis, but it would impede the City of New Orleans on the last leg of its trip north to Chicago, and at some level of management up the line, so to speak, Amtrak and Illinois Central people were debating whether to hold the City of New Orleans in Centralia and wait for the track to be cleared, or whether to detour it through St. Louis with us. We were all being held at Centralia until a decision could be made.

Soon after six-thirty, the sun rose behind scaly stratus clouds, washing the Centralia rail yard in diffuse gray light. In a scrap yard west of the tracks old brick was piled into heaps and automobile bodies lay rusting, their hoods sprung, gaping over empty engine cavities. Just before seven, a trainman came through the car to placate us with orange juice and pastries. At ten minutes before eight, an Amtrak steward announced that we would reconnect with train No. 58 and it would detour with us to St. Louis. I dozed off as the switching and coupling began. When I awoke, I saw the Gateway Arch. We were approaching St. Louis, more than two hours late.

The party of rail buffs was indignant when we reached the St. Louis station and they found that they had missed their connection to Kansas City. When the Amtrak representative, who had been dispatched there to make amends, offered the rail buffs a bus trip to Kansas City, their indignation turned to scorn. No one was happy. With much grumbling, the unfortunate travelers realized they were stuck and either accepted the bus ride or drifted out of the station to the pack of cabs that had descended with the first sounds of distress.

Two rowdy fellows, on their way to Chicago for the Sunday Bears game, realized they would never make the kickoff in Chicago after this detour so they huddled and decided to climb the hill to attend the St. Louis Cardinals game instead. Their luggage was no problem. Between them they had only a very large ice chest. But as they started out of the station one of them halted, reigned up short by a frightening thought, "They have blue laws in Missouri! What if you can't buy a drink on Sunday?" He hollered to the girl at the Amtrak counter,

"Are you sure they sell beer on Sunday at the stadium?" She had been taking abuse from frustrated travelers for thirty minutes. She hesitated; she knew this was a crucial question. She didn't want to face these guys when they came back sober and angry three hours from now. She stammered and looked around for help.

From the baggage room came a loud laugh and a man's voice, "Are you kidding? In Busch Stadium?"

4 A Sunday Stroll in St. Louis

The Amtrak station in St. Louis lies in a gully along the tracks. Instead of following the long loop of the entrance drive, I scrambled up the steep bank, climbing over tatters of cellophane wrappings and shards of pint liquor bottles and beneath the elevated superstructure of an interstate highway—the sign above the roadway read "Last Missouri Exit." Up a wide empty street that rose, more gently, toward the center of the city, I headed toward the most imposing, though not the tallest, building I could see, a granite extravaganza set off against the sky by a red tile roof. A sign at its front entrance identified it as City Hall, built in 1896 along a design modeled after the Hôtel de Ville in Paris.

Around on its north side, I found a grassy plaza where I basked in the sun on a park bench. The day that had begun overcast and gray in Centralia had been washed clean with sunshine. The temperature was in the sixties, the sun warm, the sky deep blue, the clouds benign. In Charlotte and again in New Orleans I had been meeting friends, renewing old bonds, but here I was adrift. My park lay along Market Street, a wide boulevard. It was Sunday; offices were closed. The monumental buildings along the boulevard were quiet and empty. Very little traffic moved on the streets. Yet, as I sat on my bench in the sun, I watched scores of people, in small clusters of twos, threes, and fours, some families, some couples, walk past—all headed toward the Mississippi, all walking with purpose. Some carried blankets, some carried folding seats, some stopped now and then to nip at pocket flasks. They reminded me of villagers strolling to a county fair. I wondered for a moment what drew them, and then I remembered Busch Stadium.

49

I left my sunny bench and strolled down the deserted boulevard toward the river. From beyond the horizon, one leg of the Gateway Arch seemed to rise out of the asphalt. Like the end of a rainbow, it didn't seem to touch down precisely anywhere, and I could easily imagine it disappearing in a vapor before it reached the ground. St. Louis is a city that shows a lot of sky, with a skyline still more horizontal than vertical. Nothing approaches the scale of the arch. From a half-dozen blocks away, clouds seem to drift beneath it, and, like water reflecting the sky, its mirrored skin seems to merge into the sky around it.

I wandered around downtown for a time, turning north across the boulevard and following a cross street into the commercial district of shops and storefronts, which I found deserted. Nothing moved except an occasional piece of litter, rustling in the gutter like a dead leaf. Whether by design or dearth of demand, nothing functions in St. Louis on a football Sunday save the stadium and the arch. Eventually I found myself drawn toward the latter.

The arch rises from a green lawn of manicured grass on the west bank of the Mississippi River. The riverfront park around it, called by the National Park Service the Jefferson National Expansion Memorial, was teeming with life of the tourist sort; young families with prancing children moved quickly along the walkways, past mothers pushing infants in strollers and slow-moving pensioners. The shining silver-gray skin of the arch and the uncompromising geometric purity of its shape lend it the air of a contemporary Stonehenge, equally mysterious, its purpose equally incomprehensible. Approached from the west, from St. Louis, it looms on a grassy crest against pure sky. The late afternoon sun, low in the west, lit that side of the arch with a cold, brilliant, phosphorescent reflection of its light, burning out all detail like an overexposed photograph. Where the sun's reflection did not bleach it bare, the mirror surface of the arch's stainless steel skin reflected a curved, twisted, distorted sliver of sky and clouds. I stepped off the concrete walkway and moved to the center of the grass, where all I could see was the green of the lawn, the blue of the sky, the white of the clouds, and the reflection of it all in the arch. A minimalist landscape.

The entrance to the arch is in the lobby of a museum dug into the earth between its two legs. As I came down the ramp and through the glass doors into the lobby, I saw more people than I had encountered on the streets of St. Louis all afternoon. Without hesitating, I joined the line that snaked toward the ticket window and purchased one of the last remaining tickets of the afternoon. That left me with twenty minutes or more to kill, so I wandered back to the information booth and asked the friendly, slightly pudgy woman behind the counter, "Where is everybody? Except for the football game and the park here, I didn't see a soul downtown."

"The blue laws," she said. "Only the big department stores can stay open on Sunday. It's not really fair to the smaller shops or to the city since we're surrounded by suburbs where people can go to shop on Sunday. It's a good day to see the arch, though. Do you have a ticket yet?"

I told her that I had one of the last of the day.

She was interested in my train trip. "My mother loves trains. She is eighty years old and still takes every train trip she can. I haven't been on a train in years, though. Where do the trains stop in St. Louis now?"

"Amtrak has a little cracker box down by the tracks. Strictly utilitarian. What's become of the old St. Louis Union Station?" I asked.

"It's been empty for years now. I understand that it's being refurbished as an Omni Hotel. At least it hasn't been torn down. I don't think the trains will ever come back to it though."

St. Louis Union Station was the first of the several great railroad stations built in the United States between 1890 and World War I, preceding the Union Station in Washington, D.C. (1907), Pennsylvania Station (1910) and Grand Central Terminal (1913) in New York City, and the Kansas City Union Station (1914). When the St. Louis station opened in 1894, it served twenty-two different rail lines, thirteen from the east and nine from the west. For decades between the days of the prairie schooner and the jet airplane, the eleven-acre train shed of Union Station, the largest in the world, was the true Gateway to the West. In the heyday of train travel, after World War I and the Depression jarred Americans loose from their roots and set them moving, nearly one hundred thousand people a day passed through the portals of Union Station. But times changed, train traffic dwindled, and the station was abandoned in 1974. It was, indeed, refurbished in 1985 to house a luxury hotel and complex of shops and restaurants, in one of the largest historic restorations ever undertaken in the United States.

• • •

They called for the last trip up the arch and I followed the crowd down a long hallway to wait for the tram. The proprietors of the arch call it a "capsule-transporter." It is a strange device: half elevator and half midway ride. Along a flight of steps, elevator doors at different levels opened into each of the several compartments of the tram and we loaded ourselves, five to each compartment. Each compartment resembled a barrel with seats and we sat, knee to knee, ducking our heads beneath the low ceiling. The door closed and a moment later, the barrel started upward with a lurch. On my left was a couple in their fifties, each wearing polyester pants, his brown, hers red, and on my right was a young couple, probably high school students, holding hands.

As we started to ascend, the capsule gradually tilted, following the curve of the arch. Without warning, when the capsule had tilted some ten or twelve degrees away from the vertical, it ratcheted back to upright with a clank that echoed up and down the hollow shaft of the arch. None of us was prepared for the sudden movement and our barely stifled gasps gave away our anxiety. I noticed that the older couple on my left was now holding hands, too. We crept on up the shaft and below us, several seconds later, I could hear the next capsule make the same groaning adjustment and a female voice exclaim in surprise.

It took some four minutes to reach the landing platform just below the crest of the arch. From there, a few steps led to the observation room at the top, 630 feet above the ground. The viewing room followed the gentle curve of the crest of the arch; its floor and walls were carpeted and narrow horizontal windows at shoulder height reminded me of a basement apartment. The initial effect was cool, a bit confining, and, oddly, subterranean. I thought at first of a research submarine, and then, as I peered out of the row of windows at the sky all around, of the cabin of a Zeppelin.

We were the last party of the day, so the crush for space at the windows was moderate. Most of us went first to the west windows to look across the city. Just below the arch, Memorial Drive follows the line of the river. Straight away to the west, Market Street divides the streets of St. Louis into north and south. In a sloping plaza just one block from the arch sits the old iron-domed courthouse, the theatre where played the first act in a legal drama that escalated from an obscure and apparently inconsequential suit into a controversy that threatened the U.S. Constitution.

On April 6, 1846, Dred Scott, a slave born around 1800 in Virginia, and his wife, Harriet, entered this courthouse to sue their owner for freedom. As the Scotts' case proceeded over more than ten years through the Missouri state courts, the federal circuit court, and finally to the Supreme Court, it forced the nation to confront the divisive issues of slavery and federal authority in the western territories and compelled the Supreme Court to rule on questions that had repeatedly failed to yield to legislative compromise. For the nation, the Dred Scott case culminated with the notorious 1857 Supreme Court decision that imperiled the authority of the court itself and hastened civil war. For the Scotts, their struggle ended back in the St. Louis Courthouse on May 26, 1857, when a descendant of Dred Scott's original owner voluntarily freed them. Dred Scott died on September 17, 1858, after enjoying a little more than fifteen months of freedom.

Just below the arch, on the riverbank, a crowd was gathered around a bandstand. A few blocks north, almost beneath the Eads Bridge, rested the rusty hulk of the *Admiral*, one of the largest river excursion boats ever put afloat, now raised from the muck—the missing windows of its superstructure like the empty eyesockets of a skull—to be rebuilt as a floating shopping mall. Light from the setting sun skipped over the river and grazed the storage bins of the Continental Grain Company on the Illinois side. Farther south along the river, great red letters on the riverbank spelled out PEABODY COAL. Beyond, the Illinois industrial flatlands faded to the horizon.

By the time I descended and emerged from the underground exit back onto the lawn at the base of the arch, the sun had spent most of its heat. I descended the long series of steps to the promenade along the riverbank and walked toward the crowd I'd seen from above. A high school band and chorus stood in formation on risers, winding up their afternoon performance, forty scrubbed white faces with rented instruments bashing their way through a stock arrangement, singing "I've got the music in me" with an utter lack of swing. I couldn't help but compare their plodding performance with the young brass bands of New Orleans, ragtag outfits of children, some of them twelve and thirteen and fourteen years old, who, with just a tuba and a couple of hubcaps, could make music that made you want to dance in the streets.

I walked north, up the river, past the hulk of the *Admiral*, and under the Eads Bridge. From the top level of a parking deck at the foot of Laclede's Landing, a district of renovated nineteenth-century warehouses on the slope of the levee, I looked out over the river. With a rumbling from the south, a green Burlington Northern diesel rolled under the arch of the Eads Bridge toward me. It passed about thirty feet beneath me, followed by another Burlington Northern diesel, then several flatcars carrying automobiles, then tank cars, boxcars, coal hopper cars, Illinois Central Gulf cars loaded with heavy timbers, Detroit and Mackinac boxcars and flatcars, piggyback trailer cars, Mo-Pac hoppers with two neat mounds of blue gravel in each one, and Soo Line hoppers loaded with chunks of granite the size of an automobile. The cars rumbled slowly on, bearing the bones and blood of American industry. The light was fading perceptibly and still they came. I could look down into the open hoppers and see the mountains of gravel, dunes of gunmetal gray, sandpiles of granite, and I could watch the automobiles on their flatcar platforms bob on their springs and tug at their moorings, like boats lifting against their lines as a gentle wake washes under them. I watched the last of the freight cars and the green Burlington Northern caboose curve north and west along the river and disappear in the dying light. To the south, above the Eads Bridge, I could see a delicate quarter moon over the tip of the arch.

After dinner in one of the franchise nostalgia mills that filled the old warehouses of the Landing, I was headed up Clamorgan Alley when I heard the rapturous sound of an alto saxophone. Echoing off the brick walls of the warehouses and the brick paving stones in the narrow streets, the quick notes were burnished smooth and bright. I recognized the tune immediately; it was one of the several standards that became bop anthems—"How High the Moon," "When Your Lover Has Gone," "All the Things You Are"—one of those tunes that has been rewritten a hundred ways by every working jazz musician until the changes come like breath.

Someone knew what he was doing. The improvisation never strayed too far from the melody, holding close enough not to lose a casual listener, and hewed conservatively to familiar intervals, but I listened for a full minute and the inventiveness never lagged. The saxophonist played around his imaginary rhythm section, leaving space where their beat would have been so I could feel it there and I knew he could feel it too, a small syncopated implosion of missing sound. But it was the tone that turned me back to follow the sound. It was a tone that reminded me of Benny Carter or even Johnny Hodges, an organ tone, rich and round and easeful, even when it danced quickly over arpeggios.

I walked back past the old warehouses recently converted to bars, restaurants, and precious, frivolous shops, to the end of the block. In a little alcove off the sidewalk, a bearded man wearing a tweed sportcoat and an open-collared shirt was playing a saxophone, calmly, without display or self-consciousness. He was too old to be playing the streets for adventure, too young to be there out of desperation. His beard was neatly clipped, his coat fit well; there was about him none of the usual pandering showmanship of the street musician. He played comfortably, relaxed and without any of the intensity and anguish affected by inferior musicians to make their playing seem difficult.

I stopped ten paces away and leaned against a lamppost to listen. Back from the street, in a tiny courtyard off the sidewalk, midway between two of the lampposts that puddled yellow light along the street, he stood in the shadows. As he played, he kept a casual eye on the flow of couples issuing from the restaurant across the street. Most hurried on, barely glancing at him, as if the sound was issuing from a sewer grate. When an occasional stroller crossed the street and dropped a bill or some change in his open instrument case, he nodded almost imperceptibly and played on. Absorbed, he spun out long variations on familiar changes, returning every few choruses to within a layman's reach of the melody and then wandering idly away again. Now and then, in the middle of a chorus, he would stop and fiddle with the keys of his instrument, still listening to the rhythm section in his head, and when he was ready, he would commence again in mid-chorus, unperturbed.

He played "Body and Soul" and a Charlie Parker tune, slower and gentler than I was used to hearing it, and by then the fire was well down in the bowl of my pipe and my legs were growing stiff from standing. In twenty or thirty minutes, not more than four people had tossed a consideration into his saxophone case and only two had stopped to really listen for a couple of minutes. He didn't seem to care much one way or the other. When he took his instrument from his lips and looked at his watch, I looked at mine and noticed that it was well past nine and I remembered my 10:45 train. I knew I would have to begin the long walk back to the terminal soon, so I stepped over to compliment him on his playing.

He smiled gently and asked, "Are you a musician, then?"

"Only in my dreams. I do a jazz program five nights a week for a radio station in North Carolina."

"I haven't been in North Carolina since the army. Some nice people there, as I remember, but that was a long time ago. What's it like now? Any work for musicians?"

"More than there used to be. There are a handful of working jazz musicians who stay busy. A few stations keep jazz on the radio and that helps build an audience, but it's tough to make a living playing. Most of the players teach or have a day job. It's not a bad place to live, though."

"Maybe I'll get down that way sometime. I like to stay in the sun as much as I can."

"What, then, may I ask, brings you to St. Louis? This is hardly Sun City."

"I'm living in Kentucky now and I've got a couple of club dates here this weekend. Nothing special, but it's not far from home and I've got friends here." He glanced again at his watch and said, almost apologetically, "I'd better start packing up. I'm playing with a blues band tonight and we figured to hit about ten or a little after. Why don't you come on over. It's not exactly swank, but it's not too rough. Have a few drinks. You got a car? I'll give you a lift. Just give me a minute to fold my kit here." He was starting to pack away his saxophone.

"I wish I could, but I've got that train to catch. . . ." I really did.

"That's right, you did say. Just passing through. Just passing through. Business or pleasure?"

"Tonight has been strictly pleasure."

"I guess I'd better look at it that way myself," he laughed as he fished a couple of bills and a pocketful of change out of the bottom of his instrument case. "I didn't do much business. Downtown is dead, but I really thought I might pick up some change here with all the restaurants. What'd I do wrong?" It wasn't really a question. "Doesn't matter though. It's a beautiful night. Did you see the moon? Real nice quarter moon, right down the street there." He started to tuck his saxophone away. "This thing gives me fits, but it sounds pretty good, doesn't it?"

I told him that it was the tone that had first caught my ear and turned me around.

"It fights me all the time. You heard me have to stop every now and then and free it up. It's older than I am and I've had it a long time. I'll get it worked on someday. It's embarrassing to have to fumble and stumble around on it, but I just love to listen to that sound." The horn was worn and dented and a couple of rubber bands were strapped around it. But he was right; it sounded like velvet feels.

He latched his case, picked it up and another beside it, adjusted his coat and looked again at his watch. "If you'll excuse me, I'm late already. Sure you won't come along? There'll be another train tomorrow."

"Not 'till Tuesday, I'm afraid. It wouldn't matter, though. I'm expected. You know how it is."

"Seems like it's always that way. Well, enjoy your trip. I wouldn't mind catching a train again myself someday." He extended his hand and as we shook hands, he said, "I enjoyed the chat, though."

"You made my evening." It was what I had been missing. I knew that he had been struggling with a wreck of an instrument and I knew that the brick all around us had amplified and rounded his tone, but that night, on that street corner, if he had been Johnny Hodges playing "Warm Valley," I could not have enjoyed it more.

I started up the street and rounded the corner with a little swing in my step. At the newsstand in the Clarion Hotel I bought a newspaper and magazine so I could read myself to sleep on the train. As I walked through downtown, the streets were wide and empty, with only an occasional passing car and no one else on foot. Few of the buildings were even lighted. From the gutter I picked up a heavy steel bolt and carried it curled in my hand as I walked past Busch

Stadium, fenced and grim-looking in the darkness, and on up a half-dozen blocks of empty street. Where two cars idled at the curb, I stepped off the sidewalk and walked half a block in the street. There was no traffic, no noise, such quiet I could hear the clicking of the stoplight switches. I sang "Body and Soul" softly to myself, but I forgot the words, so I whistled it, but then I forgot the melody.

From the west end of Walnut Street, I could see the Romanesque tower of the old Union Station, and then I turned south and hurried under the expressway and down the grubby embankment to the Amtrak terminal, dislodging a muddy pint bottle that tumbled down ahead of me in the dark like a stone down a well. At the bottom of the bank, I tossed the bolt next to the bottle.

5 The Eagle to Austin: Dry Counties and Strong Beer

The train had been clattering along now for ten minutes and the little girl ... whispered: "Mamma, I want to see ... "

The mother asked: "But what do you want to see? You can see everything, can't you?"

The little girl burst into tears: "I can't see the train."

Borlini let out a laugh, and the child's parents laughed too. ... Only Aghios was touched. Only he felt and knew what sorrow there was in not being able to see oneself while traveling.

—Italo Svevo, *Short Sentimental Journey*

T rain people refer to a train not by its name, which, after all, denotes only a route, but by its number. Train No. 21 is the Eagle headed south from Chicago to San Antonio; train No. 22 is the Eagle headed north from San Antonio to Chicago. Names are easier to remember for occasional use. Names encourage passengers to identify with their train. Names create an image. The work is done by number. If a market research firm suggests that the "Limited" would be more warmly received as the "Chief," the name can be changed. It doesn't matter. As long as the numbers stay straight, the schedule works.

By the time I boarded train No. 21, the Eagle, I was exhausted. My bags were dead weight as I made my way toward the rear of the train, past coach after coach, looking for my sleeping car. At every platform, the porter would call out, "Where to?" I would answer, "Austin," and he would point to the rear.

There were several Superliner coaches in the Eagle consist, but my sleeper was one of the traditional single-level coaches, similar although not identical to the sleeping car I had occupied on the

Crescent. The bed was already lowered and made when I reached the roomette. My last conscious thought was of gratitude—gratitude for clean sheets, for whatever prescience and sense of self-indulgence or self-preservation had induced me, when I had plotted my schedule weeks before, to allow myself a sleeping compartment for that long night.

I slept soundly as we passed through the Ozark plateau of southern Missouri and into Arkansas. The Eagle follows a northeast-to-southwest line through Arkansas, skirting the eastern slopes of the Boston and Ouachita mountains and cutting across the watersheds of the White, Arkansas, Saline, Ouachita, and Red rivers that drain down from the mountains and across the prairies of southeastern Arkansas. All of the state, however, is lost to the Amtrak traveler, since the Eagle, the only train to serve Arkansas, passes through at night in both directions.

We had been in Texas for a couple of hours and the morning was well along before I made it to the lounge car for my morning coffee. Later my car attendant told me that he had tried to wake me earlier that morning with a cup of coffee and had heard only low growling noises from my compartment that he took to mean, "No thank you." I had no memory of the exchange.

The lounge car was one of the Superliner coaches, which by their sheer mass seem to dampen vibration from the track, making it much easier to read, write, or drink hot coffee. They are double-decked coaches and their upper level seems to sway with a motion akin to the gentle pitch of a sailboat in undulating waters.

By the time I had attained baseline brain function, the Eagle was rolling due west across Texas, headed for Dallas. As we passed through Mesquite, Texas, I saw the first pair of cowboy boots on a fellow passenger. He had long slick sideburns, a deep leathery tan, and brown hair swept up in the front; he was wearing a blue knit shirt and dark blue pants, with a sharp crease that would last as long as the polyester. His boots were unpretentious brown cowhide with minimal stitching, a low heel, and a chisel toe. They were not working boots, but neither were they for show.

When we had passed through Mesquite, just about fifteen miles from Dallas, I started back to my roomette. On my way forward, as I passed the open door of a bedroom in one of the Superliner sleeping coaches, I noticed a young couple seated at the window playing Scrabble. They nodded and smiled as I passed their door, and, on impulse, I stepped back into the doorway and said, "Excuse me, forgive me for intruding, but I'm interested to see what your room is like."

She looked at him, and he looked at me and said, "Come on in. Have a look around. There's not that much to see, but it's pretty comfortable."

They were in their mid-twenties. He was thin, even frail, with a light brown mustache and glasses that gave him a studious appearance. She was pretty, in a shy, reserved way, with darker brown hair that hung in a slight curve almost to her shoulders.

"This couch opens up into a double bed," he said. "It's narrow, but it's pretty comfortable, as long as you're not too big and as long as you're fond of each other. There's a single bunk that folds down out of this wall up above. There's a closet over there near you, and you should see the bathroom. Go ahead, open the door."

I opened the door to a stall about the size of a shower and saw a toilet that was built into the interior wall. I noticed a small drain in the floor and a nozzle on the wall above the toilet seat.

She laughed and said, "It's tricky. The first time I used it I hit the wrong lever and got myself soaked, but it's wonderful to have a shower."

"I believe that." I was beginning to feel a bit sticky myself. "What inspired you to take the train?" I asked.

"I take the train fairly often," he said. "I'm a cellist, with the Minneapolis Symphony now, but whenever I travel to engagements or auditions I like to travel on the train with my instrument."

I glanced around. "Where's the cello?"

"At home. This is our honeymoon," he said. He glanced at her and she smiled. It might even have been a blush.

At Dallas, we made only a skid-stop. There were no passengers to board our car, but the attendant opened the door and set out the blue steel stepstool anyway. I stood in the vestibule and felt the day's heat rise from the platform. A haze hung over the city. Between Dallas and Fort Worth, we passed the Century 4 Drive-In, where four screens all faced inward on a dirt and gravel parking area. Of the eight movies listed on the billboard, about half were of the chain saw and mayhem school.

Impatient travelers are pleased with the short stops on Amtrak routes; I found them a constant frustration. Seldom was there time even to climb down and look over the station. Almost never was there time to walk even a few blocks into town. At Fort Worth, where the Eagle would wait for twenty minutes for service and a crew change, I warned my coach attendant to look out for me before pulling out, and I went for a quick stroll. Even the short walk along the concrete platform was dizzying in the bright sun. Still squinting, I walked through the dim interior of the station and out the front door. A half block away from the station I turned around to see it from Fort Worth, even if just barely.

A pink line ran along the edge of the curb, like a lipstick smear on a china cup. The sky was a thin, milky blue and the station, two stories of deep red brick, stood out in bold relief. An awning threw a curtain of shade down the front wall, over the faded pink swinging doors. Above the first floor, a decorative band of geometric brickwork in contrasting shades of red ran around the midline of the station like a fancy hatband. Across the front wall, bright white lines radiated outward from the doors and windows and cut through the dark red brick like the medallion stitching on a dress boot. I had just enough time to walk back through the pink doors, through the station, and back to the train.

At Fort Worth, the Eagle switched from Missouri Pacific track to the Santa Fe line. I asked the new conductor about our route. "Don't we run on some Missouri–Kansas–Texas track farther on down?" (The Missouri–Kansas–Texas is the "Katy," as in "She caught the Katy and left me a mule to ride.")

"Yes, sir, we sure do," he said. "My tour of duty takes me over four railroads. We ride the Santa Fe to Temple, then we bridge over on the Missouri–Kansas–Texas to Taylor. The Katy actually has track all the way from St. Louis to San Antonio, but it's pretty rough for a passenger train, so we just use it as a link back to the Missouri Pacific. At Taylor we're back on Mo-Pac to San Antonio."

"That's only three," I pointed out.

"There's a short stretch of Southern Pacific track we use into the depot. That's your fourth."

An hour south of Fort Worth, we stopped at Cleburne, named for a Confederate general, and later in the afternoon the conductor came to the lounge car to remind the attendant to close the bar until we reached McGregor, Texas, at 4:30. Amtrak is bound to obey local liquor laws even as it passes through, and in the counties of East Texas that means some dry afternoons.

I was still content to drink coffee, but some of the other patrons began to grumble, and after a while most of them drifted off to other parts of the train to pass the time. When I went back for my third cup of coffee of the afternoon, the Amtrak attendant at the snack bar refused payment. "I've got enough of your money. I'd just have to throw this pot out, anyway. Nobody but you's gonna drink coffee this afternoon."

He obviously liked to talk and I was happy to linger at the counter as long as he kept the coffee coming. We talked about politics and about Lebanon and Central America and he seemed to relish the opportunity to sound off, but then, abruptly, he said, "I could lose my job for talking to you like this."

"Doesn't seem like a hanging offense to me, talking to the passengers."

He laughed, as if to say, How little you know. "We got a guy who worked for Amtrak got fired for wearing the wrong pair of socks."

"You are kidding," I said. "Must have been another reason behind it."

"I wish I was." He seemed more resigned than angry. "Amtrak is this type of organization. You take our supervisors. Here you are, a man who has been working for the company for ten, eleven years; but rather than upgrade your position, they'll go out on the street and give somebody a position over you with no, with *no*, knowledge of the train. They'll take someone who knows absolutely nothing—I mean this is right now, this is how it is today—and hire him to dictate to me about my job."

A woman stepped up to the counter window where we were talking and asked for a soft drink and a bag of potato chips.

He put a bag of chips on the counter and set a canned drink beside it. With his hand still on the can he asked brightly, "A Diet Coke did you say, ma'am?" His voice was polite, friendly, with no hint of the urgency of our conversation. I stepped aside and leaned against the wall, waiting awkwardly.

He watched her walk back down the aisle of the lounge car, stumbling once or twice as the train lurched. Only when she was out of earshot did he speak again. He did not want to be overheard. "It's the kind of company that will go out and hire sixty or seventy supervisors to ride the trains, just to make sure we're doing everything Amtrak's way, whereas we might need another waiter, or a cook, or an assistant barman. We won't get that help. And you won't see an Amtrak chief helping out there, either. They'll say, we want everything done uniformly nationwide; then you'll get a supervisor from here to here who says 'We do it this way,' and then you'll get on another train and you'll get a supervisor who'll say, 'No, we don't do it that way over here, we do it this way.'"

"I like the way everyone does his job with a personal touch to it," I said. "With personality."

The lounge attendant smiled genuinely at that. "Well, I know. My thing is people. I enjoy my job because I am around people. But Amtrak makes it hard."

We were getting closer to McGregor. The conductor arrived to supervise the lifting of prohibition and a few disgruntled patrons circled around, badgering him to open the bar early. At 4:54, a bit more than twenty minutes behind schedule, the train rolled slowly by the old station at McGregor and the bar opened—beer and wine only in Texas. As I left the lounge, I passed the young newlyweds from Minnesota, sitting quietly and gazing out of the window.

While we held for a few minutes at Temple, Texas, where we would pick up the Missouri–Kansas–Texas track for thirty-nine miles to Taylor, I stood in the open vestibule door admiring the station, a graceful Spanish-style structure of red brick and cream-colored stucco, with a red tile hip roof, an enclosed portico, and a broad brick platform. A couple embraced under a bedraggled, fading palm tree, the tatters of its browned fronds hanging down like a thatched hut.

"Pretty thing, isn't it?" the coach attendant remarked. "Not many kept up that way anymore. Someday I mean to have a look inside. As many times as I've been on this run, I've never gotten down. That's the way it is, I guess."

When we heard the highball from the conductor, the attendant closed the door and went forward into the next car. I lingered in the vestibule as we crept out of the Temple yard. The land was flat, with occasional hills—too few to break the monotony, just enough to make plowing tricky. Small white frame houses stood at the far end of the fields. We slowed for level crossings at several small towns. At each there was a fertilizer and feed store next to the tracks, with farm implements parked on the grass. As we passed a small cemetery not far from the right-of-way, I noticed that the grass inside its low granite wall was poorer than outside, parched brown with only the faintest bloom of green. All afternoon, the sky over East Texas was light, bleached blue, like curtains faded by the sun.

I rode for an hour in a nearly empty coach, listening to an Amtrak porter and a compact, weathered Texan in his sixties, who was saying, "When I was farmin' it was cotton and corn, from here on up to Fort Worth. Oh, they used to raise a lotta cotton down here. Taylor had a big gin and down here in this other little ol' town they had a gin. Every fifteen miles there'd be a cotton gin." He shook his head. "People back in those days ruined their ground. They never fertilized or nothin' else. They just wore it out."

The soil in the fields was freshly plowed and as dark as fresh dung, with cotton lying scattered at the end of the rows like a dusting of snow.

From Fort Worth to Austin, the Eagle travels through the Grand Prairie and the Black Prairie of Texas, where the soils are black, calcareous, and fertile, and at least fifteen inches of rain falls almost every year. This is the western end of the Coastal Plains, where the crops come early, cotton and then winter wheat. Just a few miles west of the Eagle's route, the land rises in a jumble of ridges, mountains, and plains that form the Texas hill country. On the Eagle from Austin southwest to San Antonio and then due west, on the Sunset Limited, from San Antonio to the Rio Grande River at Del Rio, I would follow at the foot of the rugged Balcones Escarpment, where the southernmost plateau of the Great Plains crumbles away.

I listened through the afternoon to the steady swinging groan of the coach, swaying from side to side, and the rhythmic low-pitched squeak from the undercarriage, like a sailing ship on the ocean, only more metallic. Although we were moving along well enough, perhaps fifty or so, the long, slow cadence of the coach's rocking and the lullaby of its undercarriage seemed to slow us down to a lazy lope.

The Eagle was due in Austin at 7:08 in the evening. Back in my compartment, I took out my timetable, already tattered around the edges and about to shed its stapled paper binding like last season's snakeskin, and did a quick calculation. Allowing for stops at Temple, where we switched to the Katy, and at Taylor, where we switched back to the Missouri Pacific, I calculated that an average speed of about forty-seven miles per hour would get us into Austin on schedule. I wouldn't have cared but for the fact that I had friends waiting for me, friends I had not seen in a long time.

W hen I began planning my trip, I decided at the outset to resist the temptation to make of it a sentimental journey, a grand tour of old friends settled in venues around the country. I was out simply to see what travel by train was like in our time in this country, where trains have been, admittedly, so much debased recently and are so often vilified. (Paul Theroux has called Amtrak the worst railroad in the world, and he should know.) My plan was to see just what sort of journey one could have by train these days, provided only that he could pay the fare, had a few dollars left over to arrange for shelter and food, and remained open to whatever fortune, good or bad, turned up. Friends at every stop are not part of the bargain. To make of my trip a constant reunion with familiar faces would be to skew the equation. I also looked forward to the opportunity to recast myself. Encountering an old friend is to encounter yourself as he knew you, and I intended to enjoy the opportunity to shed, or at least reconsider, myself as I had been. That is what solitary travel is for.

And yet, in several instances my itinerary took me near old friends, friends whom the urge to see again overawed all those considerations, and there I made exceptions. I also counted it in their favor if they had a washing machine.

As I approached Austin aboard the Eagle on Monday evening, the first of October, I needed not only the use of a washer and dryer, I needed a bath. In the few minutes before we reached Austin, I had swabbed myself down in my roomette, filling the stainless steel basin with warm water that swirled and sloshed with the motion of the train and running a wet washcloth over my neck and chest again and again. I put on my last clean shirt. I achieved a certain minimal acceptability, and that would have to do.

David was expecting me, but I did not know exactly what I would find there. I have known him for more than twenty-five years. For the past decade, David has been living in Texas, first in Houston and now Austin. Even though it has been some years since we have enjoyed one of the long evening's conversations that we both used to relish, and even though we have not had much in common in recent years, we share a bond that will endure—we were fishing buddies.

Fact is, I still haven't found anyone to replace David. He and I had some of our best fishing days when there wasn't a single strike to interfere with our talk, and yet, when there were fish to be caught, David could manage the boat, catch more than his share, and keep out of my way while doing it. He raised simple competence to a high art. For now, David is committed to his work, both as the chief psychologist at the Texas state mental hospital in Austin and in his private practice, but if the bottom falls out of psychology, which seems unlikely given the increasingly chaotic lives we live, he would make a terrific fishing guide.

As the Eagle throttled down for the Austin stop, I stood in the vestibule with the car attendant. It had been a long run, with few passengers, and we had become familiar.

"You got friends here?" he asked.

"One. I haven't seen him in a couple of years, though. He's married now."

"Happy?"

"I think so. I've never met his wife."

Only a few people, all strangers to me, were waiting on the platform and they quickly dissipated as soon as the train had pulled off for San Antonio. The Austin station is another of those merely adequate bus stops recently erected for Amtrak service, but at least it had a telephone. I was riffling through the Austin telephone book looking for David's number when I heard his voice.

"Sorry we're late. Have you been waiting long?" David was speaking and I was listening, and answering mechanically, but my mind was spinning, trying to remember why the woman standing at his side seemed so familiar. "George, this is Lynn. You two should remember each other. Lynn once sat in front of your fireplace." I was smiling, saying something, beginning to move toward the door, but my thoughts were back in North Carolina, trying to put images from the past together. Eight years before, when David was in his first year of graduate school, and I was back in North Carolina for the first time in five years, he had dated a fellow graduate student. We had gone out together a few times, fried bass and bream together a few times, and, indeed, spent an evening or two in front of my fireplace. Although she had made it clear to him from the start that she would return to California to marry an old boyfriend at the end of the term, David had become quite enamored of her. As the end of the spring term approached, he pleaded with her to stay, but at its end she left just as she had said she would. David received an occasional letter from her, fewer as time went on, and then, finally, no word at all. Life went on. We went fishing. I forgot about her. I thought David had. Her name was Lynn.

We ate dinner in a Mexican restaurant, hot food and cold beer. I ate fajitas set afire with a sauce of chopped tomato and chilis. After dinner, we drove leisurely through Austin on our way to David and Lynn's house in an older suburb of Austin, where most of the houses were built thirty or forty years ago and have now been engulfed by the city.

We stopped for groceries and I went with David into the supermarket to look for Shiner beer—brewed for many years by Kosmas Spoetzl, a Bavarian immigrant, and his daughter, known to all as "Miss Celie," in the small town of Shiner, Texas, between San Antonio and Houston, not far from Yoakum, Sweet Home, and Sublime. The Bavarian and Czech immigrants in that region of Texas patronized the small Spoetzl brewery and its beers were known to knowledgeable beer drinkers outside of Texas as a rare American example of Münchener beer, the dark, malty, bottom-fermented beers first brewed in Munich in the nineteenth century. Shiner is no longer a family brewery and its beers are not so robust nor distinguished as they once were, but I like to think that I can still taste in Shiner a vestige of the Bavarian tradition. When we arrived at their house, they showed me to their extra bedroom and Lynn excused herself and went to bed. David and I each had a Shiner and talked for a few minutes in his kitchen before turning in.

In the morning, after Lynn was off to school and David off to work at the hospital, I headed for the shower and launched an all-out assault on the hot water supply. Cold water would do for the laundry.

That afternoon I drove downtown to the state capitol along Lamar Boulevard. Austin, a city on a river, was in the midst of a drought. The live oaks, with their massive trunks and spreading, drooping branches, and the cottonwoods, quick-growing but short-lived, had a parched, thirsty look, a tenuous, faded green, like a color print too long in the sun or an old Ektachrome. The earth and stone had shifted beneath the terrazzo floor of the capitol rotunda, and the lone star set in its exact center, which a young tour guide said symbolized Texas's solitary struggle for independence, was cleaved by a jagged fault line.

We spent that evening drinking beer and looking at slides David and Lynn had taken on their various junkets around Texas: David and Lynn at New Braunfels, David and Lynn at Big Bend, David and Lynn amid the wildflowers along the Texas highways. I've never quite understood how vacation slides became the butt of so many jokes. I have spent twenty years trying to master the intricacies of photography. And yet I love a snapshot. And I'm not particular about technique. The most immaculate photograph, the most grainless, saturated, artfully composed image, will never mean as much as that snapshot of you at five standing on the back stoop in the cowboy boots your dad brought home from Texas. There is life in that. If I care about someone, I want to see them in the picture, front and center, grinning and goofy.

Without comment, David set before me a slim dark bottle of German beer with a label that read, "E.K.U. Kulminator Urtyp Hell Malt Liquor 28, Erste Kulmbacher Aktienbrauerei, Aktiengesellschaft Kulmbach, Bavaria." I recognized it immediately as a bottle of the second strongest beer in the world, the premier product of the Erste Kulmbacher brewery just north of Bayreuth, Germany. Kulminator Urtyp Hell Malt Liquor 28 is a relatively pale bock, it being a popular misconception that all bock beers are dark. "Urtyp Hell" means "original pale." Kulminator 28 has roughly three times the alcohol content of the typical American beer or English stout and twice the strength of the stronger British pale ales. It is an *eisbock*, a bock beer that is first brewed to a very respectable strength and then partially frozen so a portion of its water content can be removed in the form of ice (*eis*) without removing any of the alcohol. In the United States, where beers are regulated according to their alcoholic content, and each state sets its own limits, Kulminator 28 is difficult to find. I can only say that too great an emphasis on its alcoholic content does it a disservice because its salient quality is its overwhelming maltiness, balanced not so much by the tang of hops as by the nip of alcohol. I was reminded of a single-malt Scotch whisky.

David took Wednesday off and we drove west, into the hills above Austin. As we followed the chain of lakes formed in the Colorado River above Austin, David described them. "The lowest is Town Lake, right in the middle of town. It's the narrowest, and this one, Lake Austin, is a little bit longer and wider. The next lake up, the largest, is Lake Travis. That's where we're headed."

Everywhere in the dry, chalky, fossil-rich hills I saw realty signs, new roads, and construction. "This area is just recently opened," David said. "Before the bridge over Lake Austin, you had to go all the way back into town to get out to South Austin."

We could see to our left the new bridge over the river, a giant steel arch anchored in the cliffs on either side of the river—as if the St. Louis Gateway Arch had been dropped from the sky into the gorge and its ends had lodged in the cliffs on either side, and, taking advantage of the bizarre event, an engineer had strung a highway under it. "I think the bridge is one of the tallest of its kind anywhere," David said.

A few miles farther on, he suddenly pointed up into the hills. "Look over there. Longhorns. A lot of people around here keep 'em as sort of a curiosity. I guess for a time there, longhorns were pretty worthless, sort of a weed among cultivated cattle, but they have enough fanciers now to make them quite valuable, almost collectors' items. Their fanciers think that it's important to preserve them for the gene pool since they are such remarkable, tough, well-adapted animals. Did you know that a longhorn can clear a six-foot fence? Picture that."

Just past a cactus, at a sign that said "Oasis Cantina," David turned up a dusty winding drive. "Back in the fifties there was a violent rainstorm and Lake Travis rose forty feet in twenty-four hours. And we're not talking about a farm pond, either. That's kind of a reflection of how fast it can rain here when it finally gets around to it."

Lake Travis is a bloating of the Colorado River, where its flow is slowed and its surface widened for miles. From our vantage point on the cantina's patio, we could see upriver for several miles and just below us the lake curved out of our view behind the same high bluff where we sat. The water was low and the lake had retreated to the serpentine river channel, exposing bleached sandbars and baking mudflats, as though the tide had gone out. The surrounding hills, blanketed with dark green junipers, low-growing and close-cropped, looked like a well-worn wool carpet, with moth-eaten patches and threadbare veins where the gray hills showed through the green scrub.

"I think you'll probably be in rain tomorrow." David leaned back and scanned the clear sky overhead. "A tropical storm blowing up from Mexico, off the Pacific. They were broadcasting stockmen's advisories about very heavy rains. For Texas south of here. You might ride through it."

He looked around at the other tables on the terrace. "I always wondered who would be here on a Wednesday afternoon while I'm at the office." We ordered bean, cheese, and guacamole nachos. I drank a Corona beer. David drank water.

"I had to ask where the Austin station was when you came in," David said. "I've never taken the train here. Who does ride the trains, other than people with flying phobias?"

"There are more of those than you would imagine. In fact, if you wanted the trade, you could set up a traveling phobia clinic on the rails. Just rope off a corner of the lounge car and hang out a shingle that says, 'Fear of flying cured while you wait.'"

For a couple of hours, nursing our drinks and squinting in the bright sun, we sat and talked about Austin, its scatterbrained growth of recent years, about Texas, and about ourselves. At a state hospital, David was about as far from the academy as one could get. I was curious to know how several years on the front lines of the mental health war had changed him.

"We try to do as good a job as most public service companies," he said. "You plug in the lamp and turn on the juice and ninety-nine times out of a hundred, the light comes on. You've got brownouts, occasional blackouts, but most of the time the electric company does the job."

The sun and the beer took hold and we settled into the afternoon. A small child toddled in the sunlight. I remembered my last afternoon in New Orleans, in the balmy garden at Governor Nicholls Street, and wondered, with only a perfunctory twinge of guilt, if my trip might become a series of dissolute afternoons.

6 The Eagle to San Antonio: Rolling Thunder

I leave here I'm gonna
   catch that M & O
Now when
   I leave here
      I'm gonna catch that M & O
I'm going
   way down South where I ain't
      never been before

—Willie Lee Brown, "M & O Blues"

In clean clothes this time, I went to meet the Eagle again Wednesday evening, bound for San Antonio, where my coach would lay over for five hours before being joined to the westbound Sunset Limited in the early morning. David was working that evening at his fledgling private practice, so Lynn drove me to the same small, nondescript station where they had met me Monday night. The Eagle, No. 21, was late; it had been held for a freight up north, around Temple. It was my experience that Amtrak trains are more punctual than most people expect, and when they are tardy it is often not their fault. Amtrak trains run at the pleasure of the railroads over whose tracks they travel, and on those roads freight pays the bills and sometimes pulls rank.

While we waited, Lynn told me how she and David had come to rekindle their romance. She spoke frankly about the unhappy years that followed the failure of her first marriage, how she had cherished her memories of David, and, through the series of unlikely coincidences that brought them together again thousands of miles and five years from the town where they first met, how she had kept alive the hope that he also remembered her fondly. Hearing her recount their story with such unabashed pleasure made me feel closer to them both. I would leave Austin feeling happy for them and heartened that, every now and then, time can be an ally.

It was past seven-thirty when the rails began to rattle and the headlight of the Eagle appeared up the tracks, the single piercing eye of a looming crepuscular beast. My car, number 2130, was a Superliner sleeping car, and I was looking forward to my first ride aboard one of these ships-on-rails. But for a few minutes I got no farther than the vestibule while a homely little drama played out. An older man and woman had boarded my coach just before me, and their son and his wife had followed them aboard, fussing over them as if they were children. The son carried their bags aboard and his wife pushed past the three of them, saying, "Oh, let's go see the room. I want to see your room. I hope it's nice."

The four of them were crowded into the hallway off the vestibule, at the foot of the only stairs to the upper level where all our accommodations were located. I couldn't move past them, so I stepped to the other side of the vestibule and waited. The car attendant, a genial, outgoing young black woman, tried to reassure the young couple that she would take care of the old folks and gently tried to direct them off the train so we could depart. I could see one of the trainmen on the platform just outside our coach door, waiting impatiently to relay the signal to the conductor when we were clear to go. The attendant kept trying to get the attention of the young couple, with more patience than the situation warranted.

Ma and Pa grasped the situation and seemed perfectly capable of taking care of themselves. They urged their son and his wife to step off the train. "We'll be fine. Don't worry. They're waiting to go."

Finally, the son began to understand that the entire train was being held just for them and began to urge his wife to follow him off. "Come on, they'll be all right, honey. We've got to get off. They want to start the train."

She brushed him off as a mother might a small and irrational child. Finally the engineer loosed a blast from the whistle and they flushed like rabbits, stumbling, as they hurried off the train, on the blue steel step that the steward had replaced for them on the quay.

Through all of this, I stood aside, just waiting to carry my bags up the stairs to my economy bedroom on the upper level. Each Superliner coach has two complete levels. They vary somewhat in their interior configuration, but all that carry passengers, whether coaches or sleeping cars, load from a central vestibule on the first level, a hallway cut through the middle of the coach from one side to the other. On either side is a Dutch door through which passengers board. When both doors are open, which is seldom, an open passageway through the coach is created.

The train began to move out of the Austin station as I made my way up the stairs. The stairs were narrow and after only a few steps turned ninety degrees and, a few steps higher, ninety degrees again. My bags scraped against the carpeted walls all the way up and I had to turn sideways to negotiate the turns. At the upper landing was a small foyer, open from one side of the coach to the other. From the rear of the coach to the foyer a hallway followed the central axis of the coach and economy bedrooms opened off the hallway on either side. Forward of the foyer, the hallway ran along the right side of the coach, and the larger family and deluxe bedrooms stretched across the width of the coach, from its left side to the hallway on its right. The only egress from one coach to the next was on the upper level. In contrast to the older coaches of the Heritage Fleet, the Superliner coach seemed dramatically more spacious and less confining, affording the freedom to move in another dimension, up and down from the upper to the lower level. In the same sense that, to Herman Melville, a ship was "a bit of terra firma cut off from the main," a train is a bit of terra firma rolling on rails, and the Superliner coaches even more so.

I found my room and wrestled my bags inside. I did not check them through because I knew I would be occupying that room for thirty-six hours all the way to Los Angeles, and I wanted them with me, my bookbag so I could read and write, my camera bag so I could photograph the train and the desert, and my suitcase so I could change for dinner. I discovered that the economy bedrooms on the Superliner coaches did not have the overhead luggage rack I had found in the roomettes on the older coaches, and later I carried my suitcase back down to the lower level and left it on the communal rack. The camera bag and the bookbag stayed with me.

I was still standing in the small compartment, when the coach attendant, the same young black woman who had been so patient with the dawdlers at Austin, came to my door and conducted a hilarious and good-natured grand tour of the compartment for me. She showed me the various light switches, the hidden closet, the removable armrest, and the temperature controls—which I later found to be mostly decorative—and she demonstrated to me how the two facing seats slid together to form a lower berth and how the upper bunk unlatched and dropped down into sleeping position. The mattress for the lower berth, made with linen and a blanket and rolled like a pastry, was stored in the upper berth.

After she left, I dimmed the lights so I could see into the gathering dark as the Eagle passed over the Colorado River. From my small, dark warren, I could see automobiles crossing over a graceful bridge, their headlights arcing over the river. City lights glimmered on the dark water. I was reminded that Austin is, however man-made, a riverine city in a part of the world where rivers are not to be taken for granted.

With the effort of boarding over, I relaxed into a gentle melancholy, a comfortable loneliness. I dropped the little folding table into position between the two facing seats and took out my typewriter and had just begun to collect my thoughts when a sturdy, broad-faced woman in her late forties suddenly appeared at my open compartment door and asked cheerfully, "How far are you traveling?"

I was momentarily taken aback. "San Antonio, then on to Los Angeles," I answered without elaborating. I knew I should ask the same question of her in return. The unwritten rule of travelers' etiquette. I felt rude, but I left the unasked question hanging in the air. If she wanted more, she would have to ask.

"Oh, really?" she said, as if she was surprised. "So am I."

My look of surprise was halfhearted at best. I thought to myself that it was a fair bet that every passenger in our sleeping car was bound for Los Angeles.

"Did you board in Austin?" I asked her, realizing that she wouldn't go away until I said my lines.

"Yes, in Austin. I make this trip, Austin to L.A., at least once a year. I've done it for ten or twelve years."

"Always by train?" In spite of myself, I was becoming interested. So many travelers I had met had been traveling by train for the first time, or for the first time since the forties or fifties, indulging now a nostalgic memory implanted in their youth and nurtured since. I was intrigued to meet a veteran of the Amtrak era. "I hope you don't mind my asking," I said, "but are you afraid to fly?"

"Oh no! I think it's fun. But I'd miss too much if I flew. I've taken this trip in February, when the desert is covered with ice crystals and the snow is falling, and I've taken it in the spring when the desert wildflowers are in bloom, and I've taken it in the fall when the desert is parched and brown—and the beauty is always there, if you can see it. I'd feel cheated if I flew."

"Do you know San Antonio?" I asked.

"I grew up there. I lived there for twenty years."

"It's been years since I've been there, not since the HemisFair —that's what, more than fifteen years? I'm going to try to have a look around while we lay over. I guess I'll take a cab downtown. Maybe you'd like to go with me, walk around a bit?"

"I might. I'll see how I feel when we get there."

"I'll stop by on my way out." I guessed that she would go with me to have a look at San Antonio. Few people can resist a chance to show off their hometown or revisit their native soil. And I had noticed that she wore sensible shoes.

With my acquaintance from Austin, I took a taxi into the heart of San Antonio, and for an hour or more we walked along the Paseo Del Rio, the river walk. I remembered it as a bright and sunny cobbled walkway through the heart of the city, but on this night it was dimly lit, as patrons made their way to patios of bars and restaurants along the river. The day had been hot; away from the river the pavement in the streets and the stones of the buildings still radiated heat, but along the river, walking beneath the level of the streets, the dankness of the inky water was chilling.

My companion worked for the state in an Austin office. She had been in her job long enough to know she would be there until she retired, and she had a proprietary sense about it. She lived with her father. Once a year, on her vacation, she took this trip to visit relatives in California.

We climbed out of the riverbed and walked through the narrow alleys of an old quarter of the city, where eighteenth-century Spanish immigrants had settled on land belonging to the Alamo. The short, narrow streets were empty; there was nothing there for night people. A sleek white alley cat watched us from a doorway and leaped noiselessly into a window casing as we approached.

We found the Alamo, illuminated in floodlight, just off a deserted dusty square. Its scarred facade stood out against the dark sky like a cardboard cutout, the pocked stone glowing with reflected yellow light like a full moon. Time had crumbled the once-smooth face of the stone everywhere but the window casings, which must have been of some harder stone. I noticed that the floodlights were aimed to glance across the stone, accenting the damage. The tiny barred windows gave it the menace of a fortress or a prison. In the yard, through an iron gate in a high wall, I saw several sprawling live oaks, their long branches falling away from the trunk and curling down almost to the ground before sweeping upward again. Barely visible in the dark, cables supported most of the branches.

My companion seemed to be tiring of either walking or my company, I couldn't tell which, so we waited on a bench in the driveway of one of the downtown hotels for a taxi to take us back to the station. Once back, she returned immediately to the train.

When I walked inside the Southern Pacific station at San Antonio I had the feeling that I had stepped into a Fabergé egg. It was a bijou, a jewel. The main floor was serviceable and well worn, with tile wainscoting on the walls and rows of heavy carved wood pews. I sat for a minute in one of the pews and marveled at the curve of it. The wood was gouged and scraped and worn smooth again with small signs of age and authenticity like barbed-wire nicks in a cowhide. An old man worked his way languidly around the pews with a long-handled push broom.

A wide wooden staircase at one end ascended to a landing and then divided and continued upward to a balcony that ran around three sides of the station. The staircase had a wide, graceful banister that curled upward from two massive newel posts on the first floor to the landing and then the balcony. Just above the landing, filling the end wall of the station, was a circular stained-glass window in an elaborate carved casing, a five-pointed star at its center. Buttresses of elaborate, filigreed ironwork supported the balcony, and every post in its railing was a beautifully turned series of compound curves.

The vaulted ceiling arched upward the equivalent of another two stories. The entire station was perhaps no bigger than a single basketball court, but the arch of the ceiling made it seem at once vast and intimate. The ceiling was scored by carved longitudinal beams and elaborately worked transverse ribs, with a row of skylights along the crest. At night, with no daylight, the rose window and the mosaic of skylights and intricate wooden panels were lit from within by dozens of incandescent bulbs that hung over the little station like a handmade firmament. Their light soaked the wood of the ceiling and the walls with a warm yellow light, like firelight without the flicker.

Leaving the station, I had to walk around the front of the train, which was waiting through the night, while most of the passengers slept, for the Sunset Limited to arrive from New Orleans. When I stopped five feet away from the locomotive, the throb of its engine resonated in the concrete like a natural force, like the forerumblings of a volcano or the groaning of a fault line about to shear. I guessed that the motor was idling to provide power to the coaches, power for lights and water and ventilation and heating and cooling, power for the caravan, the slumbering city. I rested the flat of my hand against the side of the locomotive and let the power course through me. It was impossible to distinguish the vibration of the locomotive from the low, subsonic sound that flowed from it, but when I pulled back my hand and stepped away, my whole body came to rest, as if from some furious molecular motion.

It was after midnight. Down the platform, street lamps threw pools of light on the concrete and against the side of the coaches. Railroad men in denim overalls went deliberately about their mysterious duties, readying the train for the long run to Los Angeles. They worked singly or in pairs, hardly speaking, quietly and without haste refilling water tanks, checking running gear, poking about the undercarriages of the coaches. They slipped in and out of the pools of light, now and then crouching low and scuttling like grease-stained crabs beneath the underbelly of a car to cross from one side of the train to the other.

I walked to the rear, toward my coach, where an Amtrak attendant stood on the platform, watching the switching engines moving back and forth around the train. He was a young black man, probably in his late twenties, handsome in a smooth, stylish way that, with his narrow mustache, belied his youth.

"It doesn't create a problem for you," I asked, "my waiting around out here?"

"Most passengers would rather sleep, but no, no problem. It's a nice night. Only thing, though, if this thing should start moving, don't try to get on it. It's not going anywhere. It's not going to leave us. That's the worst thing you could do. Slide right underneath and lose both legs. There's going to be some activity now, with the train. They definitely want to take those last two cars, and do what with them, I don't know. If they put them over there, they'll be in the way of the Sunset coming in from New Orleans." A whistle sounded, but I couldn't tell if it came from one of the locomotives at the head of our train or one of the yard engines. "Tooting the ol' whistle up there. They usually come through and put our step-boxes up before they start anything." The Amtrak attendant yawned and shook his head gently, as if he was trying to clear it. It was the middle of the night.

"What are the blue lights for?" I asked.

"The blue lights? Means men at work. Means equipment stationary. It means, 'Hey, stop!' 'We're stopped.' All the above." He yawned again. "Too much dinner tonight."

A yardman, a grinning little fellow in an orange flannel shirt, an orange hard hat, and Southern Pacific overalls, was "making the cuts," stepping between the coaches to uncouple them. The Amtrak attendant called out to him, "Doing all right now?"

"Oh yeah! Detroit's taking the second game, five to three in the eleventh inning! I just heard."

When he was gone, I nodded toward the train and asked, "Who builds these?"

"The cars themselves?" the Amtrak attendant said. "You got Budd, Pullman, and another company that completed the Superliner order, when one of the others pulled out. The locomotives, though, I'm not sure. General Motors? That's a guess."

"Ever rode in one?"

"Oh yes, I've been up in them. Rolling thunder. Incredible. So much power, so much weight. We've smashed up cows, cars, trucks. I mean there's no winning when you go up against one of those things. But people try. I don't understand it. Sad situation, not long ago, at Whittier, California. Lady and three kids, went around a stop sign, no skid marks. The motor of the car went through a steel door like a hundred feet away in a factory or something like that."

He looked down the tracks. "But my first was the worst. Two years ago. Good Friday. Leaving out of Pomona, six in the morning. Sleeper was at the end and coach was in front of the lounge, OK? I'm up, working, getting my car ready, so I'm ready to go when we get to L.A. in an hour, ready to go party, or whatever. And the brakes come on. Hard. I grab onto something and I think, 'What the hell is going on?' I mean, we're going like sixty miles an hour. Shueeeeeeeeeeee [he imitates the sharp hiss of air brakes], the brakes take hold. And I go downstairs. 'What's up?' The brakeman is there, the electrician, and the conductor are all there in the rear for some reason or the other. Coincidental. And they get on the PA, and the next thing I hear, 'Well, we're gonna have to call the coroner.' And I go, 'Holy shit.' And about five hundred yards back there, a lady dove out in front of the train. I went back with 'em, and I mean, man, you just couldn't tell, it was unreal, you couldn't tell what was what. You didn't even know if there was clothes on her. And it was early morning, cool, you know, a lot cooler than ninety-eight point six, and you got the steam rising right up. Sorry, but I mean . . . it was so final. That stayed with me."

I remembered an almost forgotten incident of my childhood. Every summer, I would spend a few weeks at my maternal grandparents' home in Shelbina, Missouri, a small town west of Hannibal. Shelbina was utterly benign, a place where the long summer evenings were spent on the front porch swing. Everything was within the reach of a small boy. A short walk brought me downtown, where there was a bandshell in the park, and an even shorter walk took me out of town, into the fields that seemed to go on forever. Behind my grandparents' house, past the yard and the wormy apple trees and the chicken coop and the cornfield, were the railroad tracks, and I would walk along them, down to the end of town and back. I was always careful, and in that flat country I could see the freights approaching almost before I could hear them, so I never was afraid. Until one day I found a dog, perhaps someone's pet, perhaps a stray, lying on the gravel beside the rails. Its head was severed from its body and both were mangled and crushed, but the scavengers had only just begun their work and there was left of the flesh and fur enough to reveal the moment of death. The canine face was set in a hideous, savage growl. The jaw was shattered. I picked up a bloody, broken tooth, turned it over and over in my hand, and put it in my pocket. For the first time, there by the railroad tracks, I saw how detached, how isolated and aloof, we animals come to look when life no longer animates us. I cut through a cornfield, back to town, hurried through someone's backyard and made my way home on the sidewalk. I didn't tell anyone. I don't remember how long I kept the tooth.

7 The Sunset Limited to Los Angeles: West of the Pecos

There is every sort of light—you can make it dark or bright;
There's a button that you turn to make a breeze.
There's a funny little basin you're supposed to wash your face in
And a crank to shut the window if you sneeze.

—T. S. Eliot, "Skimbleshanks: The Railway Cat,"
from *Old Possum's Book of Practical Cats*

I left my window shade open intentionally when I went to sleep in the Southern Pacific train yard in San Antonio sometime after 3:00 A.M. I was awakened by the sun about 7:00 A.M. and from my bed I saw open sky. I raised my head and saw a wide expanse of water. It seemed a lot of water in a thirsty place.

Later, I looked at my maps of the Southern Pacific routes from an old *Railway Guide* and decided that it had been the Presa de la Amistad, the impoundment of the Rio Grande behind the Amistad Dam just west of Del Rio, Texas. When we crossed the Pecos River on a bridge over the Pecos Canyon west of Comstock, I was asleep again. I awoke again somewhere around Marathon, where the Southern Pacific tracks begin to make their way through the mountains of West Texas, climbing thirty miles to Alpine and then thirteen more to Paisano, the summit of the pass and, at 5,074 feet, the highest point on the route between New Orleans and Los Angeles. These mountains jutted abruptly from the grassland floor, but their peaks were worn to nubs and their flanks were covered with grasses and sagebrush the color of pocket lint.

Around Valentine, Texas, I saw irrigated fields that I thought might be alfalfa. A little farther on, we passed pecan groves that looked to be recently planted: long rows of small trees, not much bigger than boxwoods, stretching away in wavy lines almost to the horizon.

I brought a cup of coffee back to my compartment and spent a few minutes examining my maps and atlas, looking over our route for the day northwest along the Rio Grande valley to El Paso, through southwestern New Mexico and across southern Arizona, past the Chiricahua Mountains, the land of Cochise, and Tombstone, the town too tough to die, and on to Tucson and Phoenix. It would be dark before we reached Phoenix and the rest of the crossing to Los Angeles would be by night. In the more than four hundred miles between Phoenix and Los Angeles there would be only three stops: Yuma, in Arizona, then Indio and Pomona, in California. I would not see the Sonoran Desert this trip.

By sliding one of my seats, one-half of my bed, back to an upright position and leaving the other flat I discovered I had a comfortable seat and a broad work surface for spreading out cameras, typewriter, maps, notebooks, and my big feet. I took a few photographs through the window of my compartment, which seemed to be some sort of plexiglass. Later in the day, I could look for a better platform with a clearer view.

God sure made a lot of Texas, but he spread it mighty thin and he ran out of trees somewhere just west of San Antonio. That morning, after seeing nothing but buzzards over Texas all week, I had begun to see hawks floating over the landscape. I couldn't identify the species —the western birds were just as foreign to me as the western flora and the cultivated crops—but it flew low like a harrier, almost skimming the ground like a marsh hawk would. Another hawk, the third of the morning and the second in about ten miles, flew alongside a flock of smaller songbirds, about ten or fifteen feet above the ground. I saw small congregations of vultures silhouetted higher in the sky, circling with their characteristic wobbling flight. The hawks were taking the low ground and the vultures were cruising at altitude, watching for the leavings.

After two in the afternoon we left the mountains behind and our track converged with the river, drawing closer to the Rio Grande as we approached El Paso. We were passing through low hillocks, covered with scrub, that resembled gravel dunes more than hills or mountains. The earth became drier, still more scrubby and sandy, cut through with long dry washes. Dry sandy creek beds showed flow patterns, waves in the sand, gentle scalloped lines etched in grays and tans. The landscape looked like an ocean floor, left behind to bake when the tide went out for good and forever long ago.

After McNary, we traveled through the Rio Grande valley to El Paso. I noticed some grains being grown, and some corn, and the short stalks of cotton plants. The lush green of pecan groves stood out sharply in a landscape where every natural color was muted with the brown tint of desiccation. Here and there down the rows were gaps, a withered stalk left where a pecan tree had perished. Beyond the rows of trees, a few lonely farm buildings stood at the edge of a cloud shadow, at the foot of a range of bare, desolate mountains. Bordering the rail right-of-way was a picket fence—a breakwater in an ocean of sand—its thin slats set inches apart like the bleached ribs of an animal skeleton. The slats, wired together, offered purchase against the wind, like mangrove roots in shallow seas. Clumps of sagebrush snuggled into the fence, growing along it like a hedge. As we approached the city I could see the Franklin Mountains to the north. At 2:33 P.M. we were stopped at the station. It was October 4, Pancho Villa's birthday.

As soon as the attendant opened the coach door, set out the step stool, and helped off the few disembarking passengers, I stepped down onto the cement platform, squinting in the midafternoon sunlight. I asked the porter where I could find something to eat nearby.

"This right here," and he pointed straight down at his feet not more than a yard from the tracks, "is as much of El Paso as I've ever seen. See that man there, in the blue coat? He's from around here. He's with the local television station, doing a feature on the train. He might be able to tell you something."

"Thanks." I started along the platform, toward the rear of the train where I could see a cameraman with a minicam on his shoulder and a shotgun microphone in his hand, speaking with the man pointed out to me by the porter. I hailed the man in the blue coat, "Are you with the television crew?"

"Yes, yes I am!" He turned and extended his hand with a broad, calculated smile. It was a car salesman's greeting, hearty and personal and practiced, but it wasn't inherently phony, just the routine of a man who has to meet a lot of people in the course of his work and can't afford to offend anyone, or to waste time.

"Well, I was hoping you could help me find . . ."

"Tell me, are you enjoying your trip?" he interrupted.

"Well, as a matter of fact, I am. Why, are you doing a story here?" He was young, perhaps thirty, blond and well groomed, wearing a dark silk tie with a small ornate pattern and a gold pin in the collar, and he clutched a memo pad in his left hand. His natural complexion tended toward pink, but he was well tanned, just dark enough to make his blond eyelashes sparkle.

"Trying to wrap one up. My editor sent me out here last week to do a nostalgia piece, a stock piece. We thought we had it in the can. Had good footage, a good kicker for the close—it looked good. My editor didn't like my sound bites, though. Said, 'Go back this week and get me some poetry. I don't want to hear some old lady tell me she likes the scenery. This is West Texas. We know better.' So this is our last try. I've got to get an interview that my editor will want to run or he's going to scrap the story and he's going to come down on my case for wasting two afternoons with a camera."

He looked at his watch. "All we got last week was nothing: 'I like the train because the scenery is nice.' 'I like the train because I hate to fly.' 'I like the train because the people are nice.' That's news to nobody. I need something that sings." Then, to me, he said, "How about helping me out with an interview?"

"No thanks. This is a face made for radio."

"Yeah, but you can talk. Help me out here."

"Not much I can say. If you're really desperate, I can quote E. B. White for you—something about sleeping berths: 'A man is never so alone with himself as in a Pullman, a small green hole in a dark moving night. There is no solitude like it to be found except perhaps in a hotel room in a strange city, and hotel rooms can be depressing, they stand so still.'"

I got the quote mixed up, but his eyes lit up. "Don't go away. We're gonna shoot you and then all go home."

He turned me into the sun and signaled to the cameraman.

"What, other than all the reasons we all know, makes train travel special?" he said, once the tape was rolling. "Besides the pleasant people and the nice scenery and the leisurely pace, what makes it special? We need an authoritative answer here, fast, on camera, with poetry in the sound of it. Make my editor happy. Save my job."

"Solitude." I thought it had a nice ring to it. I didn't know where it was going, but I was willing to make a fool of myself to make his job a little easier that afternoon. So I launched into a rambling soliloquy on the spiritual nature of train travel, touching on the proposition that a man traveling by train moves simultaneously in three spheres—the larger world flowing constantly past outside his window, the smaller more social world of people and coach moving with him, and the infinite world of his own imagination—and a perfect trip is a matter of bringing all three, each with its own pace and scale, into balance. I quoted E. B. White and E. M. Frimbo, crudely and almost certainly incorrectly. I wrapped up in about a minute and a half, I guess, finishing with what I could muster of a rhetorical flourish, and waited sheepishly for another question. The reporter tossed his microphone to the cameraman and, as the cameraman shut down and started packing, the reporter shook my hand. "George," he said, "I should pay your fare the rest of the way. You saved my ass. Give me your address and I'll send a tape. You've earned it."

I scribbled my address on a page of my memo book, tore it out and handed it to him. "I'll be home in December," I told him. He never sent the tape. It's just as well.

I was still hungry. The dining car steward assured me that we carried a light load of passengers and reservations would not be required for dinner. I planned to make an early appearance.

The Sunset Limited, now traveling on Mountain Daylight Time, rolled northwest out of El Paso, through the lands of the Mescalero, Chiricahua, and Southern Apache, made a brief stop at Deming, New Mexico, and continued on toward Lordsburg. Between Deming and Lordsburg, the Sunset Limited crosses the Continental Divide at 4,587 feet, the lowest railroad crossing between Canada and Mexico. Through the afternoon and into the early evening I watched from the window of my compartment as the Sunset Limited chased the declining sun across the desert grasslands of New Mexico and Arizona. As a day, it was ordinary: no double rainbows, no thunderheads, no ominous skies. The landscape, too, remained superficially constant—mile after mile of short, wizened, brownish-green grasses, and away to the north, mountains in the distance. Even the season was subdued.

And yet the flow of the day entranced me. In the morning, clouds had filled the sky over West Texas, veiling the sky with a fibrous web, the light milky and shadowless, muting the greens of the sagebrush and the laminated earth tones of the striated bluffs. Later, the clouds broke and thinned to reveal a porcelain blue sky and began to pile into puffy cotton balls that hovered over the desert in the distance like balloons. In the afternoon, the yellow flowers of rabbitbrush and broom snakeweed were thick among the grasses. Tall spiky succulents that I first noticed in West Texas gave way to great stretches of creosote bushes, growing mile after mile evenly spaced like groves of boxwoods. For a stretch in New Mexico, the soft grass-blanketed mountains in the distance gave way to eroded buttes, like crumbling Sphinxes, with knobby knees sculpted into their flanks by washes and gulleys. They were bare and gritty and inhospitable, and nothing grew on them except small creosote bushes like clumps of green mold. Farther on, the mountains receded almost to the horizon. I thought of my window as a canvas, framed in curving stainless steel. In the background, miles away, the distant desert and the mountains were rendered in the exquisite detail of naturalism, muted colors and sharp lines drawn in bright light. In the foreground, the movement of the train blurred the dots of sagebrush and creosote and rabbitbrush into the grainy, dancing color-beads of a pointillist painting.

As the sun outpaced us to the west, falling lower in the sky, and the clouds broke into thin mares' tails, I left my compartment and went downstairs to the first level of the coach. I stood in the central vestibule, where I could hear the sound of the wheels beneath the carriage and feel the rails through the corrugated steel grating of the floor. I put my face close to the glass and longed to smell the desert air, wondering how cool it was, how much of the day's heat it still contained. Just as I was about to open the window, against all rules and regulations, the Amtrak crew chief came down the stairs and saw me standing alone in the vestibule.

"We'll be coming to Cochise Mountain in a minute. Want me to open the door so you can take a picture?"

I had forgotten my camera bag, resting at my feet. "Yes, I would appreciate that." It was all I could say. I lifted out a camera body and lens.

He opened the window, swinging the top half of the double door inside and latching it against the side wall of the vestibule. "Don't lean out," he admonished me. "Just close it when you're finished and don't keep it open any longer than you have to." Then he disappeared around the corner into the hallway and I could hear him climbing the stairs to the upper level of the coach. When I could no longer hear his footsteps on the stairs, I put my camera back in my bag, took a firm grip on either side of the doorjamb, leaned out of the window, and inhaled the sun-warmed desert air again and again. I stood there, my face in the windstream, until the sun was finally down and the desert was dark.

When the steward called the seven o'clock seating for dinner, I climbed the stairs. The dining car was less than half full, but the steward seated me with a neat, attractive woman in her late fifties, after asking each of us if we minded dining together. I was glad for the company, and she consented cordially, but a little stiffly and with an obvious lack of enthusiasm. She was certainly better dressed than I: she wore a conservative suit, a dark blue jacket and skirt, and a light gray blouse that looked like silk and probably was. Her gray hair tended toward silver and was tailored as stylishly as her suit.

We both ordered lasagna. We waited silently, idly breaking and buttering rolls and watching the faint glimmer of afterglow in the desert. When I sensed that she had begun to relax, I asked her if she had taken this trip before.

"Yes." She paused to think a moment, performing calculations in her head. "Thirty-two years ago."

"Was it something you've always wanted to do again, or was it such an ordeal that you couldn't face it again for thirty years?"

"Both, in a way," she said. "My husband and I took this trip thirty-two years ago when we first moved to Arizona with our baby daughter. My husband was a pilot during the war, stationed at San Antonio and at Lubbock. We thought we would always want to go back home to Illinois. It was all we dreamed about all through the war, but, I don't know, maybe we had just come to expect too much, maybe we were spoiled for the same old life. I think that must have happened to a lot of young people during the war. The world changed. Or maybe it changed us. So we moved to Phoenix. It was a young city and growing. We never went back to Illinois and we've never been sorry."

As we talked, her dinner arrived. I received an assurance that mine would be up from the kitchen in a few more minutes. She hesitated politely, until I urged her to go ahead and eat.

"In all this time, we've never been back. Most of the family stayed on there in Illinois, and I don't think they ever understood why we left and I'm not sure they ever forgave us. And then last month my husband's brother died and we decided it was time to go back, so we flew back. It was a trying few days. None of us is young anymore, and you know how families can be, hard on one another sometimes. It was hard on my husband, losing his brother. His own health hasn't been good. So we thought about it, and said to ourselves, 'No one's waiting for us back in Phoenix. Let's take a few days and go by train again, just like that first time.'"

"How has it been?"

"My husband had triple-bypass surgery two years ago, and he hasn't been the same since. Traveling is hard on him. He said he just didn't feel up to dinner. I wanted to stay with him, but he told me to come ahead and eat dinner, said he'd be all right. I think maybe he's feeling a little better, at least I hope so."

She finished eating, somewhat embarrassed that I was still nibbling on bread and waiting for my meal, but, after finishing her coffee and pushing her plate away, she asked, apologetically, "Do you mind? I'd like to see how my husband is feeling . . ."

"Not at all," I said. "Why don't you take him a roll, at least?"

"That's a thought," she said. She split a roll, buttered it, wrapped it carefully in a paper napkin, and tucked it in her bag. When she had gone, I looked at my watch. It was 8:02 P.M. I had been waiting nearly an hour. I reminded myself again that I had nowhere to go. I took out my memo pad and pen and scribbled to pass the time.

I was the last remaining customer in the dining car by the time the waiter came back to my table, leaned over, and asked, in a confidential voice, "What was your order again, sir?"

"The lasagna. I ordered the lasagna. Was that my mistake?" I tried to keep the irritation out of my voice.

I wished that someone would just admit that tonight the lasagna was not to be, at least for me. Serve me another entrée. Dish up some leftovers. Reheat some hash. Fix me a tuna sandwich. Let's just agree it's been a long day for us all. Railroad dining car service has been a problematical undertaking since George Pullman built the first dining car in 1868. Tomorrow we can begin again and do better, but for tonight let's cut our losses and go home. I was about to do just that, when the waiter brought my lasagna. No explanation; no apology. At least it was hot. It was 8:18 P.M. I made a note.

After dinner, frustrated by the long wait for my meal and suffering indigestion from its subsequent hurried consumption, I returned to my sleeping car. I was too ill at ease to sit and read, the night was dark and there was nothing much to be seen from my window, and I didn't feel sufficiently convivial to join the after-dinner crowd in the lounge car, so I went downstairs and paced in the vestibule. There I talked awhile with the Amtrak car attendant, whom I had first met on the quay in San Antonio and had talked with as we stood in the upstairs hallway of the sleeping car that afternoon and looked out on the cotton fields and pecan groves east of El Paso. He was a thin black man, probably in his late thirties, with a reddish complexion and a neat mustache. He had kept a coffeepot brewing in one of the spare bedrooms all morning and well into the afternoon and so had brightened my day considerably.

We stopped for several minutes at Tucson, which is a division point, and I stepped down to stretch my legs and savor the warm night air. We were behind schedule, but not by much.

The conductor walked by as I stood on the platform, next to my coach, and said to the attendant, "San Diego took the Cubs today, 5 to 3. That means a fourth game. Should be really something!" The baseball playoffs had become a currency of casual conversation among the train crews as the World Series approached. Many of the Amtrak on-board crew were based in either Chicago or California, so for them the Chicago–San Diego best-of-five series had the flavor of a local contest.

When the conductor had passed on, the porter smiled and said to me, "I don't follow sports much."

"No sports at all?" I asked. "What do you like to do when you're not working?"

"I like to travel and I like to fish. I really love to fish. Fishing relaxes me." His face brightened with the mention of it.

On board again, leaving Tucson, I asked him where he lived.

"I live in the Bay Area now. I'm from Chicago, originally. Well, tell the truth, I grew up on the Gulf at Biloxi, Mississippi. That was a lovely place, but it wasn't right for us, you know? So we went on to Chicago, a hard town, a hard city. I had to get out of that city, so I was a seaman. That was a hard life, too, but I like to travel and it got me around the world. It got me out to California, and the very first time I saw it, I said to myself, 'Son, this is as close as you're ever gonna get to it, here on this earth!' Been there ever since."

"Do you do much fishing in California?"

"All the time. I love to surf fish. Grew up doing it, you know? Out here, though, they got some strange and ugly fish."

After a particularly rough stretch of Southern Pacific track in southeastern Arizona, the rails smoothed out. By 9:50, we seemed to be picking up speed. The rail joints no longer thumped one by one as before, but clicked quickly by with a smooth ratcheting sound like the winding of a watch stem. By five minutes to ten, I saw lights from one end of the horizon to the other as we approached the environs of Phoenix. Along the tracks the desert was still dark. I doused the lights in my compartment and watched the nebula of lights twinkling on the horizon.

The city lights diffused in the clouds over the desert and brightened the night sky, like a shine in a cheap blue suit. The thin band of light suggested that all life teemed along the horizon, but I couldn't help thinking that day or night, roasting sun or killing chill—I could feel the heat being sucked up into that deep night sky—this was country for Gila monsters, scorpions, scaly little lizards that keep furtively to the shady side of the cactus, and horned frogs that burrow into the sand by day and emerge at night. This is country that comes alive at night with nightmares. Deadly little visions on the prowl, feeding off one another because there is precious little else to sustain life. There is no slack in the food chain out here—except perhaps for those creatures that have evolved so bizarre a form that they disconcert even their fellow desert dwellers: the taloned creatures, the stinging and biting and poisonous creatures, the grossly unpalatable, and the simply toxic creatures. That men would put a city here is a testament to optimism—or hubris.

L ate in the evening, somewhere west of Phoenix, I was sitting by myself in the nearly deserted lounge car when its only other inhabitant put his glass and his ashtray on my table and sat down across from me.

I remembered noticing him drinking alone in the lounge that morning, sitting by himself at a corner table. He was not a large man: it was obvious, even when he was sitting, that he was well short of six feet. I wondered how he had come to look like this. Once, he had probably been trimly muscled, but he no longer filled his shirt. He had sandy, disheveled hair, cut short and then neglected while it had grown shaggy. I guessed that he was still in his early forties but that his leathery face was prematurely aged. His skin had once been fair; now it was reddened and creased, and it lay on his boyish features like the mask of an older countenance. The sun had weathered his face from the outside and alcohol had loosened its underpinnings. Only his eyes seemed firmly moored to something deeper. His eyes were blue, and when he talked he looked at me steadily, straight into my eyes, the way drunks and simple people do.

"Where you from?" he asked me. He introduced himself only as Chuck. He never told me his last name.

"North Carolina. Born and raised."

"North Carolina." He muttered it, slowly, and shook his head. "That's the South. That's the South." He was leaning heavily on the table, both hands wrapped around his glass and his forearms flat on the tabletop. "I'm a Southern boy myself." He blinked to clear his eyes and he shook his head slowly, quizzically, like a staggered fighter. "I was raised in Gillsburg, Mississippi. I got a double-wide over there. My daughter, I talked to her, when she got home from the hospital with the baby. I told her to take care of Terrell and the baby. And, they're doing what they can for him, for Terrell. Now Terrell, he's damn near an alcoholic, and used to be a drug addict."

"Now who is this?" I was already losing count of the cast.

"Terrell? He's my son. Now Coe, that's my son-in-law's name, he ain't gonna let 'em get in no trouble. They been knowing for two or three months that I was gonna have this surgery, and they kinda look out after everything after my wife died."

"Sounds like you've had some bad luck." I didn't know what he was talking about, but it sounded like a world of trouble.

"Nah, I've had some beautiful experiences. You hold that baby in your arms. Your grandson. And he just looks up at you. That big smile. My grandson. There ain't nothing like it." He had been drinking and smoking all afternoon and all evening, and had probably been at it since he boarded in Louisiana. The wheels slapped at the joints in the rails and the metallic two-beat rhythm resonated through the car.

"I've got five hundred thousand dollars of *in*-surance," he said, accenting the first syllable. "I took that out about three years ago. So if something was to happen to me, they'd still have the land. They could pay the taxes on the land and live in the house—the double-wide."

"What do you do?" I asked.

"The only work I do, I've already done. I'm disabled now. I draw my pension. Everything I've ever had went into my family. That's the main thing. I tell you what, there ain't nothin' like it, lookin' at your grandson, little bitty thing, tiny hands just like this."

"So that's her first?"

"Oh yeah. We was sitting there one day, she and Coe, and I said, 'You ought to have you a baby,' and she looked over at Coe and said, 'Coe, you want me to have a baby?'" He grinned at the memory. "'Course Coe's not making very much money. I paid for the baby's arrival, the doctor's bill, the hospital bill, the insurance." He started to laugh. "I paid for the wedding, come to think of it! But I've got a beautiful baby grandson."

"That's something to look forward to when you get back."

"Yeah, if I ever get back." The pleasure drained out of his voice.

I felt trapped in a conversation that could have no graceful end. The lounge attendant walked to our end of the coach and touched him on the shoulder, "Chuck, I've got to close up now. I've got to get some sleep."

"Go on, you need some sleep," Chuck said, and then, almost as an afterthought, "Thomas, would you get me a couple more before you close up?"

We sat listening to the piston sound of the wheels. "I only been to San Francisco once in my life," he said. "I went to the Fillmore. After I got back from Vietnam. A long time ago. . . . I guess it's gone now." The percussion of the rails was hypnotic. Each rail joint made its own sound: most rang with a dull clatter, but each with a slightly different pitch, like a tuned drum, and the occasional loose joints clanged through the carriage like a cymbal crash, sometimes in a steady syncopation, sometimes overlaying the regular shuffle beat with a seductive, shifting pattern of polyrhythms, Elvin Jones churning behind John Coltrane.

"Well, I got eighteen hundred dollars with me," he said finally. "I figure that oughta take care of whatever the government don't. That'll bury me anyway."

The attendant set two glasses of whiskey on the table in front of Chuck and a can of beer in front of me. Chuck grinned, rummaged in his pants pocket, and handed him a ten-dollar bill. "We're all square now, aren't we Thomas? You go on to bed now." Then to me, "Thomas and me, we're good friends. He's been up since three o'clock this morning. Did you know that?"

"You look like you could use some sleep yourself."

He laughed. "I'm gonna get all the sleep I want under that anesthetic."

"So you came all the way by train?" I asked. "You don't like to fly?"

"I used to jump out of airplanes. That's what got me in all this trouble."

Just then, a lanky, livid man came into the deserted lounge car, wobbling as he walked, fighting the rocking motion of the car with shuffling steps. He was wearing a western hat of dull dun-colored felt, and boots with wide floppy tops and stretched mule-ear pulls. His cuffs collided with the boot tops and his trouser legs stacked up in loose folds above them, giving the impression that his pants were falling down. He stopped at the bar counter and bought a carton of milk from the attendant, who was closing up shop, wiping the countertop and putting away the condiments, and continued up the aisle toward the end of the car where Chuck and I sat across from each other at the last table. He sat down at the table across from us and immediately leaned over and asked, "You men spare me one of those ashtrays?"

"Yes, sir," Chuck said, "there's one." He pushed the ashtray in front of me a few inches toward the edge of the table.

The stranger reached over with a shaking hand and took the ashtray. "Where you two coming from?" he asked. "New York?"

"New Orleans," Chuck answered. I didn't say anything.

The gaunt stranger sat quietly for a few minutes. He made no move to produce a cigarette. He opened his carton of milk and poured it into his glass, slowly and deliberately. "You celebrating something?" he asked, seeing the empty bottles. "A homecoming? The kiss of the Good Life Queen or something?"

Chuck smiled at me, a forlorn grin, and, still looking at me, but speaking strongly enough to be heard over the clatter of the train, "I'm fixing to have an operation."

"Ohhhh. An operation." The stranger drew the words out, as if he had never heard them before. "You're not worried about the operation, are you?"

Chuck didn't look at him. "Do I look worried? It's too late to worry now." He took another drink of Scotch. He was still looking straight ahead. I was three feet from his face, in the center of his field of vision, but he was looking through me. Alcohol is a powerful drug and its side effects are unpredictable, but among them is a boozy intimacy that wears off in the morning like a hangover. The sense of loneliness that envelops a deserted lounge car late at night only made it more acute.

"Well . . . my name's Carl. What's yours?"

My friend across the table said, "Chuck."

"What is it you do?"

"I'm a disabled Vietnam veteran."

"A disabled veteran? What's disabled about you?"

"My brain. I got shrapnel in it."

"Your brain? How 'bout that. And it's still in there?"

"Sixteen years. But not much longer. They're fixing to take it out."

"Don't let 'em do that. Then you'll lose your disability, if they get it all out. You'll have to go back to work. Why you gonna let 'em take the shrapnel out of you?"

" 'Cause I want to live. I want to see my grandson grow up to be a real big man."

"Why, is it killing you? Really? Now tell me the truth."

"I've already told you the truth," Chuck said, with injury and irritation in his voice. This gaunt, curious stranger was conducting an interrogation, and I half expected it to end in a conflagration of temper. Alcohol can do that, too.

Perhaps the stranger sensed it. He turned sympathetic. "I know. I can see it in your eyes. I got children myself. I got a young one, he's nine years old. Then I got one that's thirty-two. That's the oldest one. He's on his own now. Good thing, too. I worked myself to death last year. Contractor friend of mine had me on one of his jobs."

"My job's still waiting on me," Chuck said.

"Yeah, but you never told me what it was," the stranger said.

"Diver," Chuck said.

"Diver?" the stranger said. "Skydiver?"

"Underwater diver."

"Oh. Underwater diver. Demolition then," the stranger said. "So that's how you got the shrapnel."

"No," Chuck said. "I got that while I was working for the army."

"Have you been diving with the injury?" I asked.

"That's when I started having pains in my head," Chuck said. "I went to Biloxi, Mississippi, to get it checked out and now I'm on my way to California."

We all took a drink, Chuck from his Scotch, me from the same beer I'd been nursing along, and the stranger from his glass of milk.

A moment later, the stranger said, "So, Chuck, you still live there in Tennessee, right?"

"No, Mississippi."

"I get Mississippi and Tennessee all mixed up. I got this friend from Martin, Tennessee? You know where that is? He works in Chicago, and this friend, he's a hillbilly and he's quite the alcoholic."

"I'm an alcoholic," said Chuck.

"Naw, you're not an alcoholic."

"Sure I am."

"Do your hands shake like that?" said the stranger. He held his quivering hand out. "I don't think you're that bad of an alcoholic. Hold your hand out. Let me see your hand."

Chuck held his hand out in front of him, over the table toward me. His hand didn't twitch but his arm rose and fell gently, like a conductor coaxing a largo passage from the orchestra.

"Look at that! Steady, right?" said the stranger. "Then you're no alcoholic. Not to me. Now a true alcoholic, when they get to where they shake, can't really control it, till maybe they get the first belt down, then they calm down a little bit. I know a little bit about alcoholics. You don't look like an alcoholic to me. Now listen to me. You get your buddy to write down where you're gonna be in California, the town and the name of the hospital, and I'm gonna come see you when they get done with the operation. My name is Carl and you can forget that if you want, but I'm gonna come see you. You can believe that."

I took out a memo pad and my pen and put it on the table. "Do you know the name of the hospital?" I asked Chuck. "I'll be gone by then, but I'll give you a call from wherever I am."

Chuck had been fading, almost nodding, but when I took my pen in hand he started and suddenly looked anxious. "No. You put down your address. I'll write you. I don't want anybody to come see me. I might be dead. Or I might not be right."

The memo book was folded open to a blank page. I wrote my name in block letters, then paused. All I really knew about Chuck was that he had been drinking for two solid days. I wrote down my address and telephone number. I tore the page from the memo pad, folded it over once, leaned across the table, and stuffed it into his shirt pocket. He was wearing a western shirt, with triangular pocket flaps and pearl snaps. He fumbled with the snap for a moment, trying to fasten it, and then left it open.

"OK, Chuck. It's your show," I said quietly. "Drop me a card when it's all over." I put the memo pad back in my jacket pocket, clipped the pen, the same black Parker ballpoint I carried with me through the entire trip, in my shirt pocket, said good night, and left them there, Chuck and Carl, the stranger.

In my compartment it was cool and dry, the air smelled fresh and clean, like desert air at night, and the clatter of the wheels on the rails sounded muffled and far away. I opened a can of beer that had been in my suitcase since Charlotte. The carbonation boiled out of the warm beer so fast that it sizzled painfully on my tongue like acid. I sipped at it slowly, waiting for some of the gas to bubble off, and looked out at the tenebrous desert, trying not to think about anything at all.

It was nearly two o'clock. The Sunset Limited was due into Los Angeles at 7:35 A.M., Pacific Daylight Time. I never heard from Chuck.

8 On Wheels in L.A.

I awoke in the suburbs of Los Angeles. My coach was awake before me, in ferment with the preparations of early risers. The Amtrak car attendant was stripping linen from the beds of those departing passengers who were up and dressed, serving coffee to those of us still struggling toward consciousness, and hustling to ready the coach for another run. As we rumbled alongside the San Bernardino Freeway into Los Angeles, I sat in my compartment, drinking coffee and watching the Friday morning traffic. Nothing could have impressed on me more the privileged pace I had enjoyed aboard.

Eager as I was to see Los Angeles, I was in no hurry to leave the well-ordered cocoon of my compartment. In thirty-six hours of habitation I had constructed my own caddis case, stuffing clothes and belongings into every crevice and molding the steel and glass planes of my compartment into a soft, enveloping environment where everything I needed resided in its own niche, within an arm's reach. I postponed the reluctant task of disassembling my cocoon until we were well into the city, and then hurried through my last-minute preparations. Busy at them, I hardly noticed our approach as we pulled into Los Angeles Union Station.

In Los Angeles, autonomy means an automobile, so from a pay telephone in the station, I called several car rental agencies and found a used car lot that would rent me a wreck for $14.95 a day, unlimited mileage. A dilapidated car would entail a few inconveniences, but I knew they would be problems I could walk away from at the end of the day. Most problems are bearable if they cannot follow you home. At that price, no pickup, indeed no amenities at all, were included, so I would have to make my own way from the station to the lot on South Figueroa. I stowed my bags in a locker and walked through the main hall of the station out into the bright sunlight. I crossed the grassy square in front of the station, where a few homeless men slumbered through the morning on makeshift cardboard and newspaper pallets, to Olvera Street, where I watched tourists milling around peddlars' stalls hung with brightly colored Mexican trinkets.

Olvera Street is the bazaar, the midway of shops, restaurants, and taco stands, at the heart of El Pueblo de Los Angeles State Historic Park, the historic plaza on the site where the city was founded. The plaza is within a stone's throw of the front drive of the railroad station, which sits squarely on the route of El Camino Real, the eighteenth-century road that connected the Spanish missions along the California coast. Each mission was one day's horseback ride from the next, and Los Angeles was founded where El Camino Real crossed the Los Angeles River midway between Mission San Gabriel Arcángel and Mission San Fernando Rey de España.

Bright plastic pennants hung from cables over the swayback steeds of the used car lot, glittering garishly in the sun. A friendly man in his fifties sat at a metal desk beneath a masonite wallboard where dozens of automobile keys hung on hooks, like room keys behind the front desk of a cheap hotel.

Out on the lot, I found a 1970 Plymouth with a yawning portal where the radiator grill had been stripped away, door locks that had been jimmied once too often and would no longer take a key, a sprung hood, and a gaping hole in the dashboard where the radio had been. Before I made two blocks, the hood lifted six inches, the brakes were squealing, and the valves were knocking. But I was on wheels in L.A.

I had no plan, no appointments, no destination—only a tank full of gas, a map of the city, and an inclination to see as much of it through my windshield as a long day would allow. I retrieved my camera bag from the station locker and packed a toilet kit, a pair of gym shorts, and a change of clothes in a small duffel bag I could easily carry. With a street map, purchased at the station, in one hand and the wheel in the other, I bumbled my way through the city, in no particular hurry, with no particular place to go. I cruised out Sunset Boulevard past Silver Lake Reservoir, with the hills away to the right, the Hollywood Hills sign almost obscured by smog in the distance, and a light tang of oxides in the air.

Soon I found myself on Hollywood Boulevard, driving past the Capitol Records tower, the Frederick's of Hollywood building (a fittingly outrageous purple), block after block of shops and eateries, and then the financial district: Merrill Lynch, Security Bank, glass-facade buildings owned by banks with Japanese names that flashed by too quickly for me to remember. Past the Plaza Suite Hotel and the Regency Hotel, the neighborhood suddenly became noticeably pricier, and then I was on Laurel Canyon Boulevard, climbing into the hills.

Up steep, twisting streets I climbed, mashing the gas pedal and pouring fuel into the fat V-8 engine of my Plymouth, to eventual effect. On abrupt slopes, I could hear the valves knocking, that metallic clatter that sounds like someone playing the spoons on the valve cover, but I knew it wasn't fatal, and, given enough gasoline, the V-8 eventually created some torque and picked up speed, lifting me into the hills. I began to notice automobiles as much as houses or hills or flora: the red Mercedes sports car behind me, the repainted blue '63 Valiant station wagon parked on a side street, the vintage Corvette half covered by a tarp in a pebbled driveway. Passing Mulholland Drive, still on Laurel Canyon Boulevard, I crested the hills and began to descend toward Ventura Boulevard, and the neighborhoods lost distinction as they lost altitude.

At Coldwater Canyon Park, I got out and walked along a winding nature trail through the hills, following the dusty footprints of joggers—chevrons, ripples, and waffles—intermingled with occasional canine paw prints. At the crest of the trail I stopped and looked over a vista of the Hollywood hills, where modest bungalows and impressive haciendas clung to improbable perches on the hillsides. The parched hills, dotted with wiry stunted trees, looked like Spain or Italy, and every peak where houses stood seemed to be a dusty acropolis. Far across a canyon I watched a hawk circle on a thermal and heard its screeching call.

Driving down out of the hills on Coldwater Canyon Drive, I passed Lago Vista Drive, Linda Crest Drive, Loma Linda Drive—and suddenly realized that I was in Beverly Hills. Through Will Rogers Memorial Park and on south on Beverly Drive, I drove past painstakingly manicured homes set behind masonry walls. The traffic flowing around me was higher priced—Mercedes, Porsches, BMWs—but I still saw an occasional Dodge Dart or Chevy Impala parked at the curb. Still, I felt conspicuous, even suspect, in my rusting Plymouth. I turned west on Santa Monica Boulevard and then north again on Rodeo Drive.

At the next red light, a woman pulled abreast on my right in a Jaguar sedan and even with her windows closed I could hear the radio blaring. Her left hand, dangling several pounds of silver jewelry, was on the wheel and her sunglasses were framed in heavy silver. As the traffic flowed past us through the intersection, she nervously daubed on lipstick, staring straight ahead and jabbing at her lips. When the light changed, she spun her steering wheel and whipped a left turn across my bow, never looking at me. I had the feeling I had encountered some unwritten but presumed rule of right-of-way, by which workboats under power are expected to yield to yachts under sail.

Back at Will Rogers Park I turned west again on Sunset Boulevard. At Monument, an ambulance came up behind me and I pulled to the curb behind a white Jaguar and a T-roof Porsche. A few blocks farther on the neighborhood was more commercial. I thought I was still on Sunset Boulevard, but I was no longer certain. Then, around a right turn, I looked ahead, past gas stations, apartment buildings, stop lights, stop signs, and overhead wires, and there, across the Coast Highway, was the Pacific Ocean. It was my first glimpse of that other American sea.

I turned right on the highway and headed north, up the coast through Malibu. A couple of old buses, converted into living quarters and decorated in the warpaint of the sixties, magic buses of the counterculture now replaced through most of their range by Turbo Saabs and BMWs, were parked on the shoulder of the highway. California was one of only a few places in the United States where the sixties actually happened before 1970. Through Malibu, the Pacific Coast Highway was a lot like beach boulevards everywhere, showing motorists the behinds of beach houses built to face the ocean and the faces of opportunistic businesses—and very little of the ocean.

At Malibu Lagoon State Beach, a flock of surfers were making the best of very tame surf. Past Pepperdine University I crested a hill and picked up some speed, and the hood billowed as air flowed under it.

Only the safety catch kept it from flying open and creating a situation with immediate implications. The Coast Highway had bent slightly inland, and now gates barred the drives departing to the west toward the ocean. I was contemplating turning back toward the city when I drove over another hill and was transfixed by the sun over the ocean, the highlights dancing on the water. So I kept on. A mile or two farther on, I turned east on a canyon road and drove up into the hills, climbing between steep cliffs with the sun and the Pacific Ocean at my back.

Up in the hills, I turned onto a dirt road and drove until I was certain I had left all the traffic behind. I pulled the Plymouth onto the shoulder and climbed up the bank of a ravine a few hundred feet and sat in the grass, listening to the birds chattering and the dry brittle sounds of insects active in the last moments of the afternoon. While I sat looking down into the ravine and over to the high peaks beyond, the sun slipped below the crest behind me and, as my ravine fell into shadow, the birds stopped calling and the jackrabbits began to move in the grass, making quick dry rustling sounds like wire brushes on a drum head. The afternoon's sweat began to cool in my shirt and the feeling, like ice water on my back, began to chill me.

It had been an aimless spin through the city that had brought me to these hills, but I was satisfied. Train travel brings a certain kind of intimacy with the countryside, as the tracks curve away from the highway and its accumulated clutter and slice directly into the American landscape, but it brings as well a certain insularity. In New Orleans, by bicycle, and here again in L.A., I had needed to bumble about a bit and rub my nose in the city.

Driving down out of the hills, I saw the Coast Highway far below me, winding down the shoreline toward the city. The twilight was fading fast now and the last glimmers of skylight caught white stucco houses on the cliffs below, showing them pink, illuminated as if from within like paper lanterns, just as the ocean and the sky turned deep purple. The moon that had seemed to be in the east over the hills a moment before now seemed to hang over Los Angeles to the south. The breakers gave off a phosphorescent glow as they tumbled on the beach. The horizon was a gun-blue smudge at the end of the ocean.

I turned onto the Pacific Coast Highway and drove toward the city. Cars crowded the parking lots of restaurants along the shore: Jeffrey's, the Chart House, the Breakers, the Jetty, and a host of others. It was Friday night. A few lonely cars remained in the beach parking lots, with their taillights glowing in the dark and their engines idling, facing the ocean like cars lingering at a drive-in movie after the feature has ended.

I returned the Plymouth the following noon, with 307 more miles on its clock. Back on foot, I started walking north on Figueroa, planning to catch a bus back to the vicinity of Union Station and spend my last few hours in the city strolling through the neighborhoods nearby.

After a few blocks I had not seen a bus stop, so I stopped at a McDonald's to have a cup of coffee and ask about bus routes. I never eat at a fast-food franchise without a sense of cultural guilt as I watch tradition evolved over generations give way to sham. The po'boy, the hero, the hoagie, and the grinder are supplanted by a sandwich drafted by a committee of admen who make it uniform, package it to travel, and market it by creating through advertising a national culture that sweeps away the local, the traditional, the idiomatic. What is lost? Only the gene pool, the diversity of good and bad, successful and unsuccessful—the fruits of evolution and the wisdom of past experience. Franchise food drives out the source of its own inspiration. Nutritionists tell me that ethnic foods are among the last traditions relinquished in the process of assimilation. It is easier to teach a man a new language, invest him with new ambitions, and accustom him to new dwellings, a strange climate, and different clothes than it is to change his eating habits. When you have done that, you have erased the culture he was born with.

There at McDonald's on South Figueroa, sipping my coffee, I watched the process at work. The customers were almost all young: black, white, Hispanic, and Asian, with enough polyglot blends to fuel the hopes of one-world utopians and the paranoia of race purists. On the wall was a poster: McDonald's Celebrates National Hispanic Heritage Week 1984—Compartiendo la Riqueza Nuestra Cultura.

A young woman, sitting cross-legged on the marble floor, with a tackle box full of art supplies at her knee and a pad resting on her thigh, was sketching the hall of Union Station. Sun streamed in slanting shafts through the tall doorways beside her. Dust, riding invisible zephyrs, drifted slowly into the sunlight, sparkled, and then drifted again into shadow. Soft yellow light from the great hanging chandeliers blended with the sunlight from the doorways and high arched windows and burnished the wood and tile with its glow. Even on such a sunny day, the hall was quiet and cool, like a limestone cave. I could hear the murmur, like a faint bubbling spring, of an old couple exchanging confidences and laughing softly together as she gently and idly rubbed his arm, and through the archway I could hear the click of heels on the floor tiles in the main hall. A few pigeons waddled about, pecking at cigarette stubs.

It is an impressive building, inheritor of a tradition. Railroad stations of the Southwest were important architectural landmarks. In the late nineteenth and early twentieth centuries, as the eastern United States was rediscovering its colonial heritage in various Georgian-inspired Colonial Revival building styles, the depots built by the Santa Fe and Southern Pacific railroads in the Southwest evoked the much different colonial past of that region in freely adapted models of early Spanish missions. At a time when the railroad was central to the life of those western cities, the stations became civic monuments to a common cultural heritage, and the Mission building style spread to other public buildings and domestic residences.

The construction of the San Diego depot for the Panama-California Exposition in 1915 broadened the definition of Spanish-inspired design, as architects began to look beyond the traditional Mission styles and to plumb the richness of Spanish architecture found in the Old World as well as the new. They looked for inspiration to Spanish buildings throughout Latin America and even to Spain itself, where Moorish and other exotic influences colored building design. The Los Angeles station, built in 1939 by the Union Pacific, Southern Pacific, and Santa Fe railroads, is the further expression of their work, which came to be called Spanish Colonial Revival, or Spanish Eclectic. It shares with the earlier Mission depots the red tile roof, the square tower, and the stucco walls, but the exotic lines of its tower roof, its elaborate decorative tile work, the round arches of its doorways, and its lack of the traditional Mission parapet, quatrefoil windows, and widely overhanging eaves distinguish it as a landmark of the newer style: at once freer, in the sense that it ventures beyond the uniform design of southwestern Spanish missions, and more traditional in that it looks back to the Spanish source for authentic details.

Scheduled trains were listed on a beautiful wood and brass toteboard, white letters on a black felt background behind glass. Fifteen arrivals and departures were listed, and five of those were trains that did not run every day. My train, the Southwest Limited, would be the twelfth and last train to depart Los Angeles Union Station that Saturday. Any major airport would dispatch more planes in a half hour.

The small gift shop just off the main concourse of the station featured a wonderland of railroadiana. Racks of postcards, an entire wall, carried photographs of trains: the Pueblo, the Mexico City train, No. 109, of the National Railways of Mexico, part of the national narrow-gauge system, photographed in the 1960s; the Norfolk and Western Powhatan Arrow photographed near Singer, Virginia, in December 1949; the Algoma Central Railway excursion train near Sault Ste. Marie, Ontario; a Santa Fe freight on Topock Bridge near Needles, California, in 1964; a Boston and Maine 1495 2-6-0 Mogul steam engine photographed near Fitchburg, Massachusetts, in 1955; No. 163 of the Bath and Hammondsport Railroad. There were hundreds of others. One could not but notice that very few of the photographs were of recent vintage; most dated from the forties and fifties or early sixties. The lithography was dated; the colors were soft and rosy like faded chintz or dried flowers. It might have been a private collection, hidden away in an attic for a generation.

Beside the photographs were more than 450 embroidered patches representing nearly that many railroads, and these were bright and bold: the orange and black insignia of the Fishing Line/Grand Rapids and Indiana Railroad; the brown and white of the Sandy River and Rangeley Lakes Railroad of Maine; the orange and black of the Colorado Midland Railway/Pikes Peak Route; the Rock Island; the Wabash Line; the Western Pacific; the Burlington Northern; the Rio Grande/ Main Line into the Rockies; the Spokane Portland Seattle; the Western and Atlantic; the Western Maryland; the Wilmington and Western; the Western Pacific; the Yreka Western; the American Short Line Railroad Association; the Birmingham Southern Railroad; the Atlantic and Danville; the Wisconsin Electric Lines; the Virginian; the Tidewater Southern; the Texas Mexican; the Uintah Railway Co.; the Virginia Truckee; the Texas and Pacific; the Toledo, Ann Arbor and North Michigan; the Strasburg; the Texas Electric; the Tag Route; the S.O.T. Ry. Co./Corn Belt Market; Soo Line; the Georgia, Clinchfield, West Point Route; the Shawmut; the Sabine River and Northern; the South Shore Line; the Sacramento Northern through the Sacramento Valley; the Rutland/Green Mountain Gateway; the Pittsburgh and West Virginia; the Northwestern Oklahoma Red Carpet Line; the Peoria and Eastern; the Midland Route; the Milwaukee Road; the New York, New Haven, and Hartford; the Nevada California Oregon/Sierra Nevada Route; the Rio Grande Western Route; the Mobile and Ohio; the Penn Central; the Reading Lines; the Colorado Central; the Colorado and Southern/"The Colorado Road"; the Bessemer Central Railroad of Georgia; the Duluth, Missabe & Northern/ Nickel Plate Road; the Rio Grande Southern/Galloping Goose Railroad; the Katy. The glorious idiomatic plurality of American railroading as it once was.

I bought a patch of the Fishing Line, the Grand Rapids and Indiana Railroad, for a friend and one for myself; I bought a patch of the Pullman Company in the shape of a sleeping car, with the legend "Travel and Sleep in Comfort—Pullman" in yellow letters across the coach; and I bought a patch of the Canadian National Railway, which has a beaver on its crest, for a friend who considers the beaver something of a talisman for hope.

Part Two

Los Angeles
Barstow
Needles
Flagstaff
Albuquerque
Lamy
Las Vegas
Raton
Hutchinson
Kansas City
Galesburg
Omaha
Denver
Winter Park
Glenwood Springs
Grand Junction
Provo
Salt Lake City
Sparks
Reno
Truckee
Sacramento
Oakland

Piercing

the

Heartland

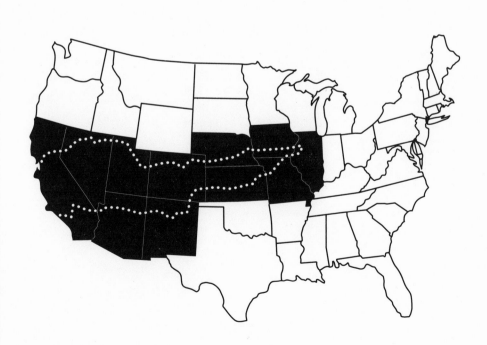

9 The Southwest Limited to Flagstaff: A Walk to the Edge

I suppose the reader has some notion of an American railroad-car, that long, narrow wooden box, like a flat-roofed Noah's ark, with a stove and a convenience, one at either end, a passage down the middle, and transverse benches upon either hand.

—Robert Louis Stevenson, who took a train west to San Francisco in 1879, in *Across the Plains*, 1892

ack in coach. The air-conditioning didn't work. The seat was lumpy. The footrest balked. My pipe was unwelcome. After two luxurious legs in a sleeping compartment, I was facing another overnight in a coach and wondering if I would literally have to sweat it out. The long walk through the tunnel and along the platform to my car had left me agitated and hot. Boarding passengers crowded the aisles, jockeying for seats and stowing their bags in the overhead racks, and I sat at a slow simmer, feeling the heat prickle my neck and the sweat bead on the backs of my hands. I wriggled out of my corduroy jacket, my all-purpose overgarment that had been too thick for El Paso and Los Angeles and would be too thin for Montana and Minnesota but had plenty of pockets and the great virtue of appearing equally disreputable in any climate. As the coach filled, the air warmed and closed in. Passengers muttered: "Isn't it stuffy in here?" "It's just awful." "It'll cool down when we get going."

When I saw a couple of grim-faced maintenance men in overalls come up the stairs to see the conductor, I had my doubts.

The conductor was impatient. "We can't hold this thing up much longer."

"Unless we can get that compressor moving again, it's gonna be a steam bath in here by the time you get to Barstow."

"Well, damn it, what do you want me to do about it? We can't wait."

"Give me just a minute," one of the maintenance men said. "I've got one more idea." He disappeared and the conductor stood and waited, looking at his watch every few seconds and trying not to notice the grumpy passengers all around him. I asked the other mechanic what the trouble was.

"The compressor's frozen. We tried everything. Don't have time to pull it, though. Might be a hot ride. Hope you're not going far."

A moment later the first maintenance man reappeared, smiling. "I think she'll go now."

With that, the conductor started up the aisle, saying, "We're out of here."

The two mechanics turned and started down the stairs to leave the coach. I asked the one who had fixed the balky compressor, "How'd you do it?" He grinned and said, "The Idiot Wrench," and held up a can of WD-40—the salvation of shade-tree mechanics everywhere. By the time we left the station it was perceptibly cooler.

Since I was going only as far as Flagstaff, a relatively short hop on the 2,200-mile run of the Southwest Limited from Los Angeles to Chicago, I was riding in the local coach, a Superliner coach but a well-worn one, with electrical tape binding tears in a few armrests and the bare steel bones showing through the rubber of well-scuffed footrests. The steward walked down the aisle, handing a polyester pillow to each passenger.

The Southwest Limited traveled over Santa Fe track from Los Angeles to Chicago, following in the path of the Santa Fe Super Chief, a storied American passenger train. Not long after I rode the Southwest Limited, Amtrak was finally able to appropriate the name as well from a reluctant Atchison, Topeka and Santa Fe Railway. Today Amtrak calls its train the Southwest Chief.

In the 1930s the steam-hauled Santa Fe Chief made the 2,223-mile run from Los Angeles to Chicago in less than two days. The Chief is among the most fondly remembered steam trains in the world, recognized for the luxuriance of its service and respected by aficionados of steam power for the sterling performance that the Atchison, Topeka and Santa Fe coaxed from its locomotives on one of the most daunting cross-country routes in the world. Only the most diligent maintenance kept the Santa Fe's oil-burning steam locomotives fit for the job. From Chicago to La Junta, Colorado, a Hudson class 4-6-4 locomotive sped the Chief over the more level half of the route; from La Junta west to Los Angeles a more powerful 4-8-4 locomotive pulled over the western mountains. The diesel-hauled Super Chief began service by 1939, made the run a little faster, and continued the tradition of first-class service, but the Chief continued in service for many years. My 1958 *Railway Guide* showed a thirty-eight-hour and fifteen-minute schedule for the Chief and a thirty-seven-hour and thirty-minute schedule for the Super Chief. Today the Amtrak schedule allows thirty-nine hours and fifteen minutes.

In the evening darkness we climbed steadily from the floor of the Los Angeles basin to the summit of Cajon Pass, the gap between the San Gabriel and San Bernardino mountains. This is one of the most celebrated stretches of track in the entire Santa Fe system. Between San Bernardino and the summit of the pass at 3,822 feet above sea level, the tracks ascend in two and three percent grades, climbing more than half a mile in twenty-five miles of travel. Just before midnight we arrived in Barstow, California, a railroad town named for William Barstow Strong, general manager and president of the railroad in the late 1800s. Now Barstow is the site of a mammoth marshaling yard where freight traffic from the east is made up into trains headed for San Diego, Los Angeles, and San Francisco, and eastbound traffic from the various points of origin in California is reassembled in block trains for the trip to Kansas City and points east.

At Barstow, I stepped down from the coach to breathe some fresh air while the crews changed. Next to the station, just opposite our coach, which was near the end of the train, was an old hotel, now in disrepair, that was once a Harvey House. Frederick H. Harvey opened his first lunchroom on the Santa Fe line at Topeka in 1876. It was so successful and its reputation for good food, a rare commodity on the frontier, so quick to spread that one reporter facetiously suggested that it might halt the westward migration and that it was "absolutely necessary for the Santa Fe to open similar houses at other points that the West might not be settled in just one spot." William Strong agreed and directed the Santa Fe to strike a bargain with Fred Harvey: the Santa Fe leased buildings, or in many cases, portions of its stations, to Harvey and gave him essentially exclusive rights to serve its patrons.

Harvey Houses were widely regarded as a civilizing influence, known for their cleanliness, reliably good service, and the Harvey Girls—"young women of good character, attractive and intelligent, 18 to 30"—who staffed them. Harvey had a firm rule that no customer without a coat would be served in a Harvey House, and each dining room was stocked with a supply of alpaca coats to lend to travelers who arrived in shirtsleeves.

In 1888 Fred Harvey put his restaurants on Santa Fe wheels. The first dinner menu on his dining cars (reproduced in *Steel Trails to Santa Fe*, a 1950 history of the Santa Fe Railroad) read like this: "Little Neck Clams on Shell; Consomme Printaniere Royale; Fillets of Sole, Tartar Sauce; Sliced Cucumbers; Pommes Persillade; Boiled Westphalia Ham with Spinach; Roast Beef; Spring Lamb, Mint Sauce; Young Turkey, Cranberry Sauce; New Asparagus on Toast; Mashed Potatoes; New Potatoes in Cream; New Green Peas; Fillet of Beef with Mushrooms; Sweetbreads Braized, Jardiniere; Spanish Puffs, Strawberry Sauce; Punch Benedictine; Broiled Plover on Toast; Sliced Tomatoes, Mayonnaise; Chicken Salad, Lettuce; Apple Pie; Pieplant Pie; Sago Pudding, Brandy Sauce; Strawberries and Cream; Assorted Cake; Vanilla Ice Cream; Edam and Roquefort Cheese; Bent's Water Crackers; French Coffee—Meals 75 Cents."

Long after his death in 1901, the name Fred Harvey continued its association with the Santa Fe and the Chief. My 1958 *Railway Guide* describes the Santa Fe train No. 17 thusly: "The Super Chief: *Completely Air-Conditioned Lightweight Streamlined Extra Fare Train* —boasts 'Fred Harvey service' in the Dining Car."

No one boarded our coach, so the attendant and I stood on the platform and talked. He was young, thin, and nervous. In his dark blue Amtrak-issue winter coat he reminded me of a rookie cop standing a street-corner beat on a chilly November night.

"Just behind ya," he said, "they got a big switching yard, a big

Santa Fe–Espee switching yard. All they move out there is just freight, only thing that's showin' a profit these days. The crews that get on and off here—lot of these guys would just as soon still be workin' freight. Rather be haulin' cabbages than people. Some of 'em figure it's about the same thing."

Between Barstow and Flagstaff lie 400 miles of brutally taxing track. The route first crosses the Mojave Desert to Needles, California, then climbs more than 6,000 feet in about 220 miles to the Arizona Divide. This is arid country, and in the days of steam power the Santa Fe had to haul water in by tank car to slake the thirst of its hardworking steam locomotives on this grinding ascent. As many as three million gallons a day were required at one point alone—the Achilles heel of the steam locomotives on this line. In the early 1940s the Santa Fe became the first railroad to replace steam power with diesel-electric locomotives on an overland freight route when it put diesels in service on this stretch.

I slept through it all, the Mojave Desert and the steep ascent to the Arizona Divide. Exhaustion had dulled my curiosity. I dreaded the miles lying ahead of me, miles I had studiously avoided counting. The distance itself was enervating. Layovers and detours that seemed so full of promise when I felt some mettle seemed only obstacles when I was tired. I really didn't know why I was stopping at Flagstaff. Sometime back in the summer, running my finger over a map and running my eye down an Amtrak timetable in my kitchen, it had seemed like a good idea. I had never been there and the train went there, and that was enough.

I awoke just at first light. I was cold, and my joints ached from tensing against the chill all night. The coach was still dark, its lights dim. In their faint glow I could see an occasional foot dangling in the aisle where a passenger slopped over his seat in a sound sleep. No one was moving about. No one had broken the compact of overnight coach passengers, the mutual pretense that our night passage is private, not communal. In my window, the landscape was just taking shape, emerging out of black into silhouette. Faint light, just that breath of pre-dawn glow in the sky that is the insinuation of morning, revealed mountains. For a moment, the mountains clashed with my last memories of the night before, Barstow on the edge of the Mojave; then my mind reeled in the miles and washed the confusion away, and I knew where I was and how I got there.

The mountains emerged first as a jagged horizon in the distance. With more light they showed sawteeth, the sharp peaks of pines. We were moving slowly, climbing gently on winding track. When the sun rose above the horizon, it burst through groves of pines, probably Ponderosa pines, on the mountainside around us. The trees scattered the light into beams, and patches of ground fog softened it around the edges like lantern light in a mist. On the slope, pines grew in pure stands on a bed of green and buckskin grasses. At first the light was too faint to penetrate into the coach. For a few minutes, it was as if I were alone in a dark room watching the day break.

My breath frosted as I disembarked in Flagstaff. The morning milkiness was clearing from the sky. By the time I had my suitcase and my bearings, the train was gone and I was alone. It was Sunday morning. I had twenty-four hours in Flagstaff. Monday morning at 6:50 the Southwest Limited would come through again and I would be on it, headed back east.

Outside the Flagstaff station, the morning sun was shining down Leroux Street toward the mountains. The stone building facades, colored by the salmon hue of the early sun, looked like rimrock. No one was going to work; it was Sunday morning. I walked for quite a while, warming myself and stepping out the overnight kinks. A little before eight a ramshackle pickup truck pulled up in front of the Weatherford Hotel, and a lanky young man got out and unlocked the front door. I watched from across the street as he turned on the lights and began to sweep up. At eight I was the first customer for breakfast.

I sat next to a window that faced east toward the street so the morning sun flooded my table. A fire burning on the hearth behind me warmed my back. The small, high-ceilinged dining room was furnished with antiques—ornately gilded mirrors, a vintage potbellied stove, and a hulk of a rusty safe still bearing the mark "Beard & Bro. Safe and Lock Co., St. Louis." The three young women who seemed to be the proprietors radiated a ruddy sort of health and well-being that I envied in my cranky and grimy state. I was expecting diner fare: steak and potatoes with plenty of grease. Instead I was served cinnamon and buttermilk pancakes with real butter, with peaches and crème fraîche on the side, followed by slices of orange and melon. The coffee came with a ceramic pitcher of real cream, and the background music was Vivaldi. Even as I enjoyed the meal and the music, I wondered why, given that we are to have classical music, it is invariably Baroque with breakfast?

My only ambition for the day was to see some of the country and to make my way to the Grand Canyon, eighty or so miles north. After breakfast I went upstairs to the youth hostel on the second floor of the hotel. Whatever inclination to hitchhike I might have had was quashed by a newspaper clipping pinned to the bulletin board that told what little was known about the last days of a teenager who had set out from his home in the Midwest to see the country and was last seen hitchhiking from Flagstaff to the Grand Canyon. The local law enforcement officer was quoted, speculating: "Looked like he'd been beaten to death. All I can figure is they killed him for his sleeping bag."

So I walked back to the station and called several car rental agencies. On my last try I found someone who would rent me a new Toyota for thirty-four dollars, unlimited mileage, and even offered to pick me up and to let me leave the car at the station Monday morning. She picked me up in front of the station in a van, gave me a map of Flagstaff and the surrounding country, and in a few minutes I was on my way. I stopped at the Weatherford and arranged for a hostel bed for the night and then headed out of town.

I drove south on Route 89-A, thinking I would take a quick run down south through Oak Creek Canyon, be back in Flagstaff for a late lunch, and be on my way north to the Grand Canyon before the sun crested. On the way out of Flagstaff, I drove past a motel and noticed "No Trains" on its marquee. For a moment I was puzzled, and then I remembered that there are those who do not hear music in the sound of a heavy freight.

Fifteen miles south I entered the Coconino National Forest. Maples were beginning to turn, and the sun shining through the pines on the grass of an alpine meadow looked warm and welcoming. Around another turn I stopped on the shoulder of the highway; below I could see the road snake down through several switchbacks out of the forested valley into Oak Creek Canyon. At my feet were low-growing purple wildflowers, configured like the common daisies of my North Carolina roadsides, but with violet petals surrounding a yellow disk.

In a few miles, I was swinging through gentle curves beneath the tall pines, following the crooked path of the creek's headwaters. There had been only a few scattered cumulus clouds when I set out and now they were getting scarce, leaving a pellucid sky. Everything seemed warm and clean, and I was beginning to feel detoxified by the fresh air.

At one point, I pulled the Toyota off the asphalt onto a bed of pine needles and walked the few steps to the creek. I sat for a few minutes on a small boulder and peered into the clear water looking for trout. Watching for small, quick trout in a clear mountain stream requires total concentration wedded to total relaxation. If your attention wanders, you've missed the telltale movement; if your vision fixes into a stare, the dance of the light and the music of the water will hypnotize you. In thin, clear waters, small trout flit from hiding place to hiding place faster than one believes possible. The natural impulse is to dismiss their movement as a glimmer of light. They can be distinguished only if one knows where to look and how they behave. I first notice a small trout not as a visceral creature but as a shadow in clear water or a ripple that moves against the flow, an otherwise unexplainable flash of light or bit of shadow or disturbance of the surface—a slight defect in the pattern of light and water. I combed through the grasses along the creek for a hopper to toss in the water, thinking that no trout, no matter how skittish, could resist showing itself for a wriggling, autumn terrestial, but I couldn't find one.

I stopped at a small general store and bought a six-pack of beer from an attractive dark-haired woman who sat behind the counter stroking a cat; she told me that a lot of people fished the creek. A few bends down the road, however, I stopped at another little store, with a couple of gas pumps in front and some rustic cabins out behind, and the crusty little man inside was less enthusiastic. "Used to be worth fishing," he snorted, "before things got out of hand. This time of year? I wouldn't bother, myself."

So I kept driving, my guilty secret still tucked away in my suitcase. There, in a cloth bag, tucked into the folds of my sport coat, I was carrying a pack rod, an old five-piece Eagle Claw fly rod that had been my very first and still went everywhere I might possibly find a use for it. Fifteen years before, I had paid twenty dollars for it one evening at L. L. Bean in Freeport, Maine. I still remember the tackle salesman trying to persuade me to spend another ten dollars for the Fenwick, which was clearly a much better rod in ways that I can now appreciate, but thirty dollars was a frightening sum to me in those days and I still had to buy a line and a reel and a few flies.

I had taught myself the art of fly-fishing in the bowels of the university library. All that winter, when I should have been researching my history papers, I had been coming home from the library with musty old tomes on fly-fishing. There was only this problem: the books I found there were yellowing copies of nineteenth-century classics. I learned how to care for a bamboo rod, how to dress a silk line, how to dry it and powder it and coil it carefully away after every use. I learned how to tie horsehair leaders and how to recognize the classic Theodore Gordon fly patterns. My authors wrote of a world before glass rods, nylon lines, and knotless leaders. My knowledge was not only archaic, but entirely bookish. I put myself in much the same spot as the scholar who fell in love with a society lady and, determined to impress her, set out to learn how to ride. In his thorough and erudite way, he retreated to his study where he read volumes on horse conformation, breeding, and care and on riding styles and techniques. Finally, satisfied that no one could know more than he, off he went with his lady friend for a ride, and within twenty paces he tumbled from his mount. Unshaken, he picked himself up and prepared to remount, saying only, "The horse made a mistake." When I ventured out of the library and into the stream, the trout made one mistake after another with me, and, frankly, every now and then they still seem a little unsure of themselves.

Farther down the canyon where the creek was wider and cut deeper, I stopped again to sit among the willows and cottonwoods along its banks. When I returned to my car, I found a big pickup with a camper on its bed parked nearby. A big, pleasant woman with an implacable face was sitting quietly in the front seat, and her husband was standing beside the truck, drinking a can of beer and looking up at the canyon walls. He introduced himself as Manuel. I fetched one of my fast-warming beers from the floor of my car, leaned on the front quarter panel of his truck, and drank it while we talked.

"We came over from Colorado in 1936," he said. "It's hard to believe how many people have come along since then. We live over in Mesa, but as often as we can we like to come back out here and camp. This is what we loved about it fifty years ago."

I told him I was driving on down through Sedona, and he scratched the rim of his beer can along his cheek and looked at me for a moment and said, "There's an old road down that way. I found it once." He looked in the cab at his wife and spoke her name. "Do you remember that road, up in the redrock?" She smiled and nodded her head slowly but didn't say anything. He looked back at me. "We took it once, it must have been 1966, before we had this truck. I haven't been able to find it since then, though. It's a dirt road, a turnoff not but a ways out of Sedona, that runs right up into the redrock. It'll take you right up high. Like a hawk."

I drove on down out of the canyon to the town of Sedona, where automobiles were parked door-to-door in front of the Olde English Shoppe, the Red Duck Pottery, the Toy Castle, Yoghurt and More, the Matterhorn Motor Lodge, the Pizza Vendor, Chez Croissant, and the Arrowhead Trading Post. Signs in front of the real estate offices advertised time-sharing deals. In Sedona, at the mouth of the canyon where spectacular sandstone cliffs widened out into a rich earthen palette of scattered buttes and gullies, families hurried from one store window to the next.

I slowed just enough to look at my map and turned left out of town. I found a dirt road that climbed back into the redrock, winding and climbing up the canyon wall. I had driven only a few hundred cautious yards up the road when a tow truck careered past me, suggesting that somewhere up ahead the road asked to be taken seriously. But the surface, even though it was rocky and rutted, seemed dry and substantially stable, and, taken slowly, my little Toyota bumped along with a sure gait. Several times, I stopped in the road —there was no shoulder to speak of, the uphill side of the road edging into the rock and the downhill side crumbling into air—and photographed the wide vista to the south, where the canyon opened into a broad dry plain relieved by dramatic rimrock ramparts. Bright yellow flowers bloomed next to clumps of prickly pear in the valley, the slopes were dotted with dark green shrubs, and the redrock monuments above jutted up sharply in fantastic shapes. It was a setting for a John Ford western: grand and pitiless. If only they still made westerns.

The road snaked higher and higher into the rimrock. My tires crunched the gravel with a sound like a coffee grinder and stones came spitting like watermelon seeds from under the front tires to ping the oil pan. The grade was steep at the last. My head fell back against the headrest in the little car and my knees seemed to be up in front of my face. Watching the valley out to my left and the road in front of me, I saw the sky grow larger and wider and the roadway ahead shorter and shorter. Around the last switchback, the road foreshortened and then crested in front of me and clouds rose off the gravel like puffs of steam. It looked as though I was set to drive over the edge straight into the lacquered sky. Ahead, the road curved around the edge of the cliff and disappeared, and where there had been roadbed there was only empty air and miles of valley.

From that vista the road turned away from the canyon and entered a grove of scrubby Ponderosa pines. Back in the hills, back from the desiccation of the rimrock, wildflowers grew among sunlit grasses. Farther along, the road entered a shady pine forest that occasionally opened into high mountain meadows—shallow basins of soft grasses ringed by tall pines. This was posted land. In a grove of pines on the edge of a wide meadow, there was a large rustic ranch house, a barn, and a corral, a spread that, had it been for sale, I would have bought on the spot and sat happily on a fence rail until my check bounced. I've always had a weakness for alpine meadows.

I emerged on the interstate highway south of Flagstaff and drove north at freeway speed, blowing off the worst of the dust. I bored through Flagstaff and came out the other end, headed north on Route 89 toward Sunset Crater National Monument and, ultimately, the Grand Canyon. I drove fast. The afternoon was already well along, and I estimated the loop that would take me along the South Rim of the Grand Canyon and back to Flagstaff at nearly two hundred miles.

By the time I turned off the highway onto the entrance road at Sunset Crater, the shadows were lengthening, the air was cooling, and I was consciously hurrying. Around a bend in the road the pine trees gave way to a black desert. It was as if someone had opened a coal chute in the sky and poured unimaginable tons of lump coal over the ground as far as I could see. These were volcanic cinders, black brittle ash coughed up like phlegm some eight hundred years before by expectorant forces at work below ground. The volcanic cones were visible in the distance: spent mountains with their tops sheared away and their slopes shrouded by cinders. Wherever a tree or shrub poked through it attained a singular dignity, set off like a marigold in a parking lot.

Walking along a flow where lava had spewed from the base of the crater and cooled into fantastic sharp-edged shapes, I met four German tourists toting walking sticks and binoculars. One of them spoke in German to another, who turned to me and asked, "These wonderful golden trees, what are they?"

"Aspens." I repeated it several times as they all listened and nodded. I walked with them back to the road as they described their itinerary to me, all the places they had been, beginning on the East Coast and making their way across the country.

I thought about their trip as I drove on, wondering if this extraordinary country might strike a European as a trifle preposterous, when I drove over a gentle rise and emerged from the volcanic debris into a vista that made me stand on my brakes in the middle of the highway. Ahead, at the far end of a sloping view that stretched dozens of miles, out to the limits of atmospheric transparency where the horizon was a long broken smudge of pink, was the Painted Desert. It was as if I had been transported abruptly to some familiar mythical land from a cherished childhood fable. I was actually looking at the variegated hues of sandstone and shale along the crumbled foot of the great Colorado Plateau, which rises over a series of escarpments up through Arizona and Utah along the western edge of the Rocky Mountains into southwestern Wyoming.

As long as I could, I delayed turning on my headlights—thinking about sitting on a porch on a long summer evening and how the world shrivels to a yellow pool of light and circling moths when the lamp comes on—but when the sky was all I could see I relented. I drove on, following my headlight beams through the desert. The temperature was falling fast. Night creatures were coming out. Ruby eyes glowed in the roadway. I bore down on them. They floated there, absorbing my headlamp beams, focusing the light into two defiant coals. I stabbed for the brake pedal, and the red eyes exploded up past my windshield and out of my vision with a hollow rush of air like a vacuum being breached. I thought about turning back, doing the sensible thing. My train left at six-thirty in the morning. The Grand Canyon was still miles away. Why drive three more hours over the desert at night? But somewhere out there on the other side of the horizon, maybe the sun was still shining on the mesas, maybe it was still warm and bright. I drove on.

I turned on the radio for company and found a San Francisco disk jockey, as he pattered along in that chummy voice that passes for friendliness, "That's Herman's Hermits, from 1965 at KNBR Sixty-Eight. In case you haven't heard what happened with the Padres and the, uh, Cubs. Well, I'll tell ya, the Padres won six to three, winning the National League pennant for the first time in their history. And I'll tell ya, I didn't get a chance to watch the game today. I was too busy giving the dog a flea bath, and if you think that was exciting, I tell ya, you haven't lived until . . ."

I spun the dial again: nothing but static. I turned it off and heard an owl calling. I've never been a regular attendant to the baseball rites, but as I traveled alone through the playoffs and the Series, the progress from game to game, from series to series, kept me in touch with the world. Wherever I came to rest, there would be at least something familiar, something ongoing, in the newspaper; there would be something to talk about with strangers.

I saw two red glints in my headlights and braked hard, but I was still traveling at least fifty when something thumped into the grill and pinwheeled in the air behind me into the dark. I stopped and walked back to the point of collision, wondering what I could do for a wounded creature. I found only an old road kill, a potpourri of fur and flesh that might once have been a rabbit and was now a bloody poultice on the asphalt.

I crested a sharp rise and the silhouette of the San Francisco Mountains loomed up in front of me so darkly, blotting out the moonlit sky, that it frightened me like a sudden upheaval of the earth. I could see for miles. Tiny pricks of light glimmered in the distance, and for ten minutes I watched them, swinging first off to my left and then off to my right as I curved with the road and they hung in the desert night as steady as stars. In the last mile, they revealed themselves to be the community of Gray Mountain: a Best Western Motel, a "Food Store" with the "d" missing from its sign, and a house by the side of the road.

A little before eight o'clock I approached the gate of the Grand Canyon National Park. The ranger station was dark and deserted. The sign said "CLOSED," but the gate was open, so I drove on through and proceeded slowly through the woods. In a clearing fifteen feet from the road, two mule deer grazed in the moonlight; they watched me, curious but unconcerned, as I drove past. I turned off at the first overlook. I could not see the canyon; I could only sense it, a looming void almost underfoot. I walked from the car to the low wall at the canyon edge and stepped up on it. The moon was luminous. The only sound was the rustle of a light breeze at my back. The canyon gaped open and the sky, without the counterbalance of earth, spun out of control. Vertigo overcame me. I stepped back. My heart was pounding. I was shivering. I felt ridiculous. That afternoon little children had probably scampered along this wall. I had driven all evening just to stand there on the precipice, and now I was reeling from it. But there was no helping it.

I followed Route 64 west along the South Rim and stopped to spend a few minutes at each of the half dozen or so overlooks along the way, edging as close as I could bring myself to each precipice, climbing whatever fences were meant to keep me away. The drive was beautiful in itself, a slow meander through an evergreen forest of pines and junipers. After driving for miles through the woods, hearing owls and stopping frequently to watch mule deer graze or amble across the road, I was satisfied just to be near the canyon, to have seen the country, to have experienced it quietly at night. I passed the last overlook by; then, swinging the car around in the road, I turned back. There was only a small turnout. I parked and walked over to the retaining wall and stepped over it onto the flat rocks at the edge of the canyon. It was like standing on the parapet of a four-hundred-story building in the dark. I felt the same impulse to shrink back from the gravitational pull of the canyon, but, instead, I took off my wool sweater, folded it, and lay down on the rock with the sweater for a pillow. I lay on my back and looked up at the sky. I could reach out with my hand and feel the edge of an abyss a mile deep. If I had rolled over twice, I would have been gone.

The sky was a shimmering, satiny blue along the northern horizon, a deep velvet overhead. The full moon shining through the clear air was almost too bright to look at; it cast a sheen across the sky that only the brightest stars shone through. An owl called from somewhere along the canyon. Half a minute later, its call was answered. The familiar sounds calmed me. I rolled my head and looked out over the canyon. The moon behind me, shining over the South Rim, illuminated the north wall of the canyon, casting sharp shadows on its folds and crenellations. The canyon was so sharply etched by the bright, full moon and yet so resolutely blue, shades and shadings of blue, that it looked like a scene from an old Technicolor western, shot in the day through deep blue filters to mimic the night, with sharp afternoon shadows pitched in blue giving away the fraud. The river channel was lost in shadow; the moon was still too low in the sky to penetrate to the bottom.

I gradually unwound. I had been traveling alone but always in crowds—on the train, in cities. The sudden solitude on the rim of the canyon was at first too absolute. The feeling was unsettling. I struggled for purchase. Reminded how big the world is and how complex, and how small is our natural role in it, insignificance is not an unreasonable feeling. One might suggest it as the only sane one. To the dilemma of scale, the Grand Canyon adds time, layer upon layer of geological time. Lying on its rim, only a fool could persuade himself that this, now, is all there has ever been or ever will be, and the slightest perspective quickly brings the realization that this, for us, will be over very fast. I tossed a pebble out into the abyss and listened. Not a sound.

10 Santa Fe: Pueblo Silver at Trail's End

The rhythm of the motion, thirty-nine hours from Chicago to Los
Angeles—what a marvel of masculinity, thirty-nine hours, power-
stroking all the way. He gave her the high ball in the Loop, stopped in
Englewood, and that's all she wrote, grinding up to ninety miles per hour,
so hot the steam was bursting out everywhere. She had fine lubrication.
You could hear her for miles, whistle-screaming, "Yes, daddy, I'm
coming, daddy!"

—Duke Ellington, *Music Is My Mistress*

The muffled rumble of a heavy freight train woke me a few
minutes after five the next morning. Out on the street, outside the hotel, the morning air was cold but the bright sun
felt warm on my face and hands. I started the car and let it
idle a couple of minutes to warm the motor even though I
was driving only a few blocks, a habit formed of a lifetime
spent driving old cars. At the Flagstaff station I felt for my
packet of tickets in the inside pocket of my coat, dropped the key on
the floor of the car, and closed the car door for the last time. I piled
my bags on the platform and waited. The sun was rising still higher,
brightening the eastern sky over the desert and grasslands, when the
Southwest Limited, full of sleeping passengers, came curling around
the mountain from the west, out of the night, and rushed into the
station. I boarded there, just at the watershed of night.

At six in the morning, back aboard the same train at the same
station, at the same hour one day later, I had a sense that I had
never disembarked, that my twenty-four hours in Flagstaff had been
a dream, a flicker of the imagination as I slumbered through the
station.

．．．

From Flagstaff, the Santa Fe tracks descend steeply, more than two thousand feet in fifty-eight miles, to Winslow, Arizona, the railroad division point that sits in a trough between the Arizona Divide just west of Flagstaff and the Continental Divide just east of Gallup, New Mexico. The tracks skirt the southern edge of the Painted Desert and the desolate reservations of the Hopi and Navajo Indians that occupy the northeastern quadrant of Arizona. The landscape is dry, brittle, and harsh, entirely different from the alpine character of Flagstaff.

The Southwest Limited was due in Lamy, New Mexico, my next destination, at 2:12 in the afternoon. By the time I made my way to the snack bar on the lower level of the lounge car, the sun was up in the sky and we were moving quickly through dry grasslands, featureless country to my eye. I drank my morning coffee and listened to the conversation between the two other men in the lounge. Every few miles, one of the men—a big, burly man with a neck like a tree stump and hair shaved to a bristle—would interject an observation on the passing country.

"Out there," he said, looking out onto the rangeland. "You've heard 'em talk about the devil's fence posts? Those are old volcanoes. Just the throats, actually. Everything else has washed away. In the twelfth century, Indians first found obsidian for tools and arrowheads in those volcanoes. Changed their civilization."

He was sitting across from me, wearing a shirt with a brown and green camouflage pattern, heavy baggy corduroy pants, and boots. He sat upright and kept his massive arms folded across his chest, and, when he wanted to point something out, he indicated it with his head, nodding almost imperceptibly. He never smiled.

"Out there," he said a few miles farther on, "you can see an old Indian trail." I looked and saw only the faintest crease in the grass.

From their conversation, I learned that he was a freight conductor, deadheading east. He swept his eyes across the grassland. "Antelope season is just over. You should see some antelope along here. We'll see if we can spot some." A few miles later, he unfolded his arms and pointed out to the south with a hand the size of a frying pan. "Look, there. Eight. And over there four more." I twisted in my seat and stared until my eyes watered and all I could see was the gray, brown, and green mottle of the range, as muddled as the camouflage pattern on his shirt. "Look for the white patch. You can see it bounce when they run." I kept my eyes moving and finally saw, at least a mile out, tiny flecks of white in the grass, like flakes of dandruff on a brown lapel. They moved, but I could not have identified them nor even counted them. Later, he pointed out two other small herds and a jet-black bird soaring over the range, "That big black bird, that's a raven. This time of year you'll see eagles migrating through."

I told him about the nocturnal birds that had flushed in front of my car on the road the night before. He told me, with certainty, that they were pygmy owls. Later, in a field guide, I found mention of the ferruginous pygmy owl, a small tropical owl found in the United States only in the desert of southern Arizona and the southern tip of Texas along the Rio Grande. Flagstaff would have been north of its usual range, but I didn't know that at the time. More likely, perhaps, would have been the elf owl, a sparrow-sized nocturnal owl of the southwestern desert and scrub.

At Holbrook we began climbing again, toward the Continental Divide east of Gallup. For miles and miles, we skirted the southern edge of high mesas and then foothills began to appear among the mesas, and higher peaks, dotted with junipers, showed in the north. At Campbell Pass, east of Gallup and just west of Thoreau, the Santa Fe tracks pass through the Zuni Mountains and over the Continental Divide. East of the pass, the land was poorer and drier, the grass more sparse. The mesas to the north, their faces scored by erosion, jutted up like a row of gnarled, twisted teeth. A hundred yards from the tracks, axle deep in dirt and sand, a rusted, stripped Plymouth station wagon rested, its doors and hood gone, another desert casualty. A line of puffy cumulus clouds rose over Interstate 40, like a procession of hot-air balloons. We would follow the interstate all the way to Albuquerque, where the Santa Fe tracks angle northeast, more or less along the old Santa Fe Trail to Kansas City.

After the freight conductor disembarked at Winslow, I talked for a while with an Australian couple, and then I climbed the winding staircase and took a seat on the upper level of the lounge car. First I faced south, then I turned around to face north—of such achievements are days of rail travel made.

Two Santa Fe trainmen sat next to me in front of the bank of windows and offered occasional comments as we looked out at the mesas in the distance. They were both old enough to be near retirement. One was gray and grizzled, his eyebrows ash white; he wore a silver and turquoise watchband. The other was taller, with gaunt Lincolnesque features, and wore a silver and turquoise bolo. Near Laguna, about midway on the long slow descent from the Continental Divide to Albuquerque, we passed a spur line that departed from our tracks at almost a right angle, heading north into the mesas through country more desolate than any I had yet seen. One of the trainmen said, "The first uranium mine in the United States is out there, at the end of that track. Nothing there now but a heap of tailings."

Farther on, I saw two riders at the foot of one of the distant mesas. By now, the mountain peaks of the Continental Divide were out of sight, replaced by a broken wall of mesas, some with sharply cleaved faces striated in shades of red, others that were only shapeless sandpiles. This was harsh country. The mesas gave it stature, but they were crumbling and as much as said: "This will be rubble." And so, I thought, will all else. Sooner or later. Out on the southern horizon, it was raining over the mesas.

My reservation for the night was in Santa Fe. The closest station on the Santa Fe railroad line to the city of Santa Fe is Lamy, eighteen miles south. When the Atchison, Topeka and Santa Fe line was laid, the rim of the Santa Fe basin was adjudged too steep to route the line through the city itself, so it was built through Glorieta Pass at the southern end of the Sangre de Cristo Mountains. To connect itself with the railroad, the city of Santa Fe had to build a spur line to Lamy, which is today not much more than a flag stop, a little town named for the historical figure cast by Willa Cather as the central figure of her masterpiece, *Death Comes for the Archbishop*.

We were just fifteen minutes short of Albuquerque when the conductor told me that the shuttle bus from Lamy to Santa Fe had been discontinued. If I traveled on to Lamy, I might be stranded there. I walked through two coaches, looking at the seat-check tags over each seat to find anyone who might be getting off at Lamy and might give me a ride to Santa Fe. I found only one family that was traveling to Lamy, and they actually lived there and so were no help to me. I didn't have time to poll the sleeper cars.

Five minutes before we were due in Albuquerque, I made a hasty decision. I went forward several coaches and found the conductor, sitting with another trainman.

"I'd like to change my ticket," I told him. "I'm booked to Lamy, but I'm going to get off at Albuquerque."

"You just change your mind?" he said, irritated.

"Just now. Sorry to bother you with the paperwork this late."

"You should have . . ."

"Oh, go on, Fred," the other trainman cut in, "what do you care where the man wants to get off? We all got things to do."

His chiding was all it took. I disembarked at Albuquerque into sunlight so bright that my pupils clamped down until they wrinkled. The Southwest Limited pauses at Albuquerque for twenty minutes, the longest layover in the 2,242 miles between Los Angeles and Chicago. The elevated concrete platform is as long as the train, and passengers spilled out onto it to stretch their legs and bask in the sun. All along the platform, Indian women set up folding tables laid with turquoise and silver jewelry and trinkets to sell. Some passengers buy, more just gawk. When I photographed her wares, a woman in a red kerchief barked at me, "Buy something!"

In the station, all the telephones were busy except one, and as I stepped up to it, the broad blue shirt at the adjacent phone turned around and I recognized John Madden, the former coach of the former Oakland Raiders who now works as a network color commentator and has simultaneously achieved wider fame in his third career as a marketable personality with an image founded largely on good-natured bluster. After flying thousands of miles every month as a football coach, Mr. Madden apparently decided that he could give up flying as well as coaching, and, when he publicly proclaimed his preference for traveling by train, he became for a time Amtrak's largest and loudest eminence. (Since then, his television network has provided him with a luxurious bus and he travels the highways like a country music star.)

He finished his call, and when he stepped out to the front portico of the station to buy a USA Today, I introduced myself. We stood on the platform and talked while the train got its windows washed. A tractor motored down the platform along the length of the train, dragging a tall mechanical arm along the side of the cars, washing and scrubbing their windows and sides. Streams of water glinted in the sunlight as they dripped from the cars and fell to the platform. It was the only time in six weeks of riding trains that I saw a window cleaned. A young bearded railroad worker from the freight yard, with sunglasses over his eyes and a pair of safety goggles riding on the crown of his yellow hard hat, asked Madden for an autograph, and several other railroad workers followed in his wake. Madden signed cheerfully. I asked him which train route was his personal favorite.

"Probably Chicago-Seattle. The one that goes across there."

"I guess you've been around the circuit. As much as you travel, do you still enjoy the trains?"

"I ride enough of 'em," he said, stopping well short of an endorsement.

The windows were washed and the attendants were shooing their passengers back into the cars. Madden boarded his sleeping car at the rear of the train, joshing as he did with the steward, a cigar clenched in his teeth.

From the south, Santa Fe is as unobtrusive, nested in the foothills at the tailbone of the Sangre de Cristo Mountains, as a cliffside pueblo. It was late afternoon when I drove my rented Volkswagen Rabbit through the narrow streets of the old town to the central square. I had reservations at La Fonda, the old hotel at the corner of the square known as "The Inn at the End of the Trail" because the plaza at Santa Fe was the end of the Santa Fe Trail. There has been an inn here since early in the seventeenth century. La Fonda, a rambling Spanish Pueblo Revival design built in the early 1920s to replace the old Exchange Hotel, became a cornerstone of efforts by the Santa Fe Railway to attract tourists to New Mexico. In the 1930s, the Santa Fe ticket office near the hotel arranged sightseeing tours to nearby Indian pueblos, billed as "Indian Detours," in a fifteen-passenger touring car.

They gave me a corner room on an upper floor. I was looking forward to my first private room since leaving home. I had either stayed with friends or acquaintances, traveled overnight on the train, or slept at inexpensive communal hostels. For two weeks I had been steadfastly cordial, the purpose of my trip being in part to meet people, and I was fast wearying of my own geniality. I looked forward to becoming reacquainted with the surly side of my nature. I longed to close a door behind me and be unfriendly, disagreeable, ill-mannered, and shabbily dressed.

The heat of the afternoon was melting away when I threw open a window in my corner room and pulled a chair over to give myself a view of the mountains. I unwrapped a hotel water glass, rummaged in my bookbag for the flask of bourbon that traveled there, and poured myself a liberal dollop. With my feet propped up in front of me, the door closed tightly behind me, the mountains in the distance reddening over the rooftops of Santa Fe, I dredged up all the unpleasantness I had been accruing and found that it was without portfolio. Motor noise wafted up from the cars in the street. After a few minutes I took it for a pleasant murmur, the gurgle of a stream, an ostinato to the approach of evening.

After a morning shower, I heated some water with the immersion heater I carried and drank some instant coffee, stirred with the handle of my toothbrush, from the hotel's water glass. After one cup, I put on my pants and thought about another cup; after a second, I put on my shirt and thought seriously about the day. I had two objectives: to wet a line in a trout stream and to get to Cimarron. Most of the drive north to Taos would follow along the Rio Grande, which I had been told was fishable water, and then the drive east over the mountains to Cimarron would take me past smaller, faster freestone streams. I could stop along the way to wet a line, which was all I had in mind, just a symbolic run-through of the fishing ritual, and still make Taos by noon and Cimarron by early afternoon. Allowing a couple of hours to unearth some old memories in Cimarron, I would still be back in Santa Fe for a late dinner.

The morning began inauspiciously. The resident fishing expert of the local outdoor shop was out of town, on his own fishing trip to Baja California, and the remaining staff seemed to regard fishing as slightly barbarous. I bought a couple of topographical maps: the Aztec and Raton sheets of the USGS 1:250,000 series. Together they covered most of New Mexico north of Santa Fe. For local fishing lore, I was referred to a sporting goods store on the outskirts of town.

I rolled my new maps into a tight tube and started walking back across the central plaza to La Fonda. The plaza itself is threadbare and scruffy, bare dirt for the most part, so I walked along the street bordering it, along the block-long veranda of the Palace of the Governors. Indian craftsmen from the pueblos gather each day under the shade of the Palace portico to sell their silver, turquoise, and bead-work jewelry. Each vendor crouches against the wall of the Palace and spreads his or her wares on a blanket. Even though many of these craftsmen clearly felt free to incorporate worldly elements of design in their work, the sensitive observer could readily distinguish the distinctive traditions of the different pueblos.

Most of the Indian craftsmen were reticent, civil but reserved. I found myself admiring the work of one man who seemed more friendly than most. Most of his jewelry was simple silver worked into clean uncomplicated shapes, with very little adornment, turquoise or oth-erwise. I asked a few questions, lingered a few minutes, and grad-ually we fell into a conversation that began with jewelry styles and techniques, as he helped me understand the different traditions I saw in the work of the other Indians. As the morning edged into the early afternoon, I sat next to him on the bricks, leaning back against the 375-year-old wall of the Palace of the Governors, and we talked about other things. His name was Glenn Paquin. He was from the Laguna Pueblo. He was stocky and wore gray slacks, a poplin jacket, and dark sunglasses with square lenses and heavy silver frames that accentuated the broad planes of his face. There were no rings on his fingers.

"I remember," he said when I told him I was riding the train, "in the forties going out with my mother to pick up coal on the tracks." A steady stream of tourists sidled past us, looking at his silver work spread out on a blanket in front of us. As we talked, he ignored their curious stares and their remarks to each other, but responded po-litely whenever one expressed an interest in his work.

"When the railroads were put through, beginning I guess in the 1870s, they came near the Laguna Pueblo, and many of the railroad workers and engineers married into the Laguna Pueblo. We have Abra-hams and Pratts and other Anglo names. These marriages actually helped the tribe. The Indian people were losing their land to home-steaders and land grabbers, and these Anglos knew the legal system and had influential friends back east, and they helped the tribe cope with challenges to their land. The railroads hired many Lagunas, and many of them followed the railroad west, forming colonies as they went." There are still colonies of Laguna Indians at Barstow, Richmond, Winslow, and Holbrook, he told me.

I asked him what other effects the railroad had on the pueblo. "Because of this contact with the railroad," he answered, "the Lagunas became one of the more outgoing, progressive tribes. The annual Laguna Feast became a famous celebration. The Zunis, who were not on the train route, kept apart more and still don't mix with non-Indian people that much. They would be the two largest of the nineteen pueblos in New Mexico."

I asked him about the rail spur I had seen from the train. He said, "In 1950, the Jackpile uranium mine began working on Laguna land and uranium was mined there until 1980. We are still battling over the reclamation, but money from that mine has made the Lagunas one of the wealthier pueblos.

"The thing most people notice about the Pueblo people is their hospitality. The Pueblo Indians weren't nomads. They settled down, built their homes, took a stand, and defended it. To survive they had to cooperate and get along with one another, so they became more diplomatic, and their techniques for getting along were friendship, respect, and cooperation. Indians share. They do not like to compete, and they don't like to succeed beyond the accomplishments of their fellow Indians. Most people don't understand this about us."

He himself had felt the conflicting emotions of living astride two dissimilar cultures. "I grew up and went on to college, in electronics first, electrical engineering, so I've had my experience with the scientific method, with analytical thinking. I eventually got my degree in public administration and I've been working on my master's. I've had my share of administrative jobs but, I don't know, I didn't find it very satisfying."

"What," I asked him, "brought you back to silver work?"

"When I reached forty, I began to wonder what sort of life it would be. I felt the stress and the money wasn't that good for my family. A few years ago, I began this, working in silver, and I began to understand what my father and grandfather knew. My grandfather was a Zuni blacksmith, my father was a Zuni jeweler. My father used to tell me, although I didn't understand when I was young—let's say it took him a week to make a ring, and in the old days, when they used charcoal, it might have taken as long as a week. When he took it to a feast and gave it to someone, he wasn't giving just a piece of jewelry, he was giving away to them a week of his life, a week that would never come again. And the person who accepted it respected that meaning and understood that value.

"I've been through the Wounded Knee thing. I organized the largest Indian march ever in New Mexico, down at Gallup. I've been through the anger. People have so many stereotypes about Indians and they don't understand. They think we are warlike and live in tepees." He pointed to the statue in the center of the plaza across the street, "You can go over there and take a photograph of that statue and you'll see what I mean. There was a big hassle over that statue. It commemorates 'Our people who died fighting the savage Indians.' Part of the inscription has been chiseled off, but you can't chisel stereotypes and racism out of people's minds.

"I think our only hope now is to educate the larger culture about Indian traditions, to bury the hatchet, so to speak, to learn to live together. And I think that other peoples are coming to appreciate the Indian view of life. The Indian philosophy tells us that everything has life: trees, rivers, even stones. People who don't understand laugh at Indians. They say that we worship rocks. We don't worship rocks. We value them and all natural things for the life that is in them. Most people who walk by here, or even buy something, don't realize this, and I can't explain it to everyone, but turquoise has meaning for us beyond its simple beauty and value as a stone. The reason I use only natural turquoise, instead of processed turquoise, is that natural turquoise changes color with time and wear. When the turquoise changes color it signifies that it has life.

"So I'm happier now than I was as a professional student or as a bureaucrat. I like to think that my work will go home with people and make them happy and that it will bring a pleasant memory. What is life when it's done but memories?"

By now it was midafternoon, and I hadn't even started out for Cimarron. The day had slipped by. I tried on one of his rings, a simple broad silver band, and asked him to hammer it out to make it a little larger. As he was sizing the ring on his mandrel, I put my money down on the blanket before he could mention it. When he was finished, we shook hands. I slipped the ring on my right hand, gathered up my pipe and the maps I had purchased that morning, which had been lying there on the bricks, and stood up to go. The briar pipe was warm from the afternoon sun.

II The Road to Cimarron

It was almost five o'clock by the time I finally left Santa Fe. At a sporting goods shop on the outskirts of the city, I purchased a one-day fishing license and asked the clerk at the hunting and fishing counter what sort of fishing I might find north of Santa Fe that time of year.

"Big trout. Not a lot of them, but good-sized trout. This would be the trophy season."

"Let me ask you this, then, what works this late in the year?" Though I had been lugging a pack rod, a fly reel and floating line, and a few leaders around the country, I had, by design, left at home the one piece of tackle that would have taken up no more space than an idle thought—a box of flies. This with the conviction that a fly purchased locally is the unofficial tariff on a traveling fisherman. I cherish local fly patterns because they celebrate diversity and idiosyncrasy. And because the right local pattern is apt to be dramatically more successful.

He didn't hesitate. "One thing. The insect hatches are over. You got to have yourself a Muddler."

Trout fishermen will know the Muddler. It is arguably the single most versatile and productive pattern devised in the long tradition of fly-fishing for trout. Not really a dry fly, nor a wet fly, nor a streamer nor bucktail, it is something of all of these, tied with mottled turkey feathers like a streamer and squirrel hair or calftail like a bucktail, with a head of spun deer hair uniquely its own. Said to have been created to imitate a species of small forage fish, its uses are legion. I so much enjoy tying Muddlers that I have boxes and boxes of them in every size and variation—Maribou Muddlers, Hopper Muddlers,

Spuddlers, tinseled Muddlers—a surfeit of Muddlers. I was amused to learn that the fly pattern I needed was one I had left at home in abundance.

I was reaching for my wallet when the clerk added, "One problem, though. I don't have any. Not a one. Sold out. Seems like we can never keep enough of 'em. This time of year, I doubt if you could find one anywhere."

The road north soon made me forget my bad luck. The air was dry and pungent as cedar shavings; the temperature ideal, warm in the sun, cool in the shade. The route follows the Rio Grande river valley, a broad grassland between high mountain ranges. Cloud shadows skimmed over the grass and drifted up the mountain slopes and over the snowfields at the top as smoothly as Zeppelins. I followed an Airstream trailer north to Espanola, watching the image of the highway, my own car, and the blue sky scroll over its mirrored curves. Two weeks out, I thought, and still no rain.

I entered the Rio Grande canyon, following a truck laden with two-by-fours. The river was bony after the summer, running in a sandy bed through autumnal cottonwoods. Farther north the road left the canyon, veering away to the east and climbing out of the Rio Grande gorge onto the broad river plain between the Sangre de Cristo Mountains on the east and the Comanche Rim of the San Juan Mountains on the west. The sun fell behind the western mountains and the wide valley fell into a summer twilight. Ahead I could make out the lights of Taos, nestled just at the foot of the Taos Mountains, house lights and car lights twinkling at the edge of the plain.

A little after seven, I parked on the plaza at Taos and walked around the dusty little square. Not much had changed in the fifteen years since I had last seen it. The change had come out along the highway, where strip development had been at work. Even though Taos is self-consciously picturesque, the dimly lit plaza on a Tuesday night in October was not much different from any other rural small town. Young men in cars with tuned exhaust manifolds cruised through the square. A motorcycle or two roared around the plaza and peeled away back to the main drag out along the highway. A four-wheel-drive pickup rolled slowly around the square, the Marcels' 1961 version of "Blue Moon" blaring from its open windows.

I drove out of Taos on Highway 64, headed east over the Fernando Mountains toward Cimarron. The highway follows Rio Fernando de Taos through a cut in the Sangre de Cristo mountain chain, and a full white moon hung over the mountain pass. As I climbed higher toward the nine-thousand-foot pass, the temperature dropped and the hardwoods gave way to pines and aspens. Descending the eastern side of the pass, I found the switchbacks even tighter, but just when I was beginning to succumb to vertigo the road straightened and flattened out and I rolled out of the forest onto the floor of Moreno Valley, a high basin in the Sangre de Cristo Mountains. East of Eagle Nest, the highway began to climb, and then it slalomed down and followed the Cimarron River through a pass in the Cimarron Mountains. Trees closed in around the road again, and a deer, dazzled by my headlights, hesitated at the shoulder and then bolted back into the woods. I was dropping from the Rocky Mountains onto the Great Plains, looking east across the high plains of west Texas and the Oklahoma panhandle, the lower Great Plains of Oklahoma, the Missouri Coteau, or Break of the Plains, and the Osage Plains of eastern Oklahoma—across more than five hundred miles of plains all the way to the Ozark Plateau.

I had been to Cimarron only once before, almost half my lifetime ago, and for only a few days, but I had thought about it many times since, walking its dusty streets in my mind. I had a personal tie to the little town on the edge of the plains that I didn't fully comprehend, but that had seemed to grow stronger as my memory transmuted it over the years. It had something to do with a short, bowlegged, mustachioed old man, with my father and myself, with how youthful self-absorption can be the enemy of curiosity —and how curiosity keeps old men young.

It was the late 1960s and I was traveling with my parents through the Southwest that summer. It was an awkward trip. I was facing the draft and, like many young people of those years, preoccupied with my own self. Too old to be a child and too young to be grown up about it, I was eager to get on with my own life and had little patience for my parents' interests.

We drove over from Amarillo, taking the scenic route up to Raton,

New Mexico, and then down through Cimarron. When we reached Cimarron in the early afternoon, I was unimpressed by the little town. Maybe a thousand people lived there, but I couldn't see why. The Kit Carson Motel, a gas station or two, a restaurant, and a bank on Highway 64 comprised the business district. Little frame houses lined a handful of streets that turned off the highway for a few blocks and trailed off into nowhere. The entire town was dwarfed by the mountains to the west and the endless plains to the east, and the hot summer winds threatened to dry it up and blow it away.

But something about Cimarron intrigued my father. Thus we found ourselves looking in at the St. James, a nineteenth-century Victorian hotel gone to seed. We wandered through, reading wall plaques and framed newspaper clippings detailing the history of the hotel and some of the more colorful incidents in the town's past. I took some interest in the bullet holes in the walls and ceilings, and some of the stories of train robberies and horse thieves and outlaw gangs and posses and hangings appealed to my typically romantic notion of the Old West, but the place was pretty dingy and I was ready to move on. My father, however, insisted that we have a look at an old mill not far away that had been converted into a museum of local history.

A stubby, bowlegged old gentleman in a western hat and boots was minding the museum that afternoon, collecting donations and greeting visitors—of which we seemed to be the full complement. I passed him by without a thought. My father, however, struck up a conversation with him that began with simple courtesies and soon became friendly and animated as my father's interest elicited a few of the little man's anecdotes of local history, about which he seemed to know quite a lot.

I was relieved when we finally got back in our car and started back through town, on our way again, and my impatience probably showed when my father stopped again in front of the St. James Hotel and insisted we have one more look around inside. He walked around the shopworn lobby of the hotel reading more of the yellowed newspaper clippings that described the capture of various criminals around the turn of the century. He pointed out to me that the lawman in each case had been the same, a deputy sheriff and later territorial ranger named Fred Lambert. Then he led me back to the car, saying only, "Come on, I have a hunch."

He drove back to the old mill, and my mother and I waited in the car while he went inside. Five minutes later I was still scanning the dial for a good radio station when he came out and led us back inside the mill. The same little man was there alone. I had never seen anyone so bowlegged before. My father said, "Mr. Lambert, this is my wife, Genevieve, and my son, George." To me, he said, "I want you to meet Mr. Fred Lambert."

Fred Lambert lived in a little three- or four-room white frame house, and that evening we sat in his living room and listened to him recollect a career as a lawman in Cimarron that began when New Mexico was still a territory. He was a born storyteller. He remembered everything in vivid detail: the names of men who had died fifty or sixty years before, the nature of his horses, the time and place and outcome of every adventure. Yet he was always just a touch reticent about his own exploits.

"Well, in the old days," he began that first night, "Cimarron was strictly a western town, built up in the year of eighteen and forty-seven on the old Santa Fe Trail leading from Clifton House to Taos. In those days, the townspeople were principally cattlemen, gamblers, miners, trappers, and two-gun men."

I remember the way he pronounced "Cimarron," accenting the first and last syllables equally and softening the last syllable until it sounded like "roan." How musical he made it sound.

"My father came west in 1863; in 1872 he built an old adobe hotel here in Cimarron, where I was born in January of 1887. During that period of time, Buffalo Bill was a very close friend of my father's and happened to be at the hotel the night I was born. He going into the bar christened me Cyclone Dick, on account of the heavy blizzard and windstorm coming down the canyon that night of January twenty-third. My mother was not disposed to letting me have that name, and compromised with Bill Cody by taking his middle name, Frederick. My parents finally chose Buffalo Bill as my godfather, and oft-times in later years when I became six or seven years old, I would watch him—he wore a wide belt with a great big silver buckle, and he had boots that were really funny boots to me in those days, they came up clear to his hips, and wore a great big heavy hat—and oft-times he would set in our parlor and have someone play the piano while he was enjoying his cigar.

"When I became about twelve or thirteen years old, I was compelled to keep bar for my father in the saloon and oft-times seeing the many rough characters and gunfights and trouble, which did not appeal to me, I would talk with Buffalo Bill and he would instruct me and tell me about the use of guns, and oft-times told me that a man shouldn't fear the other man's gun, he should fear his own, and know when to use it, at the right time and in the right place.

"It was necessary for me to have a gun when I was tending bar, 'cause different issues would come up, well, things would have to be settled, and it come natural to use a gun, as much as reaching in to get a bottle and glasses to serve a customer.

"I was just a boy when I got to know the Black Jack Ketchum gang quite well. They'd go down around Clayton, Folsom, that country, hold up a train or something, then back back in here and have a camp up the canyon where they kept the horses, one of 'em, the others stay around the saloon, drinkin', playin' poker, waitin' for another deal. They stayed there for a number of weeks, right at the hotel, and they would go out back of the old jail for six-shooter practice, and I would go along with them, see what kind of practice they were doing. Bob McGinnis showed me the way to swing a gun, how in tying back your trigger in close quarters you could thumb your gun, or in close quarters, for quick shootin', throw your gun to the left and fan the hammer.

"Well, a posse followed 'em up here and there was two or three killed here, and finally broke up the gang. Black Jack was hung over at Springer. His brother was shot through the arm and took to Santa Fe for safekeeping and died of lead poisoning down there.

"Soon after that gang was broke up I was given my first assignment as a deputy. One day the sheriff gave me the message for his deputy, 'We've had some killing down at Vegas and I want him to catch the killers in case they head that way.' Well, John, the deputy, was sick in bed, so I persuaded the sheriff to deputize me, as young as I was. I was supposed to find some man to go with me, but I just went ahead out and got my horse and pulled out.

"I went down on the high point here and I seen 'em a coming in a spring wagon and I rode around, stopped down here at the bridge, and when they crossed the bridge the man and woman was sittin' in the spring wagon, the front seat, fellow on the box in the back part with a Winchester, the only gun in sight, and I rode up on my horse and said, 'You folks are under arrest.' And the fellow raised the rifle to shoot and the end of the barrel caught on the wagon wheel, in underneath, and the shot went in between my horse's front legs. And at that, I pulled my gun and the bullet hit right there and here [he indicated his forearm and his upper arm] and he dropped the gun then, and the others, again I asked 'em to reach and they all reached. I took 'em up and frisked 'em, took 'em over and put 'em in the jail until the sheriff come and got 'em. So then I was a deputy and I went to work right then steady on different assignments.

"I think it was along about nineteen and six when I got the commission from the territory, as ranger, or Mountie we called it. We covered all this area horseback. There was just ten of us and the captain. We covered cattle rustlers, killers, anything contrary to the law. And then when the territory became a state, I went into the mounted police, the state mounted police. And it was abolished in 1912 and I went into the government service as a U.S. Deputy Special Officer in the Indian Service, Department of the Interior. It was not until 1913 we had the first car in the Indian Service."

His stories unfolded chapter after chapter. After a long, involved tale of a chase after horse thieves down toward Mexico, a chase that found him eventually tracking the thieves in a Stanley Steamer, he stopped to pet his dog for a few minutes before beginning another.

Occasionally his stories touched on memorable events, including a world championship prizefight at Las Vegas, New Mexico, between Jack Johnson and a man named Flynn. "This Flynn, he was just a rounder. He was a bouncer in a roughhouse up in Pueblo [he pronounced it "Puebla"], Colorado. He was no real boxer. He was a-farmin' then for the Santa Fe railroad, buckin' up against this here Johnson for the world's championship."

Most of Fred Lambert's stories were about the routine crimes and conflicts of early Cimarron: horse theft, robbery, murder, and mayhem. Some told of men who had committed ghastly crimes—one was about a man who had cut out another's tongue—and others were gentle reminiscences of the way life had been in the territory. He told them all in the same wry, matter-of-fact language.

He never made very much of his own courage, and he pointedly debunked the romantic impressions of popular fiction. He always began with a short, almost dismissive summary of an episode and then, with some prodding, expanded it into a rich, fully recollected narrative. His stories were fascinating revelations of a turn-of-the-century Southwest that was not yet tame but no longer primitive. Long before it became civilized in the eastern sense, the West was aware of its own mystique and even marketed it. Sitting Bull toured Canada with a Wild West show; William Cody played Madison Square Garden with his Wild West show and returned to the frontier to scout and ranch.

Could William Cody really have been present at the St. James on the night Fred Lambert was born? Could he possibly have been a friend of the family? When Fred Lambert was twelve years old and was, as he remembers it, taking instruction in gun handling from Buffalo Bill, William F. Cody was fifty-four years old and had been the star of his own Wild West show for seventeen years. A world-famous impresario, he spent his time either at his ranch in North Platte, Nebraska, attending to ranching and mining interests in Wyoming, or on tour in the East with his show, which that year featured an especially popular re-creation of the battle of San Juan Hill. In biographies of Cody I find no mention of any business that would have taken him near Cimarron in those years. Still, it is local lore in Cimarron that William Cody joined in a business venture with Cimarron rancher Lucien Maxwell in the 1860s and visited there in later years. At the time, I took Fred Lambert's stories to be true in every detail. In the years since, I have wondered. For me, finally, it didn't matter.

Eventually, I came to remember and admire Fred Lambert not so much for his heroic life as for the way he had woven his memories into a tapestry that anyone could see was a piece of art and that kept his own past, and that of his family and his home country, alive like an epic poem or an heirloom quilt with every story a pieced block.

I think of Glenn Paquin's words: "What is life when it's done but memories?"

We stayed in Cimarron several days, and after many hours of listening to his stories we began to feel like old friends. He told us of his wife, who had been dead for many years, and about his adopted Indian son and the ranch work he had turned to after leaving law enforcement. When his life had quieted down some, he had taken up poetry, writing verse about western themes, and at his wife's urging he had begun to paint. Over the years alone since her death, it had occupied his time, and now his little house was cluttered with paintings. Canvases hung everywhere and when he had tired of painting proper canvases, he had painted plates and trays and anything else at hand.

Near the end of the last evening we spent with him, he went into his bedroom and came back into the front room with a box under each arm. "I thought you might want to see this," he said. "I carried it many a day." From a square wooden box he lifted out a parcel wrapped in an old cloth that smelled of machine oil and unwrapped a single-action revolver. The bluing was worn shiny in spots and the plain wooden stocks were nicked and scarred. "I'm glad I don't have to anymore." From the other box, a big flat cardboard box, he took out a large sketch pad and handed it to my father with a mischievous, slightly embarrassed smile. On each of the first ten or so pages of the sketch pad was a careful pencil drawing of a nude woman, each one different. "I do one every year, just to make sure my memory hasn't failed me."

Our last day in Cimarron, we stopped at his house to say good-bye, and when he and his black-haired dog came out on his front porch to see us off, my father took a picture of the two of them, Fred Lambert standing self-consciously with his hands at his sides and the dog sitting at his feet, half-leaning against his leg.

Years later I was rummaging through a cardboard box of negatives in my parents' basement when I came across that roll of film shot in Cimarron, and I found the negative of Fred Lambert and his dog. With the negative in the enlarger, they were two tiny images on the easel. I racked the head of the enlarger up, refocused, and Fred Lambert's face, larger now, began to show detail. I blew up the negative until his face filled the easel and made a print, and there he was: the tight, thin lips; the brushy white mustache; the smile all in his eyes. I still have that print. Enlarged so many times, the grain of the Tri-X falls apart, washing the out-of-focus background into soft grays that surround his face, from the dark underside of his hat brim to the prickly white stubble of whiskers on his chin. It's a handsome face, gracefully aged, with bushy eyebrows that arch outward like two bucktail streamers and a bulbous nose grown prominent with age like the kype of an old salmon.

Not long ago, looking for something else in the library stacks, I found in a collection of prints from nineteenth-century magazines a drawing of his father, Henry Lambert, as a young man. The caption read: "Henry Lambert, a former chef for Presidents Lincoln and Grant, built the St. James Hotel in Cimarron in 1872." He had the same nose and the same eyes. Through a print scavenged from a forgotten frontier tabloid and a snapshot taken as a parting gesture and then forgotten, only to be resurrected from the morgue of a basement darkroom, those eyes shine across a hundred years.

I drove into town from the west on Highway 64 and turned south, the memory growing stronger like a scent in my nostrils. Like most rural crossroads, Cimarron kept farmers' and ranchers' hours. House lights were out; the streets were deserted. By nine o'clock on a cold autumn night the citizens of Cimarron had put out the cat and dropped the latch. The St. James Hotel was still standing, but it was closed and shuttered and weeds grew waist-high around its front stoop. The sign was still there, "St. James Hotel 1880." I drove on past it and, navigating again by memory, found the old mill just as I had remembered it. But where I expected to see the little frame house in which we had spent those long August evenings listening to Fred Lambert tell his stories of emprise, I saw only an adobe house with a camper parked in the front yard. I drove up to the top of the hill, where an old adobe church stood in the moonlight like a watchtower, looking over the little town on the edge of the plains. On each side of the church door was an iron urn holding withered flowers.

At the Kit Carson Inn Restaurant and Lounge on the main street, Highway 64, two men were playing pool. Both were young and wore rough clothes: work boots spattered with mud, jeans, heavy shirts, down vests, and baseball caps. Four older men at a table also wore work clothes. A couple wore baseball caps; one a hard hat. I walked around the pool table, careful to give the players a wide berth, and sat on a stool at the long bar across the back wall. The first game of the World Series was on the television mounted on the wall behind the bar.

The bartender, a stocky, red-bearded man in his thirties, paused to watch the game whenever a big play was replayed, then went on about his chores. He ignored me just enough to make me soon feel inconspicuous while I nursed my beer and watched the Padres and the Tigers. Over the weekend, the Padres had completed a surprising three-game comeback to eliminate the Cubs and, with them, the hopes of purists who dreamed of Series games played in the autumn sunlight at Wrigley Field.

A baseball trophy sat on top of the television and two or three more were lined up on a shelf behind the bar. Deer and elk racks, just the antlers and bare skulls, were mounted on the wall. A lake trout that had to go at least eight or ten pounds, a big pike, and a kokanee salmon painted its blood-red spawning color were stuffed and mounted and arrayed around the walls.

The bartender picked my empty can off the bar. "Another one?"

"Sure. I think I'll see the game out." San Diego was batting in the bottom of the third inning, leading two to one. Jack Morris was struggling on the mound for Detroit.

"You a fan?" He set a cold can of beer in front of me. "You want a clean glass?"

"This'll do fine. No, not much of a fan. I still think of San Diego as an expansion team. Still think of the designated hitter as a publicity stunt. If you get to throw at the other guys, they should get to throw at you. Guess I haven't kept up."

"Me neither. I take some interest in the World Series, but it seems kind of strange to think, I mean, we got snow already, in the mountains anyway, and they're still playing baseball."

He went on about his chores and I worked to squeeze two innings out of my second beer. It felt good to unwind after the three-hour run up and over the mountains. Detroit regained the lead in the fifth inning on a two-out two-run homer by Larry Herndon. It figured to be a fragile advantage, but Morris seemed transformed in the late innings, growing stronger with every out, seeming to drain all hope from the Padre batters. The last innings went quickly. The Tigers won, three to two.

While the announcers were recapping the game, I called for another beer, fully intending it to be my last. It was getting late and I faced a long drive, 140 miles, back to Santa Fe. In the next two days,

I was planning to drive several hundred miles and catch three trains in two states; I should have already been back in Santa Fe, asleep.

The pool players were gone. The four men who had been sitting together near the front window were getting up to go as, on the television, Johnny Carson launched into his monologue.

"Did you know of a man named Fred Lambert?" I asked the bartender.

He showed only a glimmer of recognition. "The name's familiar. Lambert is an old name around here." He called out to one of the men who was leaving, "You remember a Fred Lambert?"

The man turned and took a few steps toward the bar. His friends hesitated for a moment and then continued on toward the door. "Fred Lambert?" He had his hands in the pockets of his jeans and was looking down at the floor, trying to remember. "Wasn't he the old man used to hang around the mill, lived up there on the hill?"

"Yeah," I said. "That was him. Thanks."

I could see his three friends waiting for him in the parking lot. "See you tomorrow night, maybe," he said to the bartender and followed the others out. I was the last customer left.

"Let me settle up," I said to the bartender, "and I'll be on my way."

A mule deer, then a big jackrabbit, and then another mule deer ran across the highway in my headlights. Lightning began to burst behind the clouds over the plains ahead. Occasionally a single jagged tongue would lash down, tearing the curtain of clouds. Ten miles out of Cimarron, I slowed and stopped on a slight rise and left the engine idling while I stood in the road. I could see the lights of Cimarron behind me, and ahead of me, fourteen miles to the southeast, I could see the lights of Springer twinkling. I drove on, keeping up a steady seventy-five. When a brilliant bolt of lightning flashed, I could see all the way to the curve of the earth. Approaching Springer I saw the quick gleam of animal eyes in my lights and, as I covered the brake pedal, a house cat loped across the highway.

Just north of Springer I turned onto Interstate 25 and drove south toward Santa Fe. The big green highway sign read "Santa Fe 136 Miles." It was past midnight and I fought drowsiness, that mental fatigue that can make dying in a fiery crash seem, momentarily at least, like a small price to pay for sleep. I put on a sweater and opened the window, letting the chilly night air whip through the car. I tried slowing down, and that just lulled me into somnolence, so I kept up my speed, driving until I began to lose consciousness and my body defended itself with that sharp infusion of adrenalin that creates the illusion of alertness in the brain for a half a minute and then subsides into the stomach as simple nausea. Every twenty miles or so, the cycle would be repeated: drowsiness, resistance, surrender—then alarm, adrenaline, fear, alertness, briefly—and finally queasiness again. Then I would stop the car, not even bothering to pull off onto the shoulder, there was no other traffic, and walk around to the rear and take a leak and stand for a minute gulping the cool night air and feel better. Every time I stopped, I noticed the sky was clearer than the last time, opening up into deep space as the clouds vanished.

Unfortunately, I was not quite through demonstrating my poor judgment. As I pulled to the curb and parked in front of La Fonda on the Old Santa Fe Trail, I was thinking only of the bed that was waiting for me, and I paid no attention to the young man standing on the corner of San Francisco Street at the end of the block. I was getting my camera bag out of the back of the car when he walked up, unsteadily, and asked me for a ride. He was wearing a wool sport coat and expensive loafers of soft, crinkly black leather. He was obviously drunk, but it hadn't made him belligerent. He told me, in garbled syntax, that he had been drinking with friends in the bar at La Fonda and they had left him without a ride home. The sidewalks were deserted. I knew I had no business back behind the wheel, but perhaps because I felt a little as though some benevolent deity had seen me home safe in spite of myself, I decided I could spare another few minutes to pass the favor along.

He started describing to me which turns to take, and it occurred to me that he was more lucid than he had seemed just moments before, but I followed his directions, turning up one street and down another until I was partially disoriented. When we turned onto a street with only a few houses along it, I asked him, "Do you live on this street?"

"Uh, yeah, down here at the end. No, turn right up there, that's it, right here."

I turned where he pointed: a dirt drive that went through a small grove of trees and came out in the middle of nowhere. Suddenly, we might have been miles from Santa Fe. In my headlights I could see that the drive was just a rutted gravel lane that dipped down into a wash and came up into a loop on a low overlook. A van was parked on the other side of the wash, just off the drive in the sagebrush. I looked over at my passenger. He was grinning. Suddenly I felt very tired and very sober. I stopped the car.

"Look," I said, "I told you I'd give you a lift home. You took a wrong turn. Take my word for it."

"Oh no," he said, still smiling, very pleased, "this is just where we want to be," and he reached for my crotch. My judgment was looking worse and worse.

I slipped the car into neutral and caught his wrist with my right hand and held it while I looked very hard at the van up ahead, thinking that as long as it had nothing whatsoever to do with me this could still work out without costing me much more than aggravation. "What we have here is a misunderstanding," I said, keeping my eyes on the van and the brush around the car. "I'm very tired and a little drunk and maybe a little slow, but I was willing to give you a ride as a favor. That's it. Don't misunderstand."

He reached for me with his other hand and I let go of the steering wheel and caught his arm with my left hand and there we were, holding hands like dance partners. He was grinning and squirming like a six-year-old. "No, no, this is just right," he said. "This is just what we want."

I turned him loose and slammed the Rabbit into first gear and gunned it forward, down into the wash, but we bumped over a big stone and in my haste I stalled. When I reached for the key to start the car again, he reached for the hand brake and then reached for me again. He was not exactly suave but he was persistent. I kept cranking the car and stamping on the gas pedal and I must have flooded it. My problems were compounding. I kept grinding the starter and he kept moaning endearments and reaching for me. I let go of the key and grabbed him by the neck with my right hand and slammed his head back against the window and held it there. With my left arm I reached through the steering wheel and turned the key. The motor caught, and I engaged the clutch and we lurched forward. As soon as I reached for the wheel, he grabbed for me again. It was becoming apparent that I couldn't drive and defend my virtue at the same time. I stopped the car again.

"Listen, I've had it," I said. "You can walk back to town. Or sleep with the coyotes. I don't care. Get out."

He looked like he was going to cry. "No, please," he whimpered, "take me back with you. Don't leave me here."

"All right, then behave." I gunned the car up the hill and around the loop, bouncing over stones and deep ruts so hard that it lifted me out of my seat and I worried that I might break an axle, but the car held together and by the time I passed the van, still sitting quietly in the underbrush, I had it wound out to thirty in first gear. Let it start throwing valve stems through the hood—I wanted enough momentum to get me back into town. I roared down to the end of the block, turned, shifted, and kept going, taking the corners as fast as I could, navigating instinctively back to the plaza. I pulled up in front of the hotel and stopped, in exactly the same parking place I had left what seemed like a long time ago.

I got out and locked my door and walked around the car. He was still slumped in the passenger seat. I opened the car door and yanked him to his feet and locked the door. When I started up the sidewalk, he followed, imploring me, all the way to the hotel door. Not until I was in my room on the fourth floor, with the door closed behind me and my shoes off, did I realize that I had left my toilet kit in the car. I had no toothbrush, no toothpaste, and my mouth tasted like a waste dump. Reluctantly, I made the long walk down to the lobby and out the front door to the curb. There he was, standing under the lamp-post on the corner of San Francisco Street, where I had first seen him. I turned around and went back to my room.

12 Narrow Gauge

The youth don't talk river slang any more. Their pride is apparently
railroads—which they take a peculiar vanity in reducing to initials—an
affectation which prevails all over the West. They roll these initials as
a sweet morsel under the tongue.

—Mark Twain, from his notebook for 1882

The locomotive was huffing steam the next morning when I
rolled into the gravel parking lot next to the old depot at
Chama. I had left Santa Fe before dawn and driven nearly a
hundred miles—up the Rio Grande valley to Espanola, along
the Rio Chama northwest to Abiquiu Reservoir, and then due
north along the western slope of the Mogote Ridge to Chama,
a small town near the Colorado border named by the Spanish after the Tewa Pueblo, Tzama. I claimed my tickets at the agent's
window and, back at my car, quickly stuffed my camera, a few rolls
of Kodachrome, and an extra lens, my favorite 24 mm, in a small
duffel bag, along with a few thick rye crackers, some cheese, and a
banana and an apple that had been bouncing around in my car for a
couple of days.

Many of the passengers were taking the train, the New Mexico
Express as it was called in this tourists' consist, only as far as Osier,
Colorado, where it would turn around and return along the same
route. I was going on through: at Osier, I would transfer to the Colorado Express, which had come up that morning from Antonito, to
continue my crossing back through Toltec Gorge and on to Antonito.

From there, I would ride back over the mountains on Route 17 in a van with one of the trainmen and get back to Chama late in the day.

By the time I had gathered my duffel, the engineer and his brakeman were making a final inspection of the locomotive, a 2-8-2 K-36 class Baldwin, number 489. Steam locomotives are classified by the arrangements of their wheels and the tractive effort they produce. A 2-8-2 locomotive has a two-wheel pilot truck in front, eight drive wheels, and a two-wheel trailing truck. The "K" in the class designation stands for Mikado, the 2-8-2 design, and the 36 represents the tractive effort. Number 489 was one of ten built in 1925 by the Baldwin Locomotive Works for use as freight locomotives, but it and its kin proved equally suitable for passenger service on this narrow-gauge line where flat-out speed was not a requirement.

Form never followed function more slavishly than on a steam locomotive. To my eye, the basic steam locomotive resembles a giant tin can laid on its side, painted black, dusted with soot, and drenched in oil. I am always fascinated by their running gear—the drive wheels, their counterweights and rods. So much mass so finely balanced; the spinning complex exactitude of a pocket watch writ large, as brutal as a dredge.

This Cumbres and Toltec Scenic Railroad, from Chama, New Mexico, through Cumbres Pass to Antonito, Colorado, and another steam train from Durango to Silverton, Colorado, are the two vestiges of the Denver and Rio Grande narrow-gauge system that once laced the Colorado mountains. These two trains still travel over their original routes, which once had a purpose and now have a history; these are not toy trains traveling a pointless loop like an amusement park ride. A railroad is as much its track, its path, as its rolling stock. Out of service, standing in the grass of a museum lawn, on a few yards of track going nowhere, a steam locomotive is as hard to comprehend as a stuffed woolly mammoth. It is one thing to have dinner aboard an ocean liner moored at dockside; it is quite another to sail the Atlantic.

The standard gauge, the distance between the rails, of North American railroads is four feet, eight and a half inches, a standard inherited from England, where it had long been the customary track of carts and wagons and had thus become the general practice of English railroads. Most early American railroads in the northern states imported their first locomotives from England and adopted the English gauge, but at various times in the nineteenth century at least eleven other gauges were tried. A few railroads were even built to a unique gauge in the hope of gaining a proprietary hold on traffic.

In 1861 a trip by rail from Charleston to Philadelphia entailed changing cars eight different times to accommodate the different track gauges, and railroads with nonstandard gauges often suffered for their independence. By the 1870s, most railroad people recognized the inevitable need for standardization, and most railroads began changing to standard gauge.

But even as American railroads were changing, at monumental effort and expense, to standard gauge, dissenting voices were heard —ironically, first from England. In 1870 Robert F. Fairlie read his paper, "The Gauge for the 'Railways of the Future,'" before the annual meeting of the British Railway Association. Fairlie made the case for the specialized utility of a narrower-than-standard track gauge of three and a half feet, which, he argued, would require less earth-moving and narrower rights-of-way, would be easier to lay and maintain, and thus less expensive, and would therefore be ideally suited to operations in difficult terrain or where traffic was expected to be light.

In that same year, 1870, the Denver and Rio Grande—the D&RG —was chartered in Denver, Colorado. Denver had been shunned by the main line of the Union Pacific, and business interests there were also afraid they would lose commerce from southern Colorado to the Atchison, Topeka and Santa Fe, which was pushing through Kansas toward Colorado. When silver in abundance was discovered in the mountains around Leadville, Colorado, in the late 1870s, the first president of the D&RG, General William Jackson Palmer, snaked a narrow three-foot-gauge railroad into the mountains west of Pueblo. The first D&RG train entered Leadville to a twelve-brass band welcome, with former president Ulysses S. Grant aboard General Palmer's private car, "Nomad."

By the fall of 1880, the Denver and Rio Grande had 551 miles of track among its various extensions and 4,700 men at work laying more. Track from Alamosa, then called San Luis Park, reached Chama on the last day of 1880, and the railroad began immediately working to extend itself west to the new town of Animas City on the Rio de las Animas Perdidas. Animas City was the gateway to Silverton, Colorado, the boom town located some forty miles north among the silver mines of the San Juan Mountains. On July 27, 1881, the D&RG reached Durango, one mile south of Animas City, and within a year the track was completed north to Silverton.

Narrow gauge never amounted to a significant portion of eastern railroad trackage, but in the West, particularly in the rugged Rocky Mountain states, narrow-gauge railroads were major carriers. At one time, in the late nineteenth century, almost one-third of all the track in Colorado was narrow gauge. The San Juan Extension of the D&RG shared the silver boom with the mining towns along its route, and after bullion prices fell, it hauled lumber and coal out and returned supplies to the little towns that had taken root in the isolated mountain valleys. The narrow-gauge lines of the Denver and Rio Grande remained an important lifeline through the mountains until roads brought cars and buses and trucks after World War I. As late as the 1960s, the Denver and Rio Grande Western, successor to General Palmer's D&RG, operated trains over the San Juan Extension.

The Denver and Rio Grande is remembered because it served some of the most colorful mining boom towns of the Southern Rockies, traversing spectacular and imposing mountains, because it continued service long after most of the other narrow-gauge lines were abandoned, and because two separate segments of its narrow-gauge network survive today as tourist railroads, wriggling with life, like two severed pieces of a dismembered snake.

At Chama we boarded open air coaches, rickety wooden conversions of old D&RGW boxcars. The mountain air was cool even in the bright sunshine. On a pellucid morning in Indian summer, one couldn't choose a finer way to ride. A conductor, speaking over a bullhorn, told us that the locomotive develops 36,000 pounds tractive effort on the three-foot narrow gauge and, with its tender and four and a half tons of coal, weighs 143 tons. The fireman on this run is not featherbedding—he is shoveling some two and a half tons of coal into the firebox on the climb out of Chama. When the locomotive labored, the column of smoke from its stack grew as thick and dark as the funnel of a tornado.

The Cumbres and Toltec Scenic Railroad crosses the San Juan

Mountains in a break formed by the Rio de los Piños on the east and Wolf Creek on the west. In between the two watersheds, the railroad slips over the ridge through a narrow gap at Cumbres Pass. Surveyors for the Denver and Rio Grande minimized expensive earthwork by following the grade of the river whenever possible, always seeking the steady level grade. The railroad surveyor dreams of a route that will scarcely tilt the whiskey in his glass. So much the better if it will not require extraordinary measures on the part of the construction engineer and his crews. A detour of a few miles is a bargain if it saves the need for a tunnel or trestle, but either is preferable to a grade so steep that every ascent will require a stouter locomotive or a helper, a cost in equipment and fuel and maintenance and manpower that must be paid on every run. American railroads, particularly those that opened up unsettled territory in the West, were more free than their Old World counterparts to wander about seeking easy detours around natural obstacles instead of having to engineer ways over or through them. The major trunk lines avoided the Colorado Plateau entirely: the Santa Fe Railway skirted its southern rim, and the Denver and Rio Grande main line followed the northern edge. It was left to the narrow-gauge operations to penetrate the interior mountains of the Plateau.

We passed over the Rio Chama bridge and the Lobato Trestle and climbed up through the aspens and spruces toward Cumbres Pass. The air was cooler the higher we climbed, but the sun seemed to grow warmer in the thinner air and make up the difference. On the steeper stretches we bumped slowly through the forest at a walking pace, and the narrow, single track of light rail and short ties barely parted the woods as we passed, seeming hardly more than a footpath. Rising up the mountain slopes, the sides of the cars almost brushed the branches of the trees. There is something clean and pure about the high-altitude forest clime—the pines and aspens and spruces and firs, the delicate understory of grasses and carpet of cushioning mosses. We seemed to be passing through time, out of summer through autumn toward winter. In the meadows near Chama, the round, fine-toothed aspen leaves were just turning from their two shades of green; higher up, they were brittle and golden; and before we reached the summit, they were shedding, brightening the forest floor beneath the aspen stands. Windblown aspen leaves caught in the needles of green-black spruce trees, glimmering golden in the sunlight like ornaments on the most elegant Christmas tree. I sat dumbfounded at the careless splendor.

At Cumbres Pass we stopped for ten minutes to take on water for the locomotive. In the winter of 1906, heavy snows stranded a passenger train on Cumbres Pass for ten days before a relief train could reach it. Helper locomotives were usually required to haul working trains eastbound up the 2,100-foot climb from Chama, and so the Denver and Rio Grande built a covered wye and turntable, a repair shop, a coal house and coal bin, a water tank and standpipe, a section house, bunkhouse, and depot at Cumbres. The repair shop, bunkhouse, and tool shed are gone now and State Highway 17 crosses the tracks on the site of the old depot, which was razed in the fifties. Now it is only a lonely, windswept summit.

The track descends from the pass through Tanglefoot Curve, a long switchback that comes within a few yards of itself at the two ends of the loop, and into the broad grassy valley of the Rio de los Piños, where it crosses the stream on a long low timber trestle. Two or three miles farther on, the tracks cross the Cascade Creek Trestle, which spans the deep canyon 137 feet above the creek. The iron trestle, which replaced the original wooden structure in 1889, is now nearly a century old and, although built in an era when locomotives typically weighed thirty tons, it now supports locomotives three times as heavy.

At Osier we stopped for lunch at the head of a high meadow drained by Osier Creek. There we met another Cumbres and Toltec train that had come up the other side of the mountains from Antonito. That afternoon, each train would reverse and return to its starting point. Most passengers would return with their train, but a few of us would switch trains and travel on over the mountains.

When the other passengers herded into the old section house for their catered box lunch, I slipped away down the meadow. I walked quickly and purposefully until I was over the crest, and then picked my way leisurely along a little rivulet. It made a pleasant dripping sound and tossed off little flecks of light like a wet dog flinging water droplets, and I happily followed it down through the meadow. I sat down in the grass, surrounded by dry cowpies, and ate my apple. Up the slope behind me, I could see the stack of the idling locomotive and the smoke rising and thinning into wisps in the clear air. The curve of the hill hid the track: I couldn't see the other passengers and they couldn't see me. The pleasant drone of insects buzzing about in the dry grass was soothing and irrelevant, like cocktail-party chatter. For a little while I would be a man without worry, with a valley to myself where not even the IRS could find me.

I could see the tracks we had followed come winding up one slope of the long valley of Rio de los Piños, skirting just below the tier of trees. Even here at 9,600 feet the landscape had a gentle aspect. The mountains were smooth and round and carpeted with soft grasses: the rock showed through in only a few places, like raw patches where the hair had been shaved to the scalp to dress a wound. Something in the breeze, though, suggested to me that it could roar and bite when winter came. At this altitude, winter was not far off.

For a few minutes, the world was all warmth and light. Meadow grasses sprouted from dung heaps. The poor dumb doppelgänger who had made such a mess of things the night before had been reborn into a benign universe.

While the passengers ate, the train crews swapped locomotives. Number 489, which had hauled us up from Chama, was uncoupled and maneuvered through the wye and coupled to the other end of the string of coaches that had come up the other side that morning from Antonito. Number 488, another 2-8-2 K-36, was coupled to the New Mexico Express for the return to Chama. I watched the engineer walk along beside No. 488 and squirt globs of oil from an oil can the size of a coffee can onto the running gear, and when he climbed back into the cab I noticed the warning painted on the side of the tender: DO NOT USE THIS WATER FOR DRINKING PURPOSES.

The run through Toltec Gorge several miles east of Osier afforded dramatic vistas of the rocky canyon, and I feared momentarily for the balance of the car as every passenger leapt to the downhill side to snap pictures and exclaim. Every passenger except two. An older man and his wife, both of retirement age but looking lean and vigorous, kept their seats on the uphill side of the car and while everyone else was ogling the panorama below us, they were studying the rock cliff above us. They both wore warm, sturdy clothes—flannel shirts and whipcord trousers. Neither carried a camera. While everyone else was fighting for a window overlooking the canyon, they kept to themselves, delighting in the rock face of the cut, studying it with pleasure as if it was a wall of the Louvre passing by.

"You all look like you know something the rest of us don't," I said.

They looked around a little sheepishly and he stole a glance at her and said, "I guess I see things a little differently. I'm a geologist. I'm afraid I tend to keep my nose to the ground." He was probably in his middle-sixties, but something about him suggested that he could walk me into the ground over a day's hike. He was one of those people in whom curiosity stays alive.

Pointing at the rock face, I told him, "This makes me wish I had paid more attention in eighth-grade Earth Science."

He laughed. "Well, you know, geologists love this. We're always excited every time they cut a highway. We follow the bulldozers like prospectors. I'm retired now, but that just means I have the time to study a bit more, and my wife and I can take these trips together, and I can try to show her how exciting it can be to see the history of the earth played out in the rock."

She said, "I like the pretty rocks, and Bob explains the ugly ones to me."

He was a geomorphologist, someone who studies landforms to learn how they were created. As we talked, he pointed out geological formations. He showed me ancient streambeds in the rock face, where I could see round, waterworn stones embedded forever in volcanic ash, caught in cross section like a frozen stream flowing through the earth.

He had spent his entire career with an oil company. "We've lived all over the West: Butte and Billings, Calgary, and for the last few years we ended up in Tulsa. When we retired we moved to Durango."

She had lived in northern New Mexico as a child. "If it had been up to my grandfather," she said, laughing, "there wouldn't be a tree left in these mountains. He was a logger up here. I grew up in this country and loved it, but my family thought it was a little rough for a girl and sent me back east to school. I never got back here until now."

Waiting in the depot at Antonito for the van to take us back over Route 17 to Chama, we discovered a common interest in trout fishing.

"Anne went fishing with me once. We planned for it carefully. I schooled her, taught her how to wade, how to cast, how to select a fly. I left her to fish a nice pool and went upriver. I heard her holler and hurried back to find her standing in the middle of the stream with a fly hanging from her lip. I said, 'Come back to the cabin.' She said, 'No. I'm not moving. Take it out right now.' So I cut it out with a pocketknife."

She was smiling as he told the story. "I've never been back again," she said when he had finished.

By the time the van had ferried us from Antonito back to our cars in the parking lot at Chama, they were trying to persuade me to stay over in Durango for a day or two and visit. "We're going on to stay with some friends tonight, but we'll be back at home tomorrow night and if you could stay over in Durango we'd like for you to come out to the house. If you can find a few days, we could go up to Aspen. We've got a cabin up there with a trout stream right out the front door." It was an invitation that haunted me for months.

From the lobby of a bar on the outskirts of Chama, I called the hostel in Durango. They had one bed left for the night but would not hold it for me. It was late afternoon and getting cold. There is something about the onset of night in the mountains that makes stouter men than me want to head for the bunkhouse. The drive over from Chama, about a hundred miles north to Pagosa Springs and west to Durango, might have been enjoyable during the day. At night, I just concentrated on making the turns and ticking off the small towns like mileposts along the way: Chromo, Pagosa Springs, Dyke, Chimney Rock, Bayfield, and Gem Village. In the mountains somewhere west of Pagosa Springs, my rented Volkswagen Rabbit began to lose power, as if the fuel pump might be failing. I seemed always to be in the wake of a cattle truck or a horse trailer. Somewhere along the way I crossed the Continental Divide in the dark.

I drove into Durango around ten that night, and, just a block or so north of the train depot I found the hostel, a ramshackle Victorian house on Second Avenue, where the steep pitch of the cliff leveled out into the Animas River valley. I claimed the last bed, which turned out to be a top bunk in a rustic bunkhouse out in the backyard. There was a small, forlorn kitchen, with empty cupboards and a few battered aluminum pans, a sleeping room with four double bunks framed with rough-cut four-by-fours, and, up a couple of steps in the back, a bathroom. Accommodations for women were adjacent but separate. The only heat uttered from a sheet-steel wood stove that burned fitfully, smoldering all night and generating more smoke than heat. I slept in my clothes, under the blanket I found on the bunk, and in the chill hour before dawn I wrapped myself as tightly as I could in the blanket and was still too cold to sleep. When I got up, I was so stiff from tensing against the cold that I had to lower myself from the top bunk like an arthritic old man.

A tall, rangy young man with dark, curly hair was dressing quickly close to the wood stove. I joined him on the platform of bricks that served as a hearth and he whispered to me, "Was it any warmer up where you were?"

"I've slept colder, but only outdoors."

"Didn't you have a sleeping bag?" he asked me.

"I'm traveling light."

"We'll have a decent fire tonight. We couldn't find a thing but green aspen logs last night. I told 'em they wouldn't burn."

He, too, was in Durango to ride the Silverton train, so we walked across the street—my breath frosted in the air as we walked—and had a quick cup of coffee and went on another block to the depot, which was already crowded with people at eight o'clock. I had ordered my tickets by mail so I could avoid the long line at the ticket window of sightseers out to observe the fall colors. We boarded one of the cars—a graceful enclosed wooden coach, with clerestory windows, lights and luggage racks, bathrooms and a wood stove and coal bin at the rear.

This train was a direct descendent of the nineteenth-century Denver and Rio Grande train No. 15, the Silverton Accommodation. ("Accommodation" was a common appellation for a train in the prewar days of steam locomotion. Typically it described a train more direct than a local and less expeditious than a limited.) In 1886, No. 15 left Durango at 7:30 A.M. and arrived in Silverton at 12:40 P.M. In those days, when the Colorado mountains were laced with narrow-gauge and short-line railroads, the Silverton Accommodation met connections at both ends of its branch. Today the train of the Durango and Silverton Narrow Gauge Railroad is all alone in the San Juans. It now carries the name of the San Juan Express, which ran between

Alamosa and Durango until 1950 and was, then, the last narrow-gauge luxury-name train operating in the United States.

The route north to Silverton begins mundanely enough, wending through Durango, crossing city streets, skirting back alleys, past the Safeway, past the old hotels and new motels, the restaurants and boutiques, "Frontier Liquors" and "Summit Cleaning—The Peak in Your Cleaning Experience." For the first fifteen miles of the journey, the tracks climb gently through the broad valley of the Animas River. A few miles north of Durango, the river cuts through a glacial moraine and the tracks snake along the slopes overlooking the broad valley, where the river meanders idly along, having wound itself into oxbows.

The ardent photographers congregated in the open car at the end of the train. In the seat just ahead of me, a young couple smooched, oblivious to the mountain scenery. Mileposts along the track right-of-way are numbered with the distance in miles from Denver. Just past milepost 464, Missionary Ridge, named for the Civil War battle-field at Chattanooga, dominates the view to the east. Scrub oak, orange turning to red, Utah juniper, and scattered Ponderosa pine appeared on the hillside along the tracks, and as we climbed higher into the foothills, the pines thickened into dense stands.

The High Line is that portion of the Durango and Silverton track that creeps along the canyon wall above the deep cut of the Animas above Rockwood, almost twenty miles above Durango. The track bed is cut precipitously into the canyon wall, some four hundred feet directly above the river. As the train crawled along the ledge, curving around rock outcroppings, I could look ahead and see the mustard-yellow coaches and the locomotive skirting the edge of a sheer drop into the river.

The train negotiates the High Line under a slow order. As the cars snake along the ledge the wheel flanges squeal and groan on the railheads, giving and taking inches of lateral movement under the weight of the cars as they negotiate the curves. The earliest railways, horse-drawn colliery railways in the English mining districts, used turntables to change direction. The flanged wheel later made it possible for a fixed axle to travel around a curved track by allowing the outer wheel to travel a greater distance than the inner wheel, and later the pivoting wheel truck, or bogie, allowed cars to be lengthened to their present dimensions. Both were simple but profound solutions to fundamental problems of railroad design. Through the Animas canyon, where the tracks of the Durango and Silverton curve as much as twenty-four degrees in places, they demonstrate their utility.

The locomotive worked hard all along the High Line, where the maximum grade is two and a half percent, which means that the track rises two and a half feet in elevation for every one hundred feet of distance—stiff by the standards of main-line railroading. The sharp curves of the Animas canyon High Line aggravate the grade, because the tractive effort required to pull a train up a grade is much increased by a curve in the track. Railroad engineers have since learned to anticipate this effect. On modern "compensated" track, the inclination of the track on hills is reduced somewhat in the curves so that the tractive resistance will remain relatively constant.

On the uphill side of the track, steel cables, anchored in the red granite, looped around the rails and clasped the track like a safety chain. Farther up the line I looked down into the canyon and saw twisted lengths of rusting rail that had been swept into the river when floodwaters washed out the line some years ago. Looking at the sheer walls of the gorge, I thought of the geologist I had met in Chama and wished he were there to answer my questions.

By ten o'clock the sun was only just beginning to penetrate into the river gorge. When we stopped to take on water from a stream-fed tank, the smoke from the idling locomotive gathered over the river like a dense fog and then drifted up the canyon walls to cloud the narrow strip of sky overhead. Bronze water birches, slender as swizzle sticks, grew along the water's edge where the creek flowed into the Animas River. Between the altitudes of seven and eight thousand feet, the forest changed perceptibly. The Gambel oaks and junipers and cottonwoods and willows of the lower elevations gave way to Ponderosa pines, aspens, birches, and then, a little higher, blue spruce, more aspens, and fir.

Wildflowers—goldenrod, asters, and daisies—carpeted the meadow at Elk Park, where we stopped to let off a party of hunters, who unloaded packs, ice chests, and cased rifles and clambered down in blaze orange vests and baseball caps. As we steamed away, leaving them alone, they began gathering up their gear and hoisting their packs. I longed to be with them, watching the train disappear around the curve and listening to the deep pumping of the steam engine fade away until the quiet descended. Near the upper end of Elk Park, we passed a fishing camp at the edge of the meadow. Chest waders hung upside down from a tree limb to dry.

Along the forty-five-mile climb to Silverton, the Animas River is a constant companion. The character of the river changes with the ascent, and the mood of the trip changes with it. Through the stretches of steep river canyon, the glacial milk reflected a greenish, almost turquoise, hue, and looked cold and forbidding. Over the last five miles below Silverton, the Animas flows through open meadow in a series of shallow, sunny riffles. In the precipitous canyon, the river runs deep and fast and dangerous, slicing through sheer walls of gneiss and schist, but in the long gentle valley up near Silverton its waters are spread thin and meek, shining like a pocketful of change fanned across a tabletop so the dimes can be gleaned from the pennies.

Silverton is a mining town in a 9,300-foot-high valley surrounded by 13,000-foot peaks. More than two dozen old mines pock the slopes of Kendall Mountain and Sultan Mountain on either side of the railroad tracks south of town. Some of the old mines bear the names of other places, and if the men who staked them remembered their homes in the names they bestowed, then they must have come a long way—from Detroit, Idaho, Scranton City, New York, Shenandoah, and Iowa. Other names betrayed dreams of grandeur: King Mine, Montezuma Mine, Little Giant Mine, Black Prince Mine, Royal Tiger Mine, Mighty Monarch Mine. One, my favorite, lacks all pretense —the Legal Tender Mine. There dug a man with a literal mind.

I disembarked with a hundred or so other passengers, stepping down into a wide, muddy, unpaved street next to a small depot. I walked a block or so up a slight grade to Greene Street, where the business district of Silverton differs in only a few details from a photograph of the same street taken in 1910. In the old photograph, the street is unpaved and the only vehicles are carts and wagons; on the Thursday in October when I was there, the vehicles angled into the sidewalk were an assortment of pickups, four-wheel drives, rusty old American cars, and a few shiny sedans of recent vintage with out-of-state plates. At either end of the four- or five-block business district, the street appeared to crumble away into the glacial debris and steep mountains jutted up to high snow-filled basins and rocky, ice-encrusted peaks. Even in the shank of autumn, the town had a gravelly, gritty grayness about it.

In the quiet saloon of the Grand Imperial Hotel, a brick and stone hotel built on Greene Street in 1882, the soft patina of the cherrywood bar reflected warm yellow light. A middle-aged man in jeans and western gear drank alone on a barstool. The bartender polished his glassware. I sat at a corner table and drank a couple of cups of coffee, watching the weather turn dreary in the street outside.

I walked out of the hotel into a Scotch mist that soon turned to a cold drizzling rain. I followed the gravel street to the edge of town, where it ended in muddy ruts and the sidewalk simply stopped and the mountains began. The foot of a mountain is more mysterious to me than its peak, perhaps because it is less often clearly visible, just as beginnings are so often less apparent, harder to define, than endings. Who knows where a step will lead, what it will prove to have been the beginning of? Even looking back, how hard it is to say precisely where a career, a romance, a fear began.

By train time, the rain was falling in fat chilling drops, splatting in mud puddles along the dirt street, and rain clouds had squatted down over the town. The mountain peaks were obscured as completely as if someone had pulled a wet wool blanket over the valley. There was no thunder, no bluster. Only steady, dreary rain from an inscrutable sky. It felt as if it would rain until spring.

The brakeman was trying to start a fire in the coal stove when I boarded the coach. He was a young man with a mustache, wearing railroad overalls and heavy black work boots, and he was having a very hard time. The stove would not draw, and sooty smoke curled out of every pore of the leaky thing while the fire stagnated. I stowed my camera bag on a seat and walked back to stand with him next to the stove. "Is it going to go?" I asked.

"Not yet. But she'll draw when we get moving." He poked patiently at the grate. "Coal is slow to fire, but it burns hot."

The sweet smell of coal smoke was permeating the coach, making me a little queasy, but I stayed near the stove and even poked at it myself a time or two as we waited for the other passengers to straggle aboard in ones and twos. Almost as soon as we steamed out of the Silverton valley and back down into the narrow chute of the river gorge, the rain stopped and the sodden blanket of clouds lifted.

The early mornings and late nights, long drives and close connections, and succession of strangers—the constant effort to take it all
in—were taking their toll. Fatigue and sensory overload were slowing me down. I stuck my head out of the window every now and then
to refresh myself with cold air, trying to choose moments when the
wind was carrying away the coal smoke from the locomotive. I
thought ahead to Albuquerque, Amtrak again, and my next stop at
Kansas City, where a familiar face waited. I was ready to be with
someone to whom I didn't have to introduce nor explain myself.
There comes a time when only a deeply rooted friendship will restore
the spirit.

By the time we eased down the last gentle slope into the Durango
valley, the sun was angling low through the meadow grass, and the
horses were basking in the warmth of an Indian summer evening. As
we steamed slowly along the valley floor toward Durango, the light
of late afternoon, sliding between the clouds and the mountain ridge
to the west, struck each brown wizened weed on the banks along the
tracks, the rusting leaves of the cottonwoods and the seedheads of
the grasses, and the occasional blooming wildflower. Across the valley, a farmer on a tractor raked his mown hay. He would surely finish
in plenty of light, even there on the western edge of the valley where
the shadows of the mountains were already creeping across his field.

A fisherman looks at a river differently from most anyone else. In
the way that an attorney reads a contract, he notices where the hidden things lie. All along the Animas, from Silverton to Durango, I
had noticed still pools, delicate riffles, deep cuts, and fast runs, all
with pockets of good holding water in the scant flow of autumn, and
just as I was wondering why I hadn't seen a single fisherman, I noticed
a fly fisherman working a broad shallows on the outskirts of Durango.
I thought about the hunters we had left at Elk Park, how lonely and
peaceful the twilight must be in that narrow valley, where the sun
would set early and the chill would flow down the mountain slopes
to collect in the river bottom like rainwater into a cistern.

On the outskirts of Durango new houses, framed and roofed and
sheathed with blackboard, waited for siding, looking like packing
crates. Cordwood was stacked in open sheds or covered pens at almost
every house in the valley, and I wondered if, on still winter days when
every chimney puffed woodsmoke, the air in the valley went acrid.

I was depressed after my train ride. Having always to keep moving, I was passing by so many possibilities. My trip was beginning to feel like a cattle drive, never so fast as to walk the stock down to gristle and bone, but never slow enough to graze a second day on the good grass. So many byways beckoned. I drove through Durango in the early evening, looking for a sporting goods shop or a hardware store where I could buy a fly or two. The pack rod I had carried so many fruitless miles was beginning to haunt me. But I was too late: the shops were closed and the twilight was fading fast. So I left town, crossed over the river, and followed it north hoping to at least find a fisherman doing what I so ardently wished to do. I would watch a few minutes, perhaps strike up a conversation. Almost immediately, I came to a barrier beyond which the road was closed for repairs. Feeling defeated and dejected, I parked not far from the bridge and walked down to the river's edge. With the low water of autumn the river had grown bony, revealing the rocks in its bed. I sat on a rock and opened a bottle of beer, watching the river, now opaque in the twilight, slide smoothly around the boulders. Green and yellow cottonwoods leaned over the river downstream, and the massive humped ridge where the river turned south of town loomed forbiddingly in the fading light. A small dark bird I could not identify winged upriver, skimming the water.

The Southwest Limited to Kansas City: Stormy Weather

I never travel without my diary. One should always have something sensational to read in the train.

—Oscar Fingal O'Flahertie Wills Wilde, *The Importance of Being Earnest*

y noon the next day I was sitting on a bench in the shade of the veranda at the Albuquerque train station, the same blue wooden bench where I had waited after disembarking Monday afternoon. In the four days intervening, I had driven more than eight hundred miles across northern New Mexico and ridden the steam trains at Chama and Durango. I had spent a second night in the Durango hostel, and, although the wood stove, fed with dry fuel, had made things much more comfortable, I found myself still weary. Now I was waiting for the same train, the Southwest Limited, which would take me on across Colorado and Kansas to Kansas City.

A few minutes after noon an Indian couple drove into the station lot and parked near the quay. They unloaded a card table and what appeared to be several small suitcases and carried them to the train platform. As he left, she began setting up the folding table. With practiced, methodical motions, she shook out a white tablecloth and covered the table with it, wrapping it tightly and pinning it at the corners, as if she were making a bed, so it fitted snugly and didn't flap in the light wind. Then she opened a black sample case and took from it turquoise and silver necklaces, rings pressed into velvet-covered foam slabs in orderly rows, earrings, pins and brooches, and larger pieces, bracelets and belt buckles, and arrayed them on her table. Each piece had its place. Every movement was paced: smooth and unhurried. Somewhere down the line, the Southwest Limited was bringing her customers to her, and she would be ready.

The long concrete platform where she placed her table was warm and bright under the midday sun. Where I sat, under the portico, the coolness of early morning lingered, captured in the thick masonry walls of the station. The gentle breeze carried the heavy floral scent of her perfume to me.

As train time neared, more Indian women arrived and set up tables of wares until a colorful bazaar lined the platform. A balloonist from the balloon festival being held in Albuquerque that week, wearing a short-sleeved knit shirt emblazoned with the name of his balloon and carrying his walkie-talkie on his hip, prowled up and down the platform with his camera, calculating the best angle from which to photograph the train when it arrived. I walked across the tracks and amused myself reading the sides of freight cars parked in the yard. On the side of an Atchison, Topeka and Santa Fe flatcar: "ANCHOR FAST," which seemed good advice, and "DO NOT HUMP."

About ten minutes before one, the Southwest Limited rolled in, very nearly on time. As dozens of passengers clambered down to stretch their legs and began to gather around the tables of silver and turquoise jewelry, I made my way to the train. As I passed each attendant standing watch at his step stool, I called out, "Kansas City?" and each in turn pointed forward until I came to the one who said, "Right here for K.C.! Come aboard."

As we signaled for a crossing on the outskirts of Albuquerque, a father seated ahead of me leaned close to his daughter of four or five and whispered, "Hear that whistle? That lonesome sound, like a daddy wolf calling to his little girl who's lost?"

Through the afternoon, roughly following the track of the Santa Fe Trail, we skirted the Sangre de Cristo Mountains, climbing steeply from Albuquerque to Lamy, and on, still climbing, through Apache Canyon and over Glorieta Pass at more than 7,400 feet. Although Glorieta Pass is neither the Continental Divide nor the highest point on the line, the ascent through Apache Canyon from the west may well be the most rugged stretch on the Santa Fe. The train seems to cleave the rock. By contrast, the descent toward Las Vegas, New Mexico, on the eastern side of the pass was deceptively steady and smooth. Only my maps told me that we were descending more than a thousand feet.

For hours we raced across the high plains of eastern New Mexico, with the Sangre de Cristo Mountains occasionally visible to the west. In the late afternoon, when the lounge car was crowded with convivial drinkers and the early diners were beginning to stream through my coach on their way to the dining car, I withdrew to the lower-level vestibule. I liked to stand in the vestibule of the Superliner coaches, where I could feel some of the rattle. Riding in the Superliners is akin to riding in a 1968 Cadillac: quiet, smooth, insular, and sometimes soporific. In the vestibule, I could feel the track through the studded steel floor and hear the clack of the rails and occasionally crack the window.

We crossed the Canadian River and as the sun began to set and the light ripened we began climbing again toward Raton Pass, the highest point on the Santa Fe line between Chicago and California. Just before dusk, we stopped at Raton, New Mexico. The coach attendant opened the top half of the Dutch door in the vestibule and the two of us leaned on the sill, elbow to elbow like railbirds at the track. The residual warmth of late afternoon drifted into the car like heat from a banked furnace. We looked out on an empty, windblown street and he said to me, "I've been on this run, off and on, for two years, and I've never boarded a passenger here. Most days, I just look out there and wonder if anybody really lives here."

The advantage of Raton Pass as the best route through the mountains was recognized by the Indians, and their judgment was corroborated by the blazers of the Santa Fe Trail. Uncle Dick Wooten, an Indian fighter, trader, rancher, and opportunist, secured a charter in 1865 to establish a toll road through Raton Pass from Trinidad, Colorado, to Red River, New Mexico. In the contest between the Denver and Rio Grande Railroad and the Santa Fe Railway for possession of Raton Pass—whichever railroad claimed the pass would prevail south and west of the mountains—Dick Wooten's assistance probably tipped the balance in favor of the Santa Fe. Both railroads dispatched engineers on the same day to begin work in the pass: the two engineers rode the same D&RG train to the town of El Moro, arriving in the town near the pass shortly before midnight. Chief Engineer J. A. McMurtrie of the D&RG stopped long enough for a few hours' sleep before starting out early in the morning, but the Santa Fe engineer, A. A. Robinson, saddled up in the middle of the night and rode to Dick Wooten's ranch on the north slope of the pass, where together they mustered a crew of transients and trudged up the mountain to begin shoveling by lantern light. McMurtrie apparently rose early, because most accounts put his arrival at the pass no more than an hour after Robinson and Wooten, but he found the pass in the material possession of the Santa Fe Railway. By the few minutes advantage gained from one man's industry, the Santa Fe accrued to itself the most coveted route south and west to the Pacific.

From the crest of Raton Pass, you could roll a marble 650 miles down the Santa Fe line to Kansas City. Beginning at the New Mexico–Colorado border, the Santa Fe rail line surrenders gracefully almost all of the altitude it has arduously gained, lost, and gained again over the mountains of California, Arizona, and New Mexico. First in a steep drop through Trinidad and La Junta and then in a slow, steady decline across the Kansas prairie to the Missouri line, the railroad descends more than a mile.

With dinner to look forward to, I gathered up my maps and notebooks and went to the observation car to wait. My dining car reservation was for eight o'clock, so I would be called just before we arrived in La Junta, a Santa Fe railroad town where we would change crews. I found the observation car almost deserted. By seven-thirty, it was pitch dark, and with only the dim reading lights burning, the car had the atmosphere of an after-hours nightclub where just a few patrons lingered. The soft whoosh from the air-conditioning vents was the loudest sound, the gentle rocking of the Superliner the only motion.

Two middle-aged women, obviously traveling together, had taken an interest in a young woman in her twenties. In the quiet car I overheard snippets of their conversation. I heard her tell them that she was a schoolteacher who hadn't been able to find a job that fall. "I work all I can as a substitute," she said, "but it's not really teaching. I'm there mostly to take roll and keep order."

After a few minutes, the young schoolteacher left her new acquaintances and moved to a seat by herself on my side of the car. She curled up with her stockinged feet tucked under her cross-legged as she read a paperback. I looked up, saw her reflection in the dark window, and smiled. She had high, broad cheekbones, fair skin, and very fine light brown hair. Her jeans had soft gray pinstripes, like a banker's blue suit.

We might have been at ease in our own living room. I had the ridiculous sense that this entire train, or at least this one quiet car, was my private varnish. The train whistled for a crossing, the sound drifting back from far away. The night occasionally gave way to the station platforms of the small towns of eastern Colorado and western Kansas. Never more than a few travelers waited to board, a few well-wishers to see them off. From a train, every town is a small town.

On the steady, downward slope from La Junta, Colorado, to Dodge City, 325 miles along the Arkansas River, we rolled smooth and fast on track rated for ninety miles an hour. The moon rose swollen and orange in the early evening. Later it climbed behind the clouds and disappeared, turning the night sky into drifting vapors.

The schoolteacher and I fell gradually into conversation. I would say something; she would look up, smile at my reflection in the window, and respond, and we would both go back to our books. A few minutes later, I would look up at her reflection and find her staring out into the dark. Gradually, we put aside our books and began to talk and eight o'clock came and went. At last call, before we crossed into Kansas, I went downstairs to the bar and bought us two beers and later, when we were hungry, I went back to my coach seat and collected from my travel bag cheese and crackers and some fruit, an apple for her and a banana for me, and a warm beer, procured from the City Market in Durango the night before, and brought them back to the observation car.

We reached Dodge City a little after midnight, Central Daylight Time, losing an hour in the crossing from the Mountain time zone. By then the bar was closed and we were alone in the car. Past one o'clock and on toward two we talked, with little on the dark, flat landscape to distract us. A little before two we passed through Hutchinson and saw two tall, floodlit elevators, church steeples to the towns and grain counties of the Midwest, totems to the agricultural ethic. (In what small midwestern town did people begin to perceive the image of Christ on the side of a grain elevator?)

She came back to my coach seat with me and we curled up under a blanket she had brought with her and we slept through Newton and Strong City and Emporia, Carbondale, Topeka, Lecompton, Lawrence, and Holliday, slept until I awoke in the Argentine rail yards at Kansas City, Kansas, about six-thirty. In the few minutes while we eased through the yards and moved on the several miles to the Kansas City, Missouri, station, I thought about Fats Waller. In December 1943 he had just finished making *Stormy Weather*; some later would say he had stolen the film with a single tilt of his eyebrow. Suffering from bronchial pneumonia, he started from Hollywood for New York City on the Santa Fe Chief, traveling with his friend and longtime manager, Ed Kirkeby. Just outside Kansas City, on December 15, about six in the morning, he suffered a heart attack, and he was dead when the Chief reached the station.

The yards were steely in the scarce gray light. "Keep warm," I whispered. She was still asleep as I folded the blanket around her and slipped quietly away to disembark at Kansas City. Her name was Janice. I had her address in Bemidji, Minnesota, but I never expected to see her again.

Kansas City's Union Station was a ghostly place. When it was finished in 1914, some three hundred trains moved through Kansas City every day. On the day I arrived, there would be only six. Its platforms and subterranean passageways are now as quiet as catacombs. The archaic station is too monumental to abandon but too mammoth to maintain. Rather than refurbish and heat it, Amtrak had abandoned the concourse to the pigeons and erected an air-supported dome, an inflated geodesic tent, in the front lobby. Passing from the dim, dusty hulk of the abandoned station through a small vestibule into the brightly lit tent was a passage from the ruins of the once-glorious, now moribund past of railroading into its prosaic present—and its tenuous future. There, in the early morning, Susan met me.

"It's a little early for you, isn't it?" she said, smiling.

"I've changed my habits. Have you been waiting long?"

"Not long. This train, I knew that if you were on it, it would be late. You haven't changed that much," she said.

"You'd be surprised." Her car was just a few yards from the monumental facade of the station, where Kansas City gangsters had machine-gunned policemen in a famous thirties massacre. I had read that bullet scars remain in the stone, but I didn't stop to look. We drove through Kansas City quickly: there was no traffic early on Saturday morning.

"Are you hungry?" Susan asked. "I don't remember breakfast being your meal."

"Ordinarily, that's true," I said, "but yesterday was a lean day. Had a doughnut and a cup of coffee on the road for breakfast, never got around to lunch, and I missed the last dinner seating in the dining car."

"Late again?"

"Something like that."

"Well, I know where we can get a good breakfast. After that you can get some more sleep if you want."

We crossed over to Kansas City, Kansas, where the streets were wider and even more deserted. "This is the other side of the tracks," Susan said as we drove down a long street, past shops that looked like they hadn't changed in thirty years. "KCMO is fashionable, prosperous, progressive, and looks to the future. KCK is where working people and dancers live. So we can get a good breakfast at any hour."

We parked on the street, pulling diagonally to the curb in the manner of midwestern small towns where the streets are wide and parallel parking is an eastern affectation. The sidewalks were deserted, but inside Feagan's Cafe most of the booths and half of the counter stools were filled. We found a booth at the rear. While we ate, Susan told me, "When I first came to K.C., before I'd found a place to live or a studio, when I was still dreaming of moving the dance company, I'd come into this place every morning for breakfast and sometimes I'd stay for hours, reading the classifieds and drinking coffee. They made me feel more welcome here than I did over in KCMO where they think they know all about culture."

That afternoon, Susan took me out to purchase a few necessities and we spent the rest of the afternoon browsing through thrift shops looking for costumes for her dance company. Late in the afternoon she persuaded me that I needed a Panama hat I found in a tiny junk shop. With a few exceptions, it is the rare man under forty who looks anything but a fool in a hat, but Susan appealed transparently to my vanity and the old woman who ran the shop was her ready accomplice. I haggled for ten minutes and finally paid her twelve dollars for the Panama, which was just enough to keep me from discarding it in the snows of Montana weeks later.

On the way home we browsed through a bookshop, where I bought a copy of Steinbeck's *Travels with Charley*, a book I had fallen in love with as a child and hardly thought of since. I had not brought anything to read, intending to avoid any distraction, any way of passing the time that would interpose itself between me and my travels, but after three weeks I had come to realize that occasionally I would need company, and at that moment I couldn't think of a better companion than Steinbeck.

I spent the night on the sofa in the front room of her small frame bungalow on Valley Street, where she lived with John, the man who would become her third husband. Sunday about midday, Susan and I drove an hour or so southwest of Kansas City to Baldwin City, Kansas, and ate a late breakfast at the Blackjack Cafe. Driving back to Kansas City we talked about her work. The night before, she had shown me videotapes of some of her dance pieces. It had been my first opportunity in years to see her choreography, and it had been like finally meeting the family of someone I had known for a long, long time. Revealing but not surprising. I had always known that her dances would be good, known it since watching her teach awkward beginning dancers when we were still teenagers, known it before she had dared to dream of choreographing her own work and long before she had built her own company.

"A work like 'Trio' took two and a half to three years," she said. "I see so much choreography that just isn't finished. Somebody didn't take the time, or more likely, they couldn't buy the time. The economics of it."

I asked, "Isn't that always true in the performing arts, though? Rehearsal time is a rare and dear commodity."

"It's true," Susan agreed, "I've been really lucky. I think of choreographers in New York who put on their one concert of the year, hoping that *Dance* magazine will review it, and they sink in two to three thousand dollars of their own money, renting studio space. They know when they start exactly how many studio hours they have;

they know exactly how many dancers they can afford; their piece is shaped from inception by those economic factors. When that happens to me I'll get out of the business.

"When I agreed to set a new work on the students at Kansas State, I did it to find out how I would function under that kind of deadline, and it was horrifying. There was no innovation. All I did was craft, the little tricks of the trade that I've learned over the years.

"I'm really convinced that the time pressure has a lot to do with what I see, or don't see, in choreography today. There's no heart to it at all. And it encourages the public appetite for showy tricks.

"Did I tell you I went to see the San Francisco Ballet the other night in Manhattan [Kansas]? This woman was doing an adagio section, on point, and she did the most beautiful thing: she would start a turn on point at a quick speed and then slow it down. I have no idea how she did it. I was captured. And there was no audience reaction at all. And yet when she did a triple pirouette, which she should have been able to do when she was sixteen, the audience perceived that as a trick—she completed it, so they clapped. I was heartbroken."

As she talked, she grew more animated, admitting that regional artists all too often allowed themselves to be patronized. "I think it's a trap for regional artists—even the term is a trap—to have to constantly think of themselves in reference to New York. In November, three weeks from now, I'm supposed to go back there. This national consulting firm has picked us up, we're one of two midwestern companies they've picked up. Well anyway, they've strongly advised me to go to New York to see what's being done. The truth is, I'm not really interested."

The two pieces on tape she had shown me the night before were sharply different in their tone and technique. "Spring Fever" was a gentle comic piece for two dancers that derived much of its humor from juxtaposition with its music, a dramatic duet from Verdi's *La Traviata*; "Trio" was a long, complex, acutely visual unfolding of patterns for a changing cast of dancers set to hypnotic music by composer Steve Reich. I had been stunned by the density of detail in the choreography.

Yet Susan was most serious about her humorous pieces, and about the need for humor in dance. "I used to apologize for dances like 'Spring Fever,'" Susan said. "I even did it to you last night, 'it's just a funny little dance' and so on, but they are the pieces that are closest to my heart because they are the most human.

"I hope you get to see the new work tomorrow," she said. "It's very different from what I've done. Unfortunately, I can't find an ending." She laughed. "You know, I thought we'd be talking about something else today. Just the same, I'm glad we came out."

I pulled the car over into the grass and we crossed the road, climbed a four-strand barbed wire fence posted with dead tree limbs, and walked through a field of grain stubble to sit under a spreading oak tree on the bank of a narrow, meandering creek. The dark water moved imperceptibly and at each elbow in its deeply eroded channel decaying oak leaves blanketed the surface. The ground around the oak was covered with small yellow oak leaves newly fallen, pliable and soft. A woodpecker hammered the trunk of a nearby oak and a squirrel nosed about under another. A light rain, almost a mist, fell, and the air smelled rich, like mulch. Sitting in the leaves against the trunk of the big oak, we talked, in quieter voices now, shorter sentences, longer pauses, softer words.

"Still friends?" she asked, finally.

"I say yes. How about you?"

"Yes," she said.

"Well," I said, "then we go on." The afternoon was almost over. Since I had left home in September, the days had gotten shorter.

Walking back through the stubble to the car, we flushed a rabbit that bounded away through the field in that zigzag pattern ingrained in all rabbits, the evolved defense mechanism that enables them to elude faster, but not so nimble, predators.

That night after Susan, John, and I watched Goose Gossage give up a three-run homer in the ninth that sealed the World Series for Detroit, we headed for Brooklyn Street and Arthur Bryant's rib joint. The restaurant was small and noisy, with a side room where a band, the Kings of Jazz, was packing up after the night's gig. The juke box blared soul music, and the pagan odor of burning meat wafted from the back where racks of ribs were broiling in a brick furnace. We bought a slab and an order of fries, heavy and greasy with the skins. Both were wrapped in kraft paper and the ribs, slathered in sauce, began immediately to ooze grease into the brown paper.

When we unrolled the paper on their kitchen table the ribs were still hot. We drank beer and ate ribs for an hour, wallowing in grease and barbecue sauce, and then John and I took the bones out to the backyard and tossed them to the dogs and talked about fishing.

It rained during the night and all the warmth went out of the wind. A front had moved through: the rain stopped before morning and left the sky filled with low gray clouds. I awoke first and found a two-pound can of Hill Bros. coffee in the kitchen and made a big pot of coffee. Later in the morning, I dropped Susan off at her studio, where her company was rehearsing for its Kansas City debut, and took her car to the Westheight Laundromat in an alley on the corner of 18th and Minnesota. While my clothes washed, I read the *Thrifty Nickle Want Ads*.

Susan's studio was the third floor, the upper floor, of an old stone firehouse on the top of a hill in a working-class neighborhood of Kansas City, Kansas. When I arrived just before two, the company was in motion. The dancers, working on the final section of "Trio," gasped for breath in the chill air. Sweat flew off their faces as they danced, making and unmaking complex patterns. There was none of the glitz of a juice-bar exercise studio: the women wore faded leotards and turtlenecks, a couple of the men wore football jerseys, and they all wore tattered sweatpants, blue, gray, and black. They worked intensely, each concentrating on the cut of his or her own body while trying not to lose the intricate pattern of the piece. Susan, who on the street, in conversation, sometimes lapses into a vacant, open-mouthed moment, was unremittingly focused, intent, missing nothing, even as she stepped in to cover for a missing dancer for a complete run-through of the piece. With the presence of a quarterback who sees the whole field and just senses the rush, she intuitively danced her part and still saw the whole, catching with a wry smile the occasional uncertainty and breaking into a genuine smile of joy as the patterns unfolded.

After a complete run-through, the dancers broke down into groups, ironing out details, subtleties in specific parts of the complex piece. Working with the women's trio section, Susan danced one of the parts and when she came out of a complicated pattern too far downstage, one of her dancers said, "Susan, I know you want to distance yourself, but this is a dance." The dancer laughed, but there was a barb to her jest.

Most criticisms were strictly technical. Working from her notes, Susan corrected small, almost imperceptible details. To one of the men: "When you leave that back leg, make sure it's not a pose. It's as though the leg is being carried by your momentum." She demonstrated, and her leg seemed to flow a fraction of a beat behind her as she turned out of the spin, like a leaf settling out of a whirlwind. Watching her, he mimicked her movement, repeating it several times as I would repeat a phone number to commit it to memory.

The dancers broke for a few minutes and gulped water, fighting dehydration even in the chill winter air. The company ran through other new pieces. Sweatpants, sweaters, and worn tennis shoes were discarded and retrieved as the dancers heated up and cooled down. A fire alarm rang downstairs. It was Monday and by three in the afternoon the dancers were beginning to really work, to dance at full speed. They began to smile as they moved. The sunlight, piercing the gray, cloudy sky for the first time all day, cut through the dance space horizontally, lifting spirits.

"Let's take a final run-through," Susan called out. "We're working toward a sense of arrival in space."

The company rehearsed the new work for the first time with props and mock-ups of costumes. The effect was rough, but dramatic. And then, for the company as a whole, the day's work was over. The eight dancers sprawled in chairs, on the risers, on their backs with their feet elevated, talking about motivation. Finally, all but three gathered their sweaters and shoes and bags and drifted away. Three dancers remained to run through a quartet piece for two couples with Susan. As they danced, little girls in pink tights began to arrive for a five o'clock ballet class. The little girls, timid but fascinated, huddled together near me on the risers and watched, dumbfounded, as Susan and her three dancers ripped off a final run-through to the pulsating, hypnotic music.

I was booked on the morning train, the Southwest Limited, at 6:55 Tuesday morning. So Monday night, I put on a tie and Susan put on heels and we went out for a drink. "There's this place on Main," she told me, "where Count Basie used to hang out when he came back to Kansas City. I've always wanted to go, but I've been waiting for you."

So we went to Milton's, 3241 Main, and sat at the bar and passed an enjoyable couple of hours talking to the young man behind the bar and the slightly older woman who told us she was Milton's daughter and seemed pleased that we were curious about her father. "It's true," she said, "Count Basie was a good friend to my dad. One time a thief broke in here and stole all Pop's jazz records, he had hundreds, and Bill Basie replaced them all when he heard about it." Signed photographs of Basie hung on the walls. Only two or three other patrons came in while we were there. They sat quietly in a booth, keeping to themselves, watching the Monday Night Football game on the television over the bar. Denver was playing at home and the field was almost obscured by swirling snow. We hardly noticed the game.

As we walked back to our car later that night, the city looked dark and empty and worn out. We walked past an adult bookstore where a pair of motor-driven teddy bears fornicated in the window, humping mechanically under the neon.

14 Turnaround in Galesburg

The morning dawned cold and furious. I awoke a little past five and lay on the sofa listening to thunder rattle the windowpanes. Susan drove me to the station in the pounding rain. The radio said it was snowing all across the Rockies and raining east to the Appalachians. It was a morning as grim and depressing as any I'd seen in three weeks on the road.

I found a seat in coach and watched the industrial skyline in the dim gray morning light as the Southwest Limited eased through Kansas City. I couldn't bear to stay in the coach, so I walked through to the observation car. In every coach I passed through, the passengers, huddled beneath coats and blankets and sweaters, still trying to sleep, looked lonely and forlorn. The hard rain blew into the vestibules, soaking my jacket as I passed. I took a seat, looking out into the faint gray morning, a dim, ambivalent twilight with the promise of day held in abeyance. The rain streaked the windowpanes in front of me and spattered on the skylights above me, seeping through and running in thin streams along the ceiling. A big cold drop fell on my thumb.

The symmetry of these train stops, leaving each town the same time I arrived, was beginning to seem unreal. Here I was back on the Southwest Limited, as though I had dreamed about Kansas City.

The Missouri land, fertile and open and promising under other circumstances, was colored by the rain and my dark mood. I saw it as a sea under a storm sky, rolling and heaving in great swells, miles long and miles deep. I thought to myself, the weather will change, better days will come. At least I had privacy. Most of the passengers were still asleep and I was alone in the observation car. At seven-thirty we were rolling through flooded fields under heavy clouds. Soundless lightning flickered behind the clouds like a guttering candle. As the morning light came up, the clouds thickened and it never seemed to brighten.

About seven-forty, just as I could make out the first color in the monochrome of gray sea and sky, the faint green of soggy fields, the parade to the diner began to bring the voices of hearty early morning geniality through the car, cheering me not at all. Two ladies took seats on either side of me, waiting for breakfast. One said to the other, "Those must be corn cribs." She was reading a paperback that said on its back cover, "How Twins Become Triplets." "The corn crop fizzled this year," she said to her friend. "And the bean crop. They got twenty-five bushels to the acre."

The voice of the trainman on the intercom intruded with random facts: "The world's tallest woman was born here in Missouri. She stood eight feet, four inches tall, wore a size twenty-four shoe, and lived to the age of forty-one. The Sears Tower in Chicago is the world's tallest building. Passengers who have the time in Chicago should consider going up in the Sears Tower." It sounded like "Sears Tire" —passengers should consider going up in the Sears Tire.

All morning I sat and watched the Missouri and Iowa countryside, looking for something to lift my mood, something to reignite my interest. At 1046 A.M., twenty minutes late, we stopped in the Santa Fe yards along the Mississippi River outside Fort Madison, Iowa. The rain had stopped falling, but the sky remained gray, and out on the river the wind whipped up whitecaps on the turbid water.

We moved on, across the Mississippi on a steel bridge three-fifths of a mile long, into Illinois—shining wet roads and subdued fall colors in the hills across the fields; the pitch black dirt of plowed cornfields with broken bits of stubble protruding here and there like old bones that will not stay buried.

After the West, Missouri, Iowa, and Illinois seemed so fertile, so ordered, so clear in purpose and meaning. Another hard rain began to fall, bursting on the windows and the roof in little explosions like popcorn. Mist obscured distance and detail, limiting vision to black earth, brown cornstalks, green grass, clumps of trees, white farmhouses through the rain. Simple images. When one travels by train the country dictates the mood, and the weather, although one is protected from its hazards, colors the country.

This was the midpoint of my trip, and I hadn't found what I was looking for. I hadn't found any purpose, any theme. I was despairing, and I was lonely.

A little after eleven that morning, the Southwest Limited passed through Surrey, Illinois, where a Santa Fe special set a speed record in 1905. On July 8 of that year, a wealthy eccentric who called himself "Death Valley Scotty" walked into the Los Angeles office of the Santa Fe and asked the passenger agent if the Santa Fe could get him to Chicago in forty-six hours. He began to peel thousand-dollar bills from a big roll and, for $5,500, the Santa Fe agreed to try. News of the attempt spread fast, and by the next day a crowd estimated as large as twenty thousand gathered to see the special depart. The Santa Fe assigned its best engineers to the run. A Fred Harvey chef prepared special meals of Broiled Squab on Toast, Porterhouse Steak à la Coyote, and other delights. Death Valley Scotty reveled in the attention. He occasionally rode in the cab and assisted in the firing. He tipped crew members generously. From Dodge City, Kansas, he sent a telegram to President Theodore Roosevelt: "An American cowboy is coming east on a special train faster than any cowpuncher ever rode before: how much shall I break the transcontinental record?" Between Cameron and Surrey, Illinois, the special covered 2.7 miles in ninety-five seconds, averaging more than 100 miles an hour on the fastest part of the run. Over the entire trip, the "Coyote Special," as Scotty called his train, averaged 50.4 miles an hour, and the total elapsed time to Dearborn Station in Chicago was forty-four hours, fifty-four minutes, besting the previous time by more than thirteen hours. That record survived until the diesel "Super Chief" introduced regular thirty-nine-hour service in 1936.

After ten days and more than two thousand miles I would be leaving the Santa Fe at Galesburg, Illinois. I knew I would miss it. Most Amtrak passengers, I suspect, hardly notice over which railroad they are traveling: the coaches are the same silver and patriotic colors, the train personnel with whom most passengers have contact—the car attendants, the service chiefs, the dining car waiters—are all Amtrak people, the locomotives are all Amtrak diesels, the dining car menu remains the same. And yet, not to see beneath the Amtrak livery is to miss the wealth of history and tradition reposited in the American railroads.

Each railroad is also its track, its route, and its rails. All along the Amtrak routes, the traveler sensitive to place names will find towns that witness the history of the underlying railroads. On the Santa Fe there is Coolidge, Kansas, named for Thomas Jefferson Coolidge, once president of the Santa Fe; Morley, Colorado, named for Ray Morley, one of the engineers who pushed the Santa Fe tracks over Raton Pass in 1878; Gallup, New Mexico, which is named for an official of the old Atlantic and Pacific Railroad, which originally built these tracks (now owned by the Santa Fe); Seligman, Arizona, named for the construction engineer who built the first railroad through in 1881; Kingman, Arizona, named for Lewis Kingman, who, with Ray Morley, put the Santa Fe over Raton Pass; and Barstow, California, and Strong City, Kansas, towns fifteen hundred miles apart named for the same man, William Barstow Strong.

I t was raining again when I reached Galesburg. I took a cab from the Santa Fe station on North Broad Street, a new glass cracker box, to the new but much more traditional Seminary Street station on the Burlington line. There I would catch the westbound California Zephyr when it passed through Galesburg at 5:15 that afternoon. I left my bags in a locker and set out on foot. When the rain picked up, I ducked into a Chinese restaurant on Main Street where the menu comprised mainly variations of chop suey. On the theory that native cuisine is the traveler's best refuge, I ordered the lunch special: Pork Tenderloin in Cream Gravy.

When the rain eased up a bit, I walked up to the public library and looked for a Sandburg exhibit. Galesburg, which is a Burlington division point, is the birthplace of Carl Sandburg, whose father worked in the Burlington shops. I found only a bust next to the copier in the periodicals room and some old photographs of Sandburg with his teammates in his high school sports days. Waiting out the rain, I read a *Saturday Review* article on "The Writer's Vice," F. Scott Fitzgerald's reference to alcoholism.

I walked out Main Street, stopping at the post office to mail a few cards I had written over lunch, to the Seminary Street station. In a tobacco shop across the street, I bought some pipe cleaners for my overworked pipe. The proprietor must have seen me cross over from the station. Without any provocation he launched into a tirade about the trains. "Don't know why it can't be cheaper," he groused. "All tax money paying for it."

Behind the station I crossed the railroad tracks and started walking out to the Sandburg home. The street led away from town, past a few casual businesses, auto body shops and small warehouses, and soon I was passing worn little wooden houses. The sidewalk was brick, laid without mortar directly in the soft black soil in a herringbone pattern, and tall grass, green and lush after the rain, grew over the bricks almost to the middle of the walk. I had expected to come to the Sandburg house in a few blocks, but when I walked two blocks, then two more, then five and ten more with no sign I was coming close, I had the sense that the Sandburg house was receding as I advanced. With each block, I became more concerned about the time and more frustrated.

I had walked about fifteen blocks, wearing only my corduroy jacket and the slightly ridiculous Panama hat, when it began to rain again, so, reluctantly, I turned back toward the station. It was after five when I trotted back over the Burlington Northern tracks with just enough time to fetch my bags from the locker before the California Zephyr drew up. As we pulled out of Galesburg, I stood in the vestibule and watched the rain. The Sandburg house had become just one more thing forever out of reach.

The California Zephyr, the most spectacular route on the Amtrak system, is also the longest—2,427 miles from Chicago to Oakland, California. From Galesburg, I would be traveling more than 2,200 miles on the Zephyr. I would ride all night Tuesday through Iowa, Nebraska, and Colorado, all day Wednesday through Colorado and Utah, all Wednesday night through Utah and Nevada, and most of Thursday through California, over the Sierras to Oakland, arriving at 3:30 Thursday afternoon. Along the way I would pass through three time zones.

I had originally planned to ride coach all the way as an economy, hoping I could recover in the three days I would lay over in San Francisco, but at the last minute, with a premonition of just how fatiguing all those miles might be, I tried to book a sleeping compartment on the Zephyr. There was none available, but I struck a compromise with the reservations clerk. The Pioneer, which runs from Chicago to Seattle, shares the same schedule and route with the Zephyr from Chicago to Salt Lake City. In fact, those two trains and a third, No. 35, the Desert Wind for Los Angeles, are part of the same consist over that stretch, just different cars behind the same locomotive. At Salt Lake City, late Wednesday night, the train would be broken into three separate trains. The Zephyr would continue west over Union Pacific and Southern Pacific track to San Francisco. The cars of the Desert Wind would be cut out and made up into a separate train that would turn south over Union Pacific track to Las Vegas and Los Angeles. The cars of the Pioneer would be separated and headed north on Union Pacific track to Portland and then on to Seattle over Burlington Northern track. I booked a sleeper on the Pioneer for Tuesday night, which would give me one night's rest, but Wednesday morning in Denver I would have to relinquish it to passengers boarding for the overnight trip to Portland and Seattle on the Pioneer.

However, for the moment, I had a place to hang my hat. I stowed my bags in my compartment and watched while the Zephyr–Pioneer–Desert Wind rolled across the rich farmland of western Illinois, on without stopping through the small towns of Cameron, Monmouth, and Kirkwood. When the train began the slow descent toward the Mississippi River, through marshy bottom land west of Biggsville and Connett, Illinois, I went downstairs to the loading platform of the Superliner sleeping car to get a better view. A young woman with straight blond hair was standing at the window on the north side of the vestibule. I edged up close to her to watch as we crossed the Mississippi, which is wide and serene seen from the railroad bridge. The window was streaked with rain.

She said to me, "I used to cross this bridge as a child."

When I photographed freight cars on a siding outside Burlington, she asked me if I was "one of those train buffs." I replied that, while I enjoyed traveling by train, I didn't share the obsession with numbers and statistics that consumes some rail fans.

"I work for Amtrak," she told me, "as a car attendant. I have one train buff who keeps better records than our conductors. Every train he rides, he keeps a log of how many cars are on the train and who gets off and where, and a detailed mile-by-mile account of speed and track conditions. But he never writes comments, just dry facts."

"Are you working this trip?" I asked her.

"No, I'm just traveling. Out to Seattle and then back to Chicago. Are you going to Seattle?"

"Not yet. Now I'm taking the Zephyr on to San Francisco." I explained to her why I was temporarily lodged on one of the cars of the Pioneer. When she pressed for details, I explained that I was making the Amtrak circuit. "You must wonder why anyone would pay to spend so long on a train."

"Oh, no," she said, "I have a friend who does it every year. He's a geologist and he leaves Chicago every year and makes a big loop around the West. I always thought it sounded like a great way to see the country. They told me in Chicago that the colors were at their peak out in Seattle just now."

As we left Burlington, Iowa, headed west, we passed over the stretch of track where the final, conclusive tests were made of the Westinghouse air brake, the innovation that perhaps advanced the safety of railroading more than any other. Railroading in the last half of the nineteenth century was a rough and dangerous business. In 1881 some thirty thousand railroad employees were injured in accidents in a single year. Two devices in particular, the link-and-pin coupler and the hand brake, cost the life and limb of innumerable railroad men. To couple two cars together, a man had to stand between them as they rolled together, steer a link into its socket, and drop in a pin to secure the coupling. The loss of fingers was commonplace, so much so that some hard-bitten yardmasters who preferred to hire experienced men liked to see a missing digit as evidence of experience.

Applying hand brakes, which were controlled by a handwheel on the top of the cars, was the other task that made railroad work so perilous. Standing on the icy roof of a swaying, windswept boxcar on a freezing winter night was a routine part of the job for a brakeman, who took pride in being able to twist a brake until sparks shot from the wheels. Strength, courage, and a reckless disregard for injury and death were required. It was not a job for the timid or the delicate, and as a group brakemen were regarded as the most profane, the most brutal, and the most degenerate of all railroad men.

George Westinghouse, a young New York inventor, finally brought brakemen down from atop their cars. After reading that French engineers had used compressed air to blast tunnels through the Alps, he devised a railroad air brake in 1868, but railroad management, which considered human life cheaper than capital improvement, was reluctant to invest in the new equipment. Undeterred, Westinghouse improved his system. His original design, which had used air pressure to apply brakes on each car, was susceptible to failure and had the shortcoming of providing more braking force to the first cars than the last. By reversing his principle, so that the air pressure released the brakes, he made the system more reliable—a failure would apply rather than disable the brakes—and equalized the force applied at each car.

Even after railroads began to install air brakes and automatic couplers on passenger cars, which were expensive and delicate investments, they refused to install the safety devices on freight cars until Congress passed the Railroad and Safety Appliance Act in 1893, mandating automatic couplers and air brakes for all trains. In the years immediately following, the number of injuries to railroaders declined by sixty percent and the number of deaths by half.

Rain contined to fall as we crossed the grainfields of southern Iowa. The afternoon subsided almost imperceptibly. The low, dark clouds just seemed to close down over the fields, snuffing out the last light. From Burlington, the Burlington Northern tracks curve gently northwest for about twenty-five miles to Mt. Pleasant, Iowa, and then bend back to a straight western course. For the next 225 miles the tracks run due west across Iowa to the Missouri River. They then take a quick turn of 25 miles or so north, up the Missouri River valley to Council Bluffs, and cross the river to Omaha, Nebraska. The Zephyr crosses Iowa in the evening, averaging about sixty miles an hour including stops at Mt. Pleasant, Ottumwa, Osceola, and Creston, and arrives at Omaha about eleven at night.

Somewhere west of Mt. Pleasant, when it grew too dark to see anything from the vestibule, I said good night to Carol, the Amtrak attendant on her way to Seattle, and climbed the stairs to my compartment where I wrote a few notes before dinner. I stopped in the lounge car, which was quiet, for a beer and walked on to the dining car for dinner after eight. The coaches were almost empty and the train seemed deserted. By nine-twenty I was back in my sleeper compartment. The Zephyr was somewhere just west of Creston, Iowa, a division point on the Burlington Northern built on the high point between the Des Moines and Missouri rivers. As the Zephyr rolled onto the long steady downgrade of eighty or so miles toward the Missouri River, I lay in my bunk and read again the initial chapters of *Travels with Charley*.

The next day I would travel through the most spectacular scenery on the Amtrak system over sections of the first transcontinental railroad, and I hoped that my spirits would lift in the Rockies, but for a couple of hours I just stretched out under the reading light and revisited the book I had read as a child. For years I had regarded it as a transient pleasure of that romantic period of childhood when travel seems so exciting. Rereading those first few chapters I realized what I had missed before. It was not, as I had remembered it, a book about youth nor about travel, but about growing old, gracefully, not gently.

Those were the happiest moments of what had been a long, dispiriting day. It might have been simply the weather: from the morning thunder in Kansas City to the gray afternoon in Iowa, I had seen only moments of sunshine. Although the turnaround at Galesburg had worked just as I had planned it, the long day and the change in direction had made my traveling seem aimless. While other passengers were traveling to or from home or family or business I was going in circles. It had been my hardest day—the first day I had wanted it all to be different.

Because most long-distance Amtrak trains run only once a day (and in a few cases only three times a week) they always travel through the same country at the same time of day. For instance, you will never see Nebraska from an Amtrak train, since only the California Zephyr crosses Nebraska and always at night. These limited schedules leave the traveler with a distorted image of the nation, something like an early map of a partially explored continent, with blank regions where no man has been. The inner map, drafted from the traveler's memory of the country he has seen, becomes a checkerboard with every other square, separated by one turn of the planet, always in darkness and forever unmapped.

While the Zephyr waited in the Omaha station, I followed on my maps the route it would take while I slept. Overnight the Zephyr would travel southeast across Nebraska, crossing the Platte River about halfway to Lincoln sometime before midnight. Near Hastings the Burlington tracks leave the valley of the Platte River and turn southwest, dropping down into the Republican River valley near Oxford and following the Republican River and the North Fork upstream into Colorado. As the Zephyr climbed up the bluffs outside Omaha, out of the Missouri River valley, I fell asleep.

I awoke about six in the morning, chilled in my bed. Huddled under the single wool blanket issued by Amtrak, I shivered through the early morning hours until the sun, rising behind the train in brilliant striations of light, roused me. My compartment was on the north side, the right side, of the train, and every time the train curved to the north, I could see the silver cars following behind, shining like new dimes in the bright sunlight. By seven I began to notice snow gathered in ditches, in grainfields, on the roofs of feed stores and houses.

My trip, which had started in the torpid heat of New Orleans and the dry sunshine of the Southwest, would end in the northern winter. I could have chosen to start out in early autumn on the northern leg of the journey, catching Indian summer through New England, the northern Midwest, and the Northwest, and then turn south when the weather turned cold, but I had decided instead to travel through the South when the weather was warmest and flirt with the onset of winter up north. The purpose of travel is change, I had thought. Why try to freeze time?

By seven-twenty, as the Zephyr climbed closer to Denver, the snow was thicker, covering the fields, and water in the trackside ditches was glossed with ice. Grain stubble, glowing golden in the pink morning light, was set in clean fields of white. Cattle trotted along the fence line, a calf following its mother through the snow. Clumps of ducks huddled in a patch of open water on a small roadside pond. As the Zephyr continued climbing toward the city, we rose through a bank of clouds and the colors muted. We burst through. The sun moved up another notch. We moved slowly past acres of stockyards.

On the hillock at the center of each pen the cattle huddled pathetically together in the snow, their breath frosting in the morning air, shrouding them in steam.

I should have been evicted from my sleeper in Denver, since I was paid up that far and no farther, but my steward, that unlikely official who sees past regulations to common sense and clear through the other side even to consideration, told me that since the new occupants would not be boarding until Glenwood Springs I was welcome to remain until we neared that stop. In return, I offered to go ahead and move my bags forward to a coach seat in the Oakland/San Francisco section of the train while we were in the Denver station.

It was sharply cold in the open air of the station platform. The air stung my lungs and my hands stiffened around my bags. I was walking straight on into winter. But the light and the air were exhilarating, and the dreariness of Kansas City was far behind.

15 The California Zephyr from Denver to the Bay: The Golden Spike Route

Never make excuses, never let them see you bleed, and never get
separated from your baggage.

—from Wesley Price's *Three Rules of Professional
Comportment for Writers*

When Grenville M. Dodge built the Union Pacific Railroad
west from Omaha to link up with the Central Pacific to
form the first transcontinental railroad, the mountains
west of Denver were considered impassable, at least for a
standard-gauge railroad, so he routed the Union Pacific
line far north of Denver. For four more decades Denver
remained isolated, until David Moffat, who came to Denver as a young man and made his fortune there, decided late in life to
put Denver on a main line by building a railroad over the mountains
to Utah. Although his railroad, the Denver, Northwestern, and Pacific, never quite reached Utah, it crossed the mountains successfully
and was absorbed in 1947 by the Denver and Rio Grande. Moffat's
route survives as more than a hundred miles of the most spectacular
track traveled by a passenger train anywhere in the world.

From Denver, the Zephyr begins a long, slow grind up toward the
Moffat Tunnel on the Continental Divide, about fifty miles away
and four thousand feet up. For the first fifteen or twenty miles, the
tracks climb a natural escarpment called the Leyden Ramp, and at
the top they swing through a sweeping curve to the south and back

again to the north to attack the Front Range. Its degree of curvature, ten degrees, gives the curve its name, the Big Ten.

As we left Denver, a few passengers were standing in the corridor of my sleeper glancing over the morning newspaper headlines. A woman asked, "When do we get into the mountains?" Her answer came quickly. Within minutes of leaving the Denver station we were climbing steeply through snow-dusted foothills. Within thirty minutes, Denver became just a mist-shrouded cluster of skyscrapers below us on a white snowbound plain.

I moved downstairs into the vestibule, where I could be alone, and where I could open the window occasionally to look forward and back, along the length of the train, and up into the mountains ahead. The Zephyr climbed to the edge of the high plain, winding through groups of snowy flat-topped foothills that, but for the snow, looked like the buttes of West Texas, and then on into higher, rounded foothills dotted with evergreens. The train swung through long arcs, snaking its way into the mountains. On the Big Ten Curve, a master stroke of railroad engineering that lifts the Denver and Rio Grande line toward the sheer face of the Front Range, giving it a leg up on the daunting climb to come, I could look ahead and see the full length of the Zephyr. Two locomotives, hitched back to back, headed it. Behind were three single-level cars, probably baggage cars or perhaps crew cars, a sleeping car, then two coaches, one of which was probably the diner, an observation car, another sleeper, a coach, then my sleeper.

The snow was deeper above Denver. We crossed a county road where the snow had been piled by the plow four or five feet high along the shoulders. Within forty-five minutes we were creeping silently along the hem of the mountains, through long open vistas of soft rounded foothills. Ahead in the distance were snow-crested peaks. Above the stratum of low clouds the sky was a pure unbroken blue.

I noticed a mule deer buck, with a good rack, alongside the tracks. As the train rolled slowly by, working on the upgrade, he looked up from his browsing. To feed he had moved down along the ledge below the tracks, where the direct sun had melted the snow away from the browse. He stood, almost immobile, in the warm morning sun as we passed, watching with just a slight twist of his head. He looked sleek and healthy: this was the first snow of the winter.

As we climbed away from Denver, we passed through a series of tunnels. The contrast was stunning, a shock to the pupils, from brilliant snowscape into total darkness, emerging again into a white sheet of light. There were once twenty-nine tunnels in the first thirty-five miles of track west of Denver, and the Zephyr still runs through a number of the shorter ones as it climbs toward the main Moffat Tunnel.

In a snowy meadow above Denver, we passed a small group of weathered stock pens standing empty. Then the Zephyr sliced into the heart of the mountains, the tracks hacked into the side of rock walls, clinging above a rushing river, with scree falling away from the tracks into the water. Rock was everywhere: rock walls, cliffs and crags, boulders alongside the tracks, and stones in the river. The river rushed among rocks still capped with snow, and the water, opaque as molten lead, had begun to freeze in the eddies. Telephone poles leaned crazily out over the steep riverbank. Some cliffs above the train had absorbed enough morning sunlight to melt patches of snow, and here and there tiny avalanches tumbled down the snowbanks, gathering little snowballs, no bigger than a child would throw, as they went. Farther on, I would see their spidery tracks everywhere below the base of rock outcroppings and dirt banks.

It once took freight trains five or six hours to crawl up the four percent grade over Rollins Pass, where the highest standard-gauge railroad ever built in America once crossed the Continental Divide 11,680 feet above sea level. Now the Zephyr cuts through James Peak in the Moffat Tunnel in ten minutes. The tunnel, at 6.2 miles long, is the third longest in the Western Hemisphere. From each end, it slopes upward to its middle, where it crests at 9,239 feet above sea level, cutting through James Peak thousands of feet below the old crossing at Rollins Pass. The western end of the tunnel opens at Winter Park, where the tracks turn to the north and enter the valley of the Fraser River, a tributary of the Colorado.

Through the Fraser River valley, the Denver and Rio Grande line passes through some of the coldest inhabited—if only barely —country in the United States. At Fraser and Tabernash, four miles up the line, the winter cold has been said to freeze a standing train to the tracks. At Granby, seventy-five miles northwest of Denver, the Fraser River flows into the Colorado River, and the tracks of the Zephyr turn southwest to follow the Colorado River for 238 miles into Utah. Between Granby and Glenwood Springs, which the Zephyr reaches in the early afternoon, are three deep canyons—Byers Canyon, where the sections of the roadbed were blasted out of solid rock, Gore Canyon, probably the most forbidding few miles of track on the Amtrak system, and Glenwood Canyon.

The bright morning sun disappeared as we penetrated another mountain range and snow began to fall. In the river gorge, the sky was lost in mist and flying snow. The water was gray as slate, and above the rails for a thousand feet the walls of this narrow defile were solid rock, forming a cold shadowy slit in the mountains. We emerged in another high valley, where the river was wider and more placid, no longer rushing, no longer strewn with boulders. We crossed over it again on a snowy railroad bridge. We appeared to be in the clouds. A small ranch house huddled beneath the only two hardwood trees in the valley. A barn and broken-down corral lay slightly up the slope. A dozen cows wandered in the underbrush along the river's edge. Farther on, ten horses stood stoically in a field, almost invisible in the swirling snow.

Through the morning and the early afternoon I prowled the loading platform of the sleeper car, moving from side to side, mesmerized by the mountains. I would open the window and lean out, careful of the mountain faces that passed within feet of the train, and the draft would suck a rush of warm air from the car past my cheek, bathing me in a warmth as unnatural as a hot spring, as the falling snow softly stung my face.

Between Dotsero, where the Eagle River flows into the Colorado, and Glenwood Springs, the Zephyr passes through Glenwood Canyon. It was in Glenwood Canyon, so the story goes, that a General Motors executive riding in a locomotive cab first conceived the idea of a dome car, with the thought that passengers would enjoy seeing the canyon as he saw it.

At Glenwood Springs, the railroad station for Aspen, the Roaring Fork joins the Colorado River. A fly fisherman was working the far bank, wearing waders, a parka, gloves, and a hooded balaclava. Only his eyes peered out. He was casting upstream, standing knee deep in water so cold that it shriveled my scrotum just to look at it.

Not far west of Glenwood Springs, Carol, the young Amtrak employee deadheading to Seattle, joined me in the center hall of the car. We exchanged greetings, and she stayed on, watching me take photographs, which irritated me at first. I had enjoyed the solitude and the chance to concentrate on the mountains. I felt obliged to make conversation, so I asked her what it was like to work for Amtrak.

"I remember my first trip to Seattle," she said. "I was so excited, taking pictures and all, and everyone else on the crew was completely blasé. Most of my trips are in the East now. New Orleans is open a lot now, especially the runs that are turnarounds, where you don't have any time to spend. There are some pretty trains in the East. It's pretty coming down the Hudson from Albany. And it's pretty on the other New York train, 40–41 [the Broadway Limited, Chicago to New York], that goes through Pennsylvania."

"So you can still enjoy the trips?"

"Uh hunh," she said. "But I don't know. These western trips are long. Three days! It all depends, who I'm working with. I've had trips where we laughed all the way. And I've had trips where the people were so dull, so burned-out. There are some that are old and just sort of . . . hanging on. I've still got to get used to that. I know that no job is going to be good all the time. Is yours? No, I didn't think so. There will always be times."

We had descended from the Front Range and Park Range, still following the Colorado River. I was becoming accustomed to sharing the small space.

"Did you grow up in the Midwest?" I asked.

"I was born in Missouri," she said, "and I've lived in Ohio and Illinois and I've been through Indiana, Iowa, Wisconsin, just a little bit of Minnesota—just barely into it, really—and Kansas. And those states, they bother me because they're in between. I don't like in-between states. I like a state to be either full of mountains or flat, like Montana—just that long horizon, all the way around, and then all that sky. I had this picture when I was a little girl, this picture of Vermont. In the picture, it's of a road, and the road sort of vanishes in the distance. It's an old road, with leaves all over the road. It's fall, birch and all, beautiful trees along both sides, and there's a cabin beside the road. I just wanted to walk into that picture. And be right there."

The Zephyr skirted the southern edge of the Book Cliffs, limestone and shale deposited on the floor of an ancient sea, now thrust up and eroded to show the layers of sediment like leaves of a book across their deckled edge. Grand Mesa, a great flat-topped table tens of miles long, appeared to the south. The landscape was undergoing a sea change, from the frozen granite mountains and plummeting river canyons of the morning to the weatherbeaten mesas of afternoon.

Carol seemed a little nervous. Whenever she heard someone coming down the stairs it distracted her, and I thought I detected a moment of relief each time it turned out to be just another anonymous passenger. Finally, sometime in midafternoon, she said, "Why don't we go sit down for a while? I know where we can be alone."

I followed her around the corner to the compartment at the rear of the coach where she had been traveling. On most of the Superliner sleeping cars there are one or two rooms on the lower level, often with private bathrooms, that are spacious and accessible to handicapped passengers. Those downstairs compartments were often unoccupied, and car attendants find them a useful work space in which to sort linen or to relax away from the passengers.

Carol told me, "I've been traveling in here, trying to stay out of the way. I don't think anyone minds."

We heard an announcement over the intercom, a woman's voice, that, to me, sounded officious and not particularly warm. "This is your on-board service chief. I would at this time like to give you your train schedule for dinner. Seatings will be at five, six, seven, and eight P.M. Please take the menu that has been distributed to you and jot down on it the time you would like to eat. I would also like you to indicate the entrée that you wish to have for dinner."

Carol said, "That's an efficient way to do it."

"To make people order ahead?"

"A lot of times," she said, "it's so irritating. People will come into the diner, and they'll sit there dawdling and trying to make up their minds, and you want to serve them as fast as you can, that's the whole thing, quickly. You've got a lot of people on board."

Out in the vestibule, two people were talking. Carol got up and closed the compartment door, and as she sat down again, as if I was not to misunderstand, she told me, "I'm just trying to be inconspicuous."

I asked, "Are you afraid that they'll put you to work?"

"They can," she said. "Those are the rules."

"We're headed out toward Grand Junction now, aren't we?" She nodded. "Are we coming down?" I asked. "There's no snow anymore. I thought the mountains would continue at least as far as Grand Junction."

Carol said, "Well, it does become more desert on toward Salt Lake City. I intended to get on the Empire Builder, but I got on the wrong train. Then after I got on, I realized I could go back on the Empire Builder. Maybe this really wasn't such a bad mistake after all. I'll get to see more country this way. You don't see much when you're working."

Just then, someone knocked. Apprehension flickered across Carol's face, and she said, "Come in."

An Amtrak attendant stepped into the compartment, looked at Carol, and then turned to me and asked, "Do you want to make a dinner reservation?"

"I believe I will. Eight for me. I'll eat late." I asked Carol, "Will you eat with me?"

"Yes. Sure. At eight."

The attendant marked the menu, handed me a reservation card marked for the eight o'clock dinner seating, and left.

About four in the afternoon we stopped for a few minutes at Grand Junction, where the Colorado River (once known as the Grand River) conjoins with the Gunnison River, known among fly fishermen for its salmon-fly hatch. The rain had stopped, and as Carol and I sat in her compartment and talked, the sun lit up the redrock formations of Ruby Canyon west of Grand Junction. We made small talk and we looked over my maps and studied the different routes that lay ahead for each of us.

Late in the afternoon, just before the Zephyr crossed into Utah, there was a sharp knock at the door. The Amtrak crew chief, the same woman I had heard on the intercom earlier, burst into the compartment. In an angry voice she said to Carol, "I want to speak to you alone." She did not look at me.

She waited, ignoring me as I gathered up my books and papers—my maps were still spread across the seat—and my camera bag. "If you will excuse me . . . ," I said, and edged past her through the door and out into the hall of the car. I heard her slam the door behind me as I climbed the stairs. I waited for fifteen or twenty minutes in the sleeping compartment I had occupied the previous night. When I went back downstairs, Carol was gone.

I collected the last of my belongings from the sleeping car and moved forward several cars to the coach seat where I would spend the night. We had crossed over into Utah, swinging away from the Colorado River. As the Zephyr turned northwest, climbing along the Price River into the Wasatch Mountains, a magnificent sunset commenced. In the southwest, the late light flared over the mesas and silhouetted the table rock against heavy, smoke-blue clouds. To the north, a range of mountain peaks lay in the far distance. Their lower slopes were layered in tones of brown, beige, and black and, up above, the high peaks were white with snow and covered with dark green conifers. It looked as though West Texas had been laid down as a foreground for the Rockies.

The coach was peaceful and quiet. The whisper of moving air from the ventilator was the only sound. The tracks seemed far below, far removed, and the coach surged forward and back as the diesels climbed steadily, relentlessly. The regular rocking, forward and back, as the coaches tugged at their couplings, gave the car a human aspect, like a weary walker leaning heavily into each step on a long uphill grade. It was on these long climbs, not on the easy downhill tacks or the fast runs across flat desert or cropland, that the train seemed to float. It reminded me of the flying dream: when I dream that I can fly, it is never effortless soaring but a slow rising on wingbeats against the pull of the earth. With that gentle pulsing, the Zephyr rose toward the clouds hanging just above the horizon.

After the sun had set, I went on to the dining car without Carol. Later, as the Zephyr followed the Jordan River from Provo north toward Salt Lake City, I walked back to the Pioneer coaches and found her sitting alone in a coach seat. I sat down beside her.

"I'm glad to see you," she said. "I was afraid to go looking for you."

"What happened?" I was worried that I had somehow caused her trouble.

"I wish I knew. I wish. I really do." She smiled, wanly, and shook her head. "You remember I told you that I got on the wrong train? I really did intend to take the Empire Builder to Seattle, but at the last minute I decided to go this way instead. I just told the conductor that I wanted to go on to Seattle, and he let me come aboard. Everything was fine. I had a coach seat and the conductor didn't mind at all. Then yesterday I was talking to the attendant in the sleeping car and he told me that he had those unoccupied compartments, so last night I stayed in the sleeping car. Somehow, the crew chief found out about it today, and you saw what happened."

"What about the conductor?"

"That was in Chicago." She was whispering. "That was on the Burlington, remember? He probably got off at Aurora or Galesburg. He's probably back home in Chicago by now. This conductor doesn't know who I am and doesn't care. This is a completely different railroad."

"Can't you square it with this conductor?"

"I thought I could," she said. "After the crew chief came down and talked to me, she said, 'Go talk to the conductor,' and I went and talked to him and he said, 'Pay for a ticket,' and I thought it was over. And then later she comes back and says it's not over yet. She says, 'The train attendant in the car you were in is going to write you up.' I don't know if you know what that means, writing someone up?"

"You mean the guy in the sleeping car?"

"Yeah, but I said, 'Well, I'll go down and talk to him,' and she said, 'I don't think it will do you any good.' But I said, 'Well, I'm going to do it anyway,' so I went down there and I talked to him. And he was real understanding. He said, 'Why don't all three, I mean all four, of us meet and talk this over and decide what we're gonna do?' He was real rational about it. And so we all got together. And they all agreed, they were just going to let it go, not do anything. And so I just went back, just now, and talked to him to make sure that everything was all right, that he was still comfortable with it. I told him, 'I know that it was your idea that we all get together and talk this out reasonably, and I really appreciate that. I think you saved my job, and I'd like to buy you dinner in Seattle.' And he said, 'No problem, you don't have to do that.' I still might buy him dinner in Seattle. Can you believe it?

"I still don't know if it's over." Carol sounded exhausted. "I should have just stayed in my coach seat. I just wish I didn't need this job so much. It's my only way out. I'm not going back to Ohio. I just have to work this out."

In the dark, the lights of Geneva, American Fork, and Riverton, towns along the corridor between Provo and Salt Lake City, flashed by. Other passengers in the coach were trying to sleep. "We're coming into Salt Lake City in just a few minutes," I said. "I guess I'd better get back to my coach. If I made trouble for you, I'm sorry."

We both got up and started through the train, she to the rear to find the new conductor when the crews changed at Salt Lake City, I forward to my seat in the Zephyr coach. Just as I reached the door, I looked back and saw that she had left the coach. I turned around and went back to where we had been sitting. Her coat was lying on the seat. I took out the eight o'clock dinner reservation we had made that afternoon and scribbled on it, "I'll be home about 7 November. Let me know what happens. Thanks for the company." I wrote my home address on the bottom, and tucked the card in the pocket of her coat.

I fell asleep in my coach seat as they made the cuts in the yard at Salt Lake City, breaking out cars for the Desert Wind, the Pioneer, and the Zephyr and heading up the three separate trains. The sounds of the yard locomotives and the shuttling railroad cars were muffled by a heavy snowstorm. The station lights were blurred by mist.

I n the night, the Zephyr would make my closest approach to the most celebrated place in the history of American railroading, Promontory, Utah, where the first transcontinental rail line was joined with the golden spike on May 10, 1869. The original Central Pacific line curved around the northern shore of the Great Salt Lake to Promontory; a Southern Pacific line crosses the lake; and the Union Pacific tracks followed by the Zephyr travel the south shore. If I had taken the Pioneer north through Ogden to Portland I would have approached a few miles closer, but no train passes through Promontory these days: the site of the original conjoining, a national monument since the centenary of the event in 1969, can no longer be reached by rail.

Historians of the railroad industry have observed that the railroads finally joined by the golden spike, indeed the entire system of American railroads of that time, were far more primitive than the achievement might suggest, still relying on mechanical brakes and link-and-pin couplings and still lacking a uniform gauge and a standard time system. The principal accomplishment of the two great railroads that came together at Promontory, aside perhaps from their ability to gobble up public lands and money, was logistical. And the final mad scramble of each railroad to claim the last miles of the route for its own typified the ambition and greed of American railroads in the nineteenth century. For a time, the two railroads, the Central Pacific building east from California and the Union Pacific building west from Omaha, actually met and continued on into the territory of the other, grading parallel roadbeds and mounting impromptu combat between their crews, each railroad trying to extend its own dominion as far as possible. Congress finally had to squelch the conflict. Promontory was declared the official meeting place as much to settle a border dispute as to stage a joyful union.

The golden spike ceremony was immortalized in a famous photograph by A. J. Russell of the two locomotives, the Jupiter of the Central Pacific and No. 119 of the Union Pacific, coming together cowcatcher to cowcatcher. The photograph, habitually reproduced in history texts, is a fascinating tableau. A man standing on the Jupiter holds out a bottle of champagne, railroad officials strike officious poses, and dozens of dusty laborers stare proudly at the camera. One man among the multitude in the photograph turned his back to the camera and, by so doing, hid his identity forever. I never look at the photograph without wishing I could stroll into it and steal a look at his face.

While I slept, the Zephyr traveled on west over the old Western Pacific tracks, now part of the Union Pacific system. It skirted Great Salt Lake, bore across the salt flats, and climbed over the Toano and Pequop ranges of Nevada. At Wells, the Union Pacific tracks join the Southern Pacific, and the two lines run together for about 180 miles. At Winnemucca, Nevada, between five and six in the morning, the Zephyr left the Union Pacific line and moved to Southern Pacific track, which it would follow to its terminus in Oakland.

A few minutes after six in the morning, now on Pacific Daylight Time, I awoke east of Sparks, Nevada. While I had slept, the Zephyr had come more than 550 miles across the deserts, through the basin and range country, and now to the foot of the Sierras. I had endured another night in a coach seat, folding and unfolding my extremities. Stiff, cold, and sore, I hobbled through to the lounge car a few minutes before seven, got a cup of coffee, and settled into a window seat on the upper level. My first cup of coffee went back neat; to oil my stiff joints, I laced the next with a dollop from the flask that traveled in my bookbag. For a half hour, until other passengers began to drift in and take up seats around me, I was alone.

The gently wrinkled mountains to the south, on my side of the train, were powdered white with snow, like loaves of yeast dough that had been left to rise and then dusted with confectioners' sugar. Just after eight-fifteen the Zephyr passed through Fernley and joined the Truckee River, which it would follow up the eastern slope of the Sierras. Mist rose like steam from the slow-moving river, which curled, forty or fifty feet wide, through the foothills.

When the lounge began to fill up with passengers, I went downstairs to the platform. A trainman walked through as we approached Sparks and said, "See those buildings we just passed back there?" I had, but I hadn't paid them much attention. A handful of ordinary buildings nestled at the foot of the mountains on the south bank of the Truckee River, they looked like any other small ranch or homestead. "That was the Mustang Ranch, the famous brothel."

"I thought that had passed on into legend."

"It's up for sale now. Twenty-five million."

"What I saw didn't look like twenty-five thousand."

"Well, there's a good deal of river frontage."

A new train crew came aboard at Sparks, and the public address system crackled, "Good morning, ladies and gentlemen. This is your conductor. Your well-rested crew will be taking you on to California. Our next stop, in just a few minutes, will be Reno. If Reno is not your stop, please stay on the train. We will be stopping only long enough to board passengers and you will be left behind. Our stops the rest of the day will be skid marks."

The Zephyr rolled through downtown Reno just as though it had swung onto a trolley line and detoured down the main street. When it came to a stop at the Amtrak station at Commercial Row and Lake Street, I was looking south down Lake Street, over the roofs of automobiles and the heads of pedestrians just as if I was sitting in a bus at a stoplight. In the western suburbs of Reno, even modest suburban houses had pole and timber ranch gates opening into their yards, like the quarter-acre "rancheros" I used to see advertised in the back pages of *Field and Stream*.

West of Reno, the Zephyr began to climb in earnest up the eastern flank of the Sierras. Back in the observation car, a woman sat down next to me and said, "This is an early snow for us, isn't it?"

I told her that I didn't know. I was from the East.

"I've been away myself," she said. "In Denver. We'll be going through the Donner Pass. That's named for the Donner party, those settlers who got stranded in the snow crossing the mountains and ate each other to survive. It was probably about this time of year. They thought they could get over before winter, but an early snowfall caught them up near Donner Lake. About half of them died."

Later that day, I looked it up in a guidebook I carried. The Donner party did indeed set out in October—October 31, 1846. Of eighty-nine settlers, forty-two died in the snows of the Sierra Nevada, and some of those who perished were consumed by the survivors in the most famous case of cannibalism in American history.

About nine-fifty in the morning, thirty-five minutes behind schedule, we climbed through the town of Truckee, where rugged little log houses lined the main street, each with a snow shovel and a broom on the front porch. From Reno, Truckee is about halfway to the crest of the Sierras. I excused myself, returned to my coach to get my camera bag, and went downstairs to enjoy the climb through the Sierra Nevada mountains. The best of it would be over before noon.

From Donner Lake, the Southern Pacific tracks climb in fewer than twenty miles to Norden, near the summit of this pass. As we neared the summit, snow began to fall and the snow on the slopes deepened, covering everything except the trees, clumps of granite, and the twin splines of track. High up, where the snowdrifts were three or four feet deep, the tracks ducked through snowsheds, dark wooden tunnels with peaked roofs. They reminded me of New England covered bridges. Here in the Sierras this first snow of the season was just a dusting. Above sixty-five hundred feet in these mountains most of the annual precipitation falls as snow—less than five percent falls during the summer months—and the snowpack deepens all winter. Until the invention of the rotary snowplow, men suffered frightful hardships to keep these mountain passes clear of snow.

The first methods of snow removal were crude: men crouched on the cowcatcher of a steam locomotive and held shovels to the rails as the locomotive crept ahead. A loose piece of iron strapping or a loose tie would catapult the unfortunate shoveler into the air. A pilot plow, a heavy piece of sheet iron fastened to the cowcatcher, replaced human hands and served well enough in the East, where snows were frequent but manageable, but when railroads pushed across the northern plains and over the Sierras, where blizzards deposited snow at a fierce rate and strong winds piled it into deep snowdrifts, winter was much more daunting. Over the first winter in the Sierras, the Central Pacific Railroad employed an army of twenty-five hundred shovelers and even so could not keep the line open all winter.

Hard-pressed railroaders in the West devised the bucker plow, a specially built steel-reinforced car constructed for weight and strength with a wedge-shaped plow at its bow. A string of locomotives, however many were necessary, drove the bucker ahead of them like a battering ram, gathering speed over clear track and colliding with the snowpack at full throttle. If successful, the bucker would part the snow and lift it away from the tracks; if not, the train crew would recover from the bone-rattling impact and withdraw to make another run. The process was not unlike a series of intentional train wrecks: occasionally the bucker would ride up over the ice and snow and derail, and might take one or more locomotives with it. In the two decades after 1865, the Central Pacific shops in Sacramento constructed some of the largest bucker plows ever built. These huge battering rams, weighted with forty or fifty thousand pounds of pig iron, were propelled into heavy snowdrifts by as many as eleven locomotives.

On the principle that it was better to keep the snow off the tracks, at least in the deepest cuts, than to have to clear it after every snowfall, the Central Pacific eventually built more than thirty miles of permanent snowsheds in the Sierras. But it was the rotary snowplow, a giant fan with cutting blades to slice through the snow and cast it aside, that finally conquered the snows of the western mountains. A Canadian invention, the rotary plow was first tested by the Canadian Pacific and was soon thereafter put into service by the Union Pacific in the United States.

A trainman came through the loading hallway to check the fusebox and stopped to talk. He noticed my cameras and asked a few technical questions. Before he moved on, he smiled and said, "I shouldn't tell you this, but you can open the window if you want a clearer shot. Just be careful. Look out for sparks, hot metal chips, any kind of debris flying up from the track. It can be dangerous."

The Zephyr swung through the curves, bending to the left, then to the right, the locomotive coming back to me and then turning away, swinging me to the outer edge of the track, out over the precipice, and then drawing me back to safety. Leaning out of the window, I tasted the snowflakes and watched them melt to droplets on the silver skin of the cars. The cars that had looked so bright and shiny crossing the desert looked dingy and soiled against the fresh white snow, just working machinery.

The Southern Pacific tracks down the western slope of the Sierras from Norden to Colfax are among the most dearly obtained railroad miles in the United States. Building from the west across the Sierras, Charles Crocker employed ten thousand or more Chinese laborers to construct the Southern Pacific line. Many of the Chinese workmen came directly from China; most were enticed here by the railroad. In 1867, they struck for wages equal to the Irishmen and black men they worked alongside and exacted thirty-five dollars a month from the railroad. They dug tunnels with pickaxes and sledgehammers, and they allowed themselves to be lowered over the cliffs in wicker baskets to plant dynamite charges. They died, in avalanches and accidents, of falls and fatigue, and were buried along the tracks when their bodies could be recovered and, when they fell into canyons and ravines, were left for the winter freeze and the spring thaw.

Dropping down the western side of the Sierras, the somber snow-clad forests of fir gave way to pines and mixed forests and then, as the snowpack thinned and finally disappeared at lower elevations, to scrub oak and chaparral, and finally we eased down into the Sacramento Valley.

A few minutes after two in the afternoon we were leaving Sacramento, moving cautiously over the Yolo causeway built in the early part of this century to keep the Sacramento Valley from flooding. Broad fields radiated away from the tracks, converging toward the horizon. After the Colorado Rockies, the arid basin and range country, and the High Sierras, the first cultivated field looked to be tilled as fine as sand and furrowed as smoothly as if it had been raked by hand. The ends of the furrows were edged as neatly as a Beverly Hills lawn, the fine crumbled dirt fluffed like a soufflé and spilling over into the grass at the end of the field in a neat line.

The conductor spoke on the public address system: "We're going slowly over here because the bridges in the causeway are being rebuilt over two years. But my head brakeman would tell you it's because a conductor never likes to run off his overtime."

I returned to my coach seat after Sacramento. Three seats ahead, a young college graduate was talking to his seatmate about expectations in the Pennsylvania coal country where he grew up. "You finish high school if you feel like it, then you go to work in the steel mills. It used to work, but about the time I finished high school, it quit working." Earlier that afternoon I had heard another rider, in another context, say, "You gotta learn discipline sometime. You get out of this world what you put into it. That's a fact." Some people, I thought, get from the world what they put into it, but some get much more, and more get a great deal less. Particularly when the world changes too fast for them.

San Francisco Bay was foggy and calm as we skirted its shore. Gentle ripples lapped at the gravel beside the track. The sky was darkening with rain clouds. The far shore was almost obscured by mist. A single workboat floated far out on the bay.

I arrived in Oakland tired and uncertain. Amtrak trains do not cross the bay to San Francisco; they stop at Oakland, and Amtrak provides bus service on to San Francisco. At the Oakland terminal I disembarked and left my bags on the platform where the bus for San Francisco was loading. From a pay telephone inside the Oakland terminal I called my hotel in San Francisco and learned that my reservation had not been held. Neither pleas nor imprecations would restore it. I slumped against the phone booth and looked around the big empty station. Most of the passengers who had disembarked with me had piled on the bus for San Francisco. I didn't know what to do next. My bags were still on the platform. I would have to make up my mind quickly whether to go on into the city as I had planned. I walked back out to trackside to gather my bags, only to see the bus pulling out of the depot and my bags nowhere in sight. I dashed after the bus, but knew it was futile and pulled up in a few strides. Fearing the worst, I went back into the station and asked one of the clerks what had happened to my bags. She asked me, "Were they on the platform with the other San Francisco baggage?"

"Yes, I left them there while I was in here making a phone call."

"Aren't you going to San Francisco?"

"I'm not sure," I said.

"Well, it looks like your bags have."

"Would you call over there for me and tell them I'll be in to claim them?"

"When?"

"Just tell them I'll get there as soon as I can. Don't hock the bags."

Finally, after thousands of miles, in a moment of weariness and indecision, I had committed the cardinal sin.

Part Three

The

Northern

Way

16 The Coast Starlight to Seattle: Under the Weather

Trains are tantalizing that way—they give you
great power, then complete forgetfulness.

—E. B. White, *Letters*

I had my camera bag with me, and my tickets; everything
else—my clothes, books, maps, notes, addresses and phone
numbers—was on its way to San Francisco. I walked out to the
street in front of the terminal and thought for a minute. The
day was gray and rainy. The weather had turned grim. Through
the South and the Southwest I had enjoyed an Indian summer
and a golden, glowing autumn, a privileged climate. The rain
in Kansas City and the blizzard in Colorado now seemed to have
been a warning that my charmed days were over.

I went back to the phone and called old friends in Berkeley. "Barbara," I said, "I really didn't want to do this, but I won't kid you, I
need a friend."

"Where are you?"

"I'm in the Oakland terminal."

"Where are you staying tonight?"

"Why don't I take you and Steve to dinner and let's talk about
that."

"I see. Steve will be home in a few minutes. I'll get some clothes
on Joseph and we'll come down and get you."

While I waited, I studied the sullied glory of the old Southern Pacific depot. The marble floors were dirty and scuffed. The vending machines were broken. The dilapidated steam radiators hissed. The gold paint on the woodwork was peeling. The massive wooden pews were gouged and scarred. The big hall was almost empty. A young girl warmed her hands at a radiator. An older woman, who had been waiting alone, smoking and pacing with her arms tightly pinned to her sides, looking as though she had no one in the world, suddenly came to life when a large red-faced man in a red windbreaker hurried in off the street. "I was fighting the traffic," he said. "I'm sorry."

"That's OK, honey, let's go home." They embraced quickly, but longingly, and hurried out. He kept one arm around her. The two bags that had seemed such a burden to her he stuffed under his other arm like a couple of shoe boxes.

Barbara and Steve took me in and, once again, I found myself relying on the kindness of friends. With an infant at home, they could not go out for dinner—boarding a lodger on ten minutes' notice was enough spontaneity for one evening—but they allowed me to assuage my guilt by buying dinner at a Berkeley Chinese restaurant and bringing it home, and before the evening was over I could not have felt more welcome if I had actually been invited. After we ate and put Joseph to bed, Steve drove me over the Bay Bridge into San Francisco to reclaim my bags from the downtown terminal.

I had known Steve since the fourth grade. From our first acquaintance he had displayed a fundamental decency that was almost dogged and a personal reticence that masked a world-class intellect. As we grew up, he was drawn into the world of mathematics, a secret service where he toiled beyond my comprehension, yet we had remained friends and had somehow never lacked for other things to talk about. In Princeton, he had met Barbara, a refugee from a career as a writer in New York City, and together they had moved to the Bay Area. When I arrived in Oakland he was in the midst of a year at a Berkeley think tank.

I spent the night at their rented house across from the Berkeley BART station, and the next afternoon, after wandering the streets of Berkeley most of the morning, I walked over to Steve's office, where we had agreed to meet. I arrived while he was still in a meeting. Like every office of his that I have ever seen, it was sparsely furnished: a desk, a chair, a blackboard. One of his recent papers lay on his desk. The first paragraph fooled me into believing that I might understand the next, so I picked it up to pass the time. Five minutes later, I was still mired in the second paragraph when I realized that I had been mistaken about understanding the first. I put it back on the desk and looked around the office again. The blackboard was covered with figures of such apparent simplicity that only a three-year-old child or a brilliant mathematician would have drawn them. The more profound mathematics becomes, the simpler it appears on the surface. An old rubber basketball lay in the corner—*that* I could comprehend. I picked it up and spun it on my fingertips until Steve walked in.

We spent Saturday touring San Francisco, a city new to me. We drove over the San Francisco–Oakland Bay Bridge, around and through the city to Golden Gate Park, and over the Golden Gate Bridge to Marin County. We climbed up to an overlook on the Marin headlands where we could see the Pacific to the west and back beyond the bridge to Alcatraz and over the bay to Oakland to the east. Sails danced on the bay like white feathers and the long wakes of powerboats trailed behind like plumes. Across the bay, the north-south streets of San Francisco rose up and over the hills of the city, looking like a field of corn rows in the late afternoon sun.

After a walk along the harbor at Sausalito, my energy suddenly drained away as though I were a broken vessel. I fought it for twenty minutes and then confessed to Steve and Barbara that I felt a little weak. We drove back to Berkeley where I fell out on the couch, so tired and aching that I couldn't imagine getting up for a week. I awoke after three hours and spoke to Steve and Barbara in what they later told me was a vaguely deranged way, clearly feverish. I slept fitfully and painfully through the night. Once I roused myself, wondering if I had the strength to walk the length of the hall. Barbara found me in the morning collapsed on top of the covers. "What happened to me?" I asked her.

"I'm afraid you caught a virus from Joseph. He brings them home from day care. I think we're immune by now, but you were vulnerable. I'm really sorry. Why don't you stay another day so we can be certain you won't relapse?"

"That's kind of you, but I don't want to bust my schedule now. I think I'll come around as the day wears on." I was scheduled to take the Coast Starlight north to Portland that evening and I was determined to make my train.

S till in a daze, I was aboard the Coast Starlight when it pulled out of Oakland at nine Sunday night. The Coast Starlight, which rides Southern Pacific track from Los Angeles up the coast to San Francisco and on north to Portland, where it switches to Burlington Northern track for its last leg to Seattle, has been the most successful Amtrak train outside of the Northeast Corridor. With a beautiful route through populous cities and a string of colleges and universities all along its way, the Coast Starlight attracts a steady ridership in all seasons and is crowded with college students at vacation periods. On board the Coast Starlight, I found for the first time a preponderance of young people. At any other time, I would have welcomed this change, but my stomach was still in turmoil and I didn't feel fit for company, so I kept looking until I found a single seat in the downstairs section of one of the coaches. It was a seat that no one wanted because it was at the front of the section and had no leg rest, which made it uncomfortable for reclining and sleeping on an overnight route.

The train was disagreeably warm. I stored my bags and went to the lounge car, where I found a more comfortable seat and watched the lights of Richmond across the bay. Students and young people quickly filled the lounge car, which came alive with chatter. The energy, the smoke, and the noise tightened the spasms in my stomach. As the Coast Starlight rolled on, the bay narrowed to a river, the Sacramento River. Rows of lights illuminated the valley slope above the bay.

At ten o'clock the Coast Starlight was still retracing the route of the Zephyr to Sacramento. At night, the bay seemed far away. A girl from Eugene, Oregon, was saying to the bearded, porcine young man beside her, "Like, my sister is still there, in Vancouver. She got married, man, like in the course of the summer. I had to split." She went on, but I tried not to listen. She was someone in whom the wonder of life had induced a perpetual giddiness that seemed endearing, until it became apparent how indiscriminate it was. The Coast Starlight turned north at Marysville and followed the Sacramento River valley north to Chico with the Coast Range on the west and the Sierras on the east. The cars began to cool down. As a Southern Pacific freight rumbled by on an adjacent track, lights in the distance flashed through the cars like strobes.

I went to my coach seat to try to sleep awhile, and finally, unsuccessful, I returned after midnight to the lounge car, walking through three cars of peaceful, sleeping people on the way. The lounge car was dark, and I thought at first it was empty. Then I noticed two figures on the floor. The girl from Eugene was sitting astride her suitor massaging his shoulders and murmuring to him. I kept overhearing the word "mellow." Joni Mitchell sang from a boom box on the floor. I ignored them and took a seat at the end of the car.

Crossing and recrossing the Sacramento River in the middle of the night, the Coast Starlight began climbing into the Cascade Mountains of northern California. The train twisted through sharp curves, the locomotive's headlight poking into the darkness ahead, first left, then right, shining on dark conifers, then a rock cliff, then a trackside signal. All beyond was a dark mystery. By three in the morning I was alone in the lounge car. I was sore, stiff, and sleepy, and my thorax throbbed from whatever virus I was still harboring. My face needed washing and my teeth needed brushing. The car had gotten cold. It felt as though a window was open somewhere. Air rushing from the vents made a steady soft roar. The couplings of the train cars, or maybe it was the vestibule fittings, groaned when the Coast Starlight negotiated tight turns through the mountains. After miles of total darkness, I began to notice street lamps glimmering on roads almost hidden in the forest. We were emerging from the thirty-mile-long Sacramento River canyon and approaching Dunsmuir, just south of Mt. Shasta and the Cascade Mountains. I had noticed an empty seat in one of the coaches on my last walk through to the lounge car, and I went back and claimed it. I slept until the sun awakened me in Oregon.

Klamath Falls is on a high, windswept plain that is the southeastern approach to the Willamette Pass for the Coast Starlight. At seven in the morning it was twenty-four degrees. We had arrived a few minutes early and had to wait in the station while the train crew changed and Southern Pacific maintenance workers refueled the locomotives and checked the running gear. The sun was up in a clear sky and it was a beautiful day, but the wind was sharp. The Amtrak attendant in my coach, a young man with neatly groomed blond hair, stood at his post in the open door cursing the cold. "I grew up in Michigan," he told me. "I loathe the cold. Then last year, I'm driving down the street in Detroit, and they're salting the street with those whirlybirds on top of the trucks. I'm being pelted with salt. Right there, I said this is it for me. I bought a house in Seattle. It never gets real hot, but it never gets real cold either, and it doesn't snow much."

I was still trying to shake the virus I had acquired in San Francisco, and a few hours of fitful sleep in a coach seat had left me feeling bruised and confused. I could see: my eyes registered images. I could move my jaw, if painfully. I could definitely hear; so, my ears and their associated brain parts functioned. I could turn my head; my cervical spine worked. But it was stiff—and below my neck it was all up for grabs. I felt like my favorite tabloid headline: "HUMAN HEAD KEPT ALIVE SIX DAYS!" ("Microsurgeons keep decapitated head alive, it communicates by blinking eyes!") I felt like that head on about the fifth day. Late in the afternoon.

But it was morning. Bright, noisy, bodacious morning. I picked up my bookbag and headed straight for the lounge car. I bought a cup of coffee, found a seat looking out upon the glorious, transcendent Oregon mountains, temporarily removed the clever plastic lid on my Amtrak-issue styrofoam coffee cup, gulped just enough coffee to clear some headspace in the cup, dug in my bookbag for my sixty-nine-cent pocket flask, and sloshed a slug of bourbon in the cup. I snapped the plastic lid back on, gave it a quick shake, and sat back to come to terms with the day. By my second cup, we had made a morning stop at Chemult, Oregon, and the world looked doable.

At Chemult, the Southern Pacific tracks bend northwest through the Deschutes National Forest toward Eugene. Here the northbound Amtrak passenger enjoys the advantage of daylight over the southbound. On such a brilliant late autumn morning, this run through Willamette Pass over the Cascades rivals any montane scenery on the Amtrak system. We passed Crescent Lake and then Odell Lake, shrouded in mist, and we crested and started down the north slope of the Cascades. Whereas the climb up the southern side of the Cascades is slow and steady, hauling up to the high plateau that stretches

150 miles from Grass Lake, California, to Crescent Lake, Oregon, the Southern Pacific tracks plummet down the north slope in less than fifty miles, down through Salt Creek Canyon to the Willamette River valley. We descended through heavily forested mountainsides of jack pine, lodgepole pine, and giant towering fir trees onto lower slopes of viney maples, adding red to the colors, and then the yellow of oaks and finally into the Willamette Valley at Oakridge.

We stopped at Eugene a few minutes after eleven. North of Eugene, I rode for a while on the platform in the downstairs hall of the Superliner coach. Since Amtrak doesn't permit smoking in its coaches, the hallway sometimes becomes an informal smokers' lounge, and north of Salem I was joined by a compact, balding man, who looked idly out of the window for a few minutes.

"These trains are really nice," he said, finally. "But they are not inexpensive. Particularly the sleepers."

"It's true," I agreed, "that you could put up at a pretty swank hotel for what you pay Amtrak for a bunk bed and a wool blanket."

"But you know," he said, "stretching out does make a difference. I never realized it. I go to Europe quite often. I get a EurailPass and just go"—he made an expansive gesture with his arm—"twenty thousand miles. The last time I got one of those couchettes and it really made a difference. On the European trains, even the coaches have compartments. Isn't it funny how American trains don't have separate compartments?"

"From what I've read," I said, "the American railroad coach evolved from the canal boat or packet boat, whereas the English and European railroad coach copied the stagecoach. If you think about it, each compartment on a European train resembles a stagecoach. Maybe the open seating arrangement of American coaches complements the American notion of egalitarianism. But that's just a guess. Who knows why things are the way they are?"

Later, as the Coast Starlight approached Portland, I was alone again when a big burly man in a gray houndstooth sports coat came down for a cigarette. His coat stretched tightly over his large frame, and he wore a checked hat that made him look something like Bear Bryant, the late and legendary Alabama football coach. His pants were tucked into brown cowboy boots, which were plain and battered with low, rounded tops. He had a face like a lava flow. I have never seen a face so deeply rutted.

When a trainman walked through, his walkie-talkie crackling, the man in the boots looked at me and shook his head, "I guess they just use the radios now. I remember when they had lanterns." He had a voice like a rockslide.

"They still use the lanterns at night," I said. "I noticed at six this morning, when it was still dark, that the brakeman was signaling with a lantern."

"That so? I thought the lantern was a thing of the past. This is the first time I've been on a train in forty-five years."

I asked if he was headed to Portland or on through to Seattle.

"I get off at Portland and go over to Spokane. That's the way I'm going home." A connecting train from Portland northwest to Spokane, Washington, enables eastbound travelers to catch the Empire Builder without going north all the way to Seattle. "Don't mind saying I'll be glad to get there, either. Had enough of San Francisco. I don't like to drive anywhere where there's five lanes of traffic all going the same way. I'm always in the wrong lane."

"I guess I'll be going through Spokane myself, from Seattle over to Chicago on the Empire Builder."

"You're going back on Amtrak? You'll go on what they call the High Line right through my hometown—Wolf Point, Montana."

"Does it get pretty cold over in your part of Montana?" My question was not entirely idle. I was contemplating a layover of a few days in western Montana.

"It's a land of extremes. It gets hot in the summer and cold in the winter. 'Bout like the desert would do. Forty, fifty below, that's not unusual. Sixty below, it has been. Then it gets hot. A hundred above, that is not unusual. It has been up a hundred and twelve, a hundred and sixteen. The big figures, above a hundred and way below zero, that's not something you get every year."

"Get pretty windy?"

"Lots of wind. Very seldom do you have any snow laying on the level. If you have a lot of snow, it piles up in the coulees. They build shelter for their cattle, so the cattle won't have to stand out in the snow. I've known the snow to drift up over the shelter and bury the cattle."

"Mostly ranching out there in eastern Montana?"

"It's high plains country. Grazing, some wheat. We've had three or four dry years in a row now. It can be a hard place."

"What about you?"

"Grow some grain, run some cattle." He said it in such a way that it could have been a mud hut and five spindly cows or a spread two days' ride from end to end.

The Portland station struck me as the most appropriate station I saw on the Amtrak system—a handsome old station, of impressive scale, stature, and tradition, but still full of light and life—not a monument to lost civilization as in Kansas City or even Los Angeles. As I walked through the waiting room, the man from Wolf Point gave me a hearty wave. With bags in both of my hands I could only nod as I walked by.

I had arranged to spend the night in the home of a couple who rented out a room through a local bed and breakfast agency, and they had agreed, for a few dollars extra, to meet me at the station. In a downtown Portland bookstore I purchased a *Golden Guide to Western Trees*. I chose it over several other more elaborate guides to the same subject for its three obvious virtues: it was small, simple, and cheap. On the way to his home, my host showed me around the city, climbing to a park on a hill from which we could see Mt. Hood in the distance. He and his wife lived on a steep slope overlooking the city. After they had eaten, I rode back down the hill into the city with his wife, who was teaching an evening class at a local school, and who was big, friendly, garrulous, and a very bad driver. I wandered around for a while, walking through residential streets of old Victorian houses that reminded me of neighborhoods I had known in New England. I ate dinner in an Italian restaurant, lingering over my plate to read the last chapters of *Travels with Charley*.

Late that night, just before midnight, after my hosts had retired, I stood on their rear deck, which was built out over a very steep hillside overlooking the city. I was standing above the treetops: only the Douglas firs reached as high as the deck, which had every sense of being a treehouse perched in the top branches of the firs. I found myself thinking of Rhode Island, of winter nights in 1970 when I would walk up to Prospect Point Park and look out over Providence in the snow, another port removed from the sea. I remembered listen-

ing to the low rumble of traffic drift up from the streets, the upshift-
ing and downshifting; how the falling snow would finally muffle the
noise until only the lights and the movement remained, and how,
late at night, the movement too would subside, slowed and then
stilled, except on the interstate, where traffic would continue to flow
steadily through on a corridor outside of time. I remembered the first
snowfall of my first winter in Providence, standing for hours watching the accumulating snow slowly muffle and then halt the city,
imposing a quiet and a stillness that seemed at first unnatural and
then revealed itself as the reassertion of natural force, like a tuft of
grass pushing up through the sidewalk or a zephyr rippling the curtain's edge at the closed window, a reminder that the city is but a
tenant with a long lease on the site.

Tuesday morning dawned cloudy and while I ate breakfast rain
began to fall. I was eager to get back on the train and keep
moving. I had come to the point where I was at ease only on
the train. I knew it well. It had come to be my home. I looked
forward to the run up to Seattle that afternoon: find a place in the
lounge car, put my feet up, have a cup of coffee, study my maps, and
watch the Cascades roll by.

In fact, the run up to Seattle was dreary. On Burlington Northern
track, the Coast Starlight travels straight north from Portland, crossing into Washington State at Vancouver, continuing to its next stop
at Kelso, and on through Castle Rock to stops at Centralia and East
Olympia, where it comes to the edge of Puget Sound, which it follows for the last seventy-five miles to Seattle. The afternoon was gray
and cloudy, appealing only to the waterfowl I saw on the sound.

In midafternoon, I made the mistake of going to the lounge car.
One problem with meeting people on the train is that one so often
meets them in the bar. That afternoon I met Ralph and Sam and
Betty. Ralph and his wife, Betty, were coming home to Seattle after a
vacation in Reno, and on the train they had chanced upon Ralph's
cousin, Sam, who was coming home for a visit from Houston, where
he was a policeman. They had stumbled into each other the night
before and by the time I ran into them they had been celebrating
their good fortune all day.

When I encountered them, they were well lit and trying with gusto to sing "El Paso," the old Marty Robbins country and western hit. "Down in the West Texas town of El Paso, I fell in love with a Mexican girl." They weren't getting past the first line. "Hey," Ralph hollered over at me, "what's the next line?"

"Something about Rose's Cantina. I'm afraid I don't remember the verse."

"Wait!" Ralph shouted. "That's it! Listen." He threw his head back, "Night time would find me in Rose's Cantina. The music would play and Felina would whirl." He sang the first few lines again, and Sam tried to join in. Sam made it as far as "cantina," where too many drinks took their toll and it came out sounding something like "Roses canned tuna." That broke up the choir.

"Damn it," Ralph said, encouraged by his progress. "I'm gonna get the whole thing before we get to Seattle!" He hummed the melody again while his friends laughed and hooted. "You know, my son, he knew I loved this song. When he was five years old he used to go around singing this song. He could sing the whole goddamned thing."

"If you're going to go on about your son," Betty said, "I'm gonna show him my daughter's picture."

Ralph shook his head. "No. No. We do not show pictures on the train."

"Let me see it, Ralph," Betty said sternly. "I bet you've got it."

"I don't have it with me. I took all the garbage out of my wallet. All my children. All your children."

"Sounds like a goddamned soap opera. All my children. All your children."

Betty was getting angry. Then they all began to talk at once and forgot about it. Ralph and Sam started singing again, the first few lines of "El Paso" over and over. Ralph didn't have a bad voice. Sober, he might have been able to carry the tune. Sam, who was several drinks ahead of the rest, kept shaking his head and muttering, "I been trying to learn those damned words for twenty years. That's always been one of my favorite songs. Hey, let me tell ya, Marty Robbins. That's a fine tune." He leaned toward me, "Do you know who Marty Robbins is?" His head tumbled forward and then he snapped back upright. He took out a pint bottle of Jack Daniel's and poured himself another drink.

Betty said, "He's probably an asshole."

"He died a year or so ago," I said.

"Then he died an asshole." She was still angry about the pictures. "I want another drink, Ralph."

Ralph ignored her and said to me, "He was the only country and western singer I ever liked, and he was in Seattle, he was in Seattle, and I was going to go, and the day of the concert I decided for some reason not to go and he died."

"Probably a coincidence," I said.

Betty said, "I need another drink, Ralph." Betty had been enjoying the flattery of both men and was hungry for new attention. My camera immediately caught her eye and she insisted on posing for a few photographs. Heedless of my protests—the light was all wrong, I had the wrong film, the wrong lens, the wrong camera—she took off her glasses, batted her eyelashes, and knocked her drink over on my coat. Ralph and Sam insisted I should take her photograph, but I demurred. It only frustrated her. She looked over at Ralph and said, "I guess he's holding out," and she began to unbutton her sweater. To placate her I gave in and fired off a few desultory rounds, but it only whetted her enthusiasm for the project. She began to toss her head and purse her lips and her admirers insisted that I capture the breathless moment, so I surreptitiously clicked off the power on my shutter and fired my flash a few times on full power, creating an impressive splash of light. After five or ten bursts of the strobe, she began to calm down and lose interest.

At the same time, I found myself rebuffing the inquiries of another woman in the lounge car who identified herself promptly as a writer and seemed determined to impress me equally with her calling and her need for a room that night.

"I'm a writer," she told anyone who would listen. "I'm going to write a novel."

She went on to tell me that she was on her way to an artists' colony in Washington but had only enough money to get to Seattle. "I'm down to four and a half dollars now. I'll just hitch from there," she said. "I do it all the time. It's the best way to travel. I'm going to write about that. Where are you going to stay in Seattle?"

"I'm not certain yet," I lied.

"Maybe we could get together."

"We'll see what happens. What's this water out here?" By then we'd been traveling along the shore of the sound for half an hour, but the question provided just the momentary distraction I needed to extricate myself from the lounge car. While I was making my way through the King Street Station in Seattle I saw her again, wandering aimlessly through the waiting room, and I kept walking.

17 Seattle and the Empire Builder: The Far Turn

Do you know what the three most beautiful sounds in the world are?
Anchor chains, plane motors, and train whistles.

—Jimmy Stewart as George Bailey in *It's a Wonderful Life*

I never got a feel for Seattle. I had no clear purpose there, as I
had been compelled by the Amtrak schedule to spend one night,
and out of vague curiosity had elected to spend two. I was still
exhausted from my bout with the flu, and my itinerary for the
next week, complicated by threatening weather and unresolved
logistical problems, was very much on my mind.

For two days I enjoyed the comfort of a grand hotel, the
Olympic—now the Four Seasons Olympic. Its accommodations were
so superior to the general level on which I had been traveling that for
the first day I was disoriented by the contrast. My original, and somewhat naive, idea had been to visit several of the hotels that dated
from the railroad age on the chance that I might gain some insight
into an earlier time and style of railroad travel. At the Olympic I
realized just how much things have changed: I would guess that few
if any of my fellow lodgers at the Olympic would be caught dead on
a train.

After checking in and cleaning up, I spent an hour or two walking
around the city, looking at the storefronts and watching the people
in the street and the nighttime traffic. For a few blocks I trailed

along behind a little band of suburban teenagers dressed in punk for a night in town. The next day was gray with a drizzling rain falling, so I took a bus tour of the city. Even at the time it seemed like an admission of a certain lack of initiative, but I thought it would at least acquaint me with Seattle in the one full day I had. Now and then, at the canal locks or the botanical gardens, the bus would stop and we'd clamber off and troop a block this way or that, all the old ladies and I. I enjoyed their enthusiasm and curiosity even after mine waned.

Later in the afternoon, I sat down in my room at the Olympic with the telephone and made a few calls, trying to figure out where to go next. I had planned from the first to spend a couple of days at Glacier National Park in northwestern Montana. The Empire Builder, the next train I would take, travels the full length of its southern boundary, with stops at Belton, Montana, on the western edge of the park, and East Glacier, on the eastern edge. My first thought had been to disembark at East Glacier, near Glacier Park Lodge, but a footnote in the timetable warned me that the Empire Builder had made its last stop at East Glacier on September 16. So, instead, I planned to stop at Belton, Montana, also called West Glacier, on the west side of the park.

After the summer season, the lodges and hotels in and around Glacier close down for the winter, so I had investigated other possibilities and discovered a youth hostel in a rustic ranch building in the little town of Polebridge, Montana, up the western side of the park near the Canadian border. I was planning to take the Empire Builder to Belton, get off at seven in the morning, and scuffle my way to Polebridge. However, by the time I reached Seattle, a blizzard was expected over on the east side of the Cascades, in Idaho and western Montana. From the Olympic Hotel I called the park office at Glacier to get a fix on the situation. I spoke to a ranger who all but forbade me to get off the train. "I can't recommend that you come to Glacier," he said in an official tone. "The weather will be severe. Everything is closed." I pressed him, but his manner as much as said, "People like you don't understand what it's like here. You just don't understand." He was right in the end. I didn't understand. Neither, however, did he understand that I had come a long way and would not be deterred, least of all by common sense.

After talking to the park office, I phoned Polebridge again and got through to the hostel. I talked to the woman who operated it, and she told me not to be frightened away by the Park Service people. "They're just trying to save themselves work." She suggested I try to rent a car at Whitefish, or, failing that, call from Whitefish and let them see if they could come down and get me. I called Whitefish and couldn't find anyone who would rent a car. I was apparently going to climb down from the Empire Builder in the midst of the season's first blizzard with very little idea where I was going and no idea at all how I would get there. I put my feet up and thought about it and came to no conclusion.

Around midnight, I riffled through my notepad and found the phone number in Bemidji, Minnesota, of Janice, the woman I had met on the Southwest Limited in Kansas. She had said to me, "I live on forty acres out in the country and if you come through, you really should see Minnesota."

Her phone rang for quite a while, and I tried to imagine the sound of the bell ringing in a cabin in northern Minnesota. "Hello?" she answered, tentatively.

"Janice? This is George Scheer. We met on the train two weeks ago?" I didn't wait to see if she remembered. "I hope I didn't wake you up?"

"No, no. I just came in." She sounded skeptical. "Where are you?"

"I'm in Seattle tonight."

"Are you coming to Minnesota?"

"I'm coming through in a few days, on my way to Chicago."

"Well?" she said, still noncommittal, but warmer.

"You did say . . ."

"Just tell me when you'll be here," she said, as if, all of a sudden, she remembered.

"I'll be coming through on the train Sunday night. But here's the thing. Do you know what time the Empire Builder comes through St. Cloud?"

"No, what time?"

"Five in the morning. If you want to hang up, I won't call back."

"I said I'd come get you, didn't I? Where else does it stop?"

"Just Staples. And that's at four."

"That's better for me. Four Monday morning at Staples. I'll be there. I don't have to teach Monday. It works out."

"I'll call you after you've had a chance to sleep on it."

Late the next afternoon, on my last day in Seattle, I found myself walking along the waterfront as afternoon traffic gave way to early evening strollers and the bars and seafood restaurants along the harbor began to fill with patrons. The sun set behind billowing clouds across Puget Sound. A big ferry moved with surprising swiftness from the horizon toward me and then beyond to its dock farther up the waterfront, booming out on its horn as it approached, a long blast, a short, and another long. As the sun declined, the air turned chilly and a stiff breeze blew off the water. Behind me, the yellow lights from the windows of the downtown towers glimmered against the gray sky. A few gulls flew with steady wing beats upward toward the city on the hill, as if to roost in the skyscrapers. A Burlington Northern freight rumbled slowly along the waterfront tracks, and every now and then the city trolley clattered past. High in the sky the contrails of two jets caught the last direct rays of the sun, and a vanguard of geese worked up the sound, the leader breaking the air and then falling back as another moved forward to take its place in a smooth rotation.

I sat on a bench on a public pier and watched four fishermen, three black men and a young Asian-American, fish from the end of the pier. As the light faded and the temperature dropped, they pulled up the hoods on their sweatshirts and parkas. One, feeling a strike, stepped back and lifted his rod to tighten his line. He froze with his rod overhead, waiting to feel the throb, but it didn't come and he lowered the rod. His friends jeered and tended their own rods. A minute or two later, he left his rod leaning against the railing of the pier with its bail open and walked off, going for food or relief, perhaps. He was halfway up the pier when his line began to pay out. One of his friends picked up his rod, tripped the bail, tightened the line, and set the hook, and then began to retrieve line, levering the rod upward and then reeling, levering and reeling, repeating the motion until he swung a fish up on the pier as the rod owner ran back.

I kept my seat and watched the small group of fishermen. Another Asian-American joined them and the five of them became a little community bound by common interest. By six forty-five, the sky was nearly dark, a deep purple with only a few cracks of violet and red.

The lights of the pier highlighted their parkas against the sky. A third Asian arrived with his rod and bait bucket and greeted the three black men with words I couldn't hear. One of the black men, called Jawbone by his friends, had a run of luck and began to haul in hake one after another, five or six in fifteen minutes, and one of the others hooked a double, but then it was over and they were left leaning against the railing of the pier, watching their lines and passing the time with joshing and idle chatter. A few minutes before seven the sky had darkened almost to black, with a single red rip in the cloud cover. Lights twinkled from the point across the harbor. I left them all at the end of the pier, smoking and talking and laughing, waiting for their luck to change again, and started back up the hill into the city.

At the hotel, I showered and put on a coat and tie and went down to the Garden Court, where important people were sitting at tables under the palm trees talking about important things. I sat at the bar and drank a Guinness or two. The next day I would be back on the train, aboard the Empire Builder to Montana.

I changed my ticket in the King Street Station. After a day of indecision, I asked the conductor to rewrite my destination to Whitefish, Montana, instead of the West Glacier stop at Belton. I was still determined to see Glacier and to make it to Polebridge, but I had not yet found the means and I decided that Whitefish, being a town, would give me more to work with than Belton. Even knowing that I might have made the wrong decision, I felt better having made it.

The Empire Builder is a name that conveys as much railroad history as any in the Amtrak system, devolving as it does from the storied Great Northern limited of that name, which was itself named after the builder of the Great Northern railroad empire, James Jerome Hill. From St. Paul, Hill's adopted city, to Seattle, the Empire Builder travels the line he built. The Great Northern was one of the most successful of the great western railroads, due primarily to Hill's vision and ability. While other railroads threw down hastily laid track to secure subsidies and land grants, he insisted on a carefully surveyed, smoothly graded line. Where other railroads passed by all but the most obviously profitable communities, Hill built branch lines to feed and nourish his trunk line and encouraged homesteading along his routes. While other railroads skimmed profits, he established a conservative financial structure and exerted prudent management. As a consequence, the Great Northern operated more efficiently and more profitably than its competitors and continued to expand, building an average of one mile of additional track for every working day between 1891 and 1907, the year Hill retired as president.

The Empire Builder entered service in 1929, supplanting the earlier Oriental Limited as the flagship Great Northern train. Although James J. Hill himself once compared passenger trains to the male teat—"neither useful nor ornamental"—his Empire Builder is, ironically, one of the most fondly remembered of the crack passenger trains, famous for transporting passengers in splendor and comfort through the most glorious country, often in the most severe weather. Today, the Amtrak Empire Builder operates between St. Paul and Seattle over the tracks of the Burlington Northern, the eventual successor to the Great Northern, the Northern Pacific, and the Chicago, Burlington & Quincy.

We left Seattle in fading afternoon light a few minutes before five, but vestiges of the light held for nearly an hour as the Empire Builder rolled north along the sound, gentle waves lapping almost against the rails. Deadwood floated on the water, like artfully deployed decoys among the ducks that strung out in long, wavering threads across the water. At five forty-seven, we stopped at Everett, a port and fishing town. A few minutes before six, the Empire Builder turned east, away from the sound, and entered the forest to climb the western flank of the Cascades. We had made the turn.

I was happy just to be back on board. I made a late dinner reservation, asking the dining car steward to hold a salmon dinner for me, and I settled in. The car attendant walked by my compartment, saw me typing, and offered to move me to a room with a table. I declined, saying that I was used to working on my knees, but the truth was that I already felt at home in the compartment. Within twenty minutes I had spread out my books and clothes and made it my own.

Early that evening he came by again, just to say hello and ask if I needed anything. He introduced himself as Julius. He was black, like most of the Amtrak car attendants, and, in his late forties or perhaps early fifties, older than many. When he found me still typing, he leaned into my doorway. "You gonna write about the trains?" he asked.

"What of them I've seen."

"You been on some others, then?"

I rattled off the list: the Crescent, the City of New Orleans, the River Cities over to St. Louis, the Eagle, the Sunset Limited, the Southwest Limited, the California Zephyr, the Coast Starlight.

"I can tell you like trains," he said.

"Doesn't everybody like trains?"

"Maybe so," he said, smiling, "but doesn't everybody ride 'em."

I left the door to my compartment open all evening. Only a few other parties were traveling on the upper level of my car and not much traffic came through. In the compartment across the aisle two women were traveling home to Cut Bank, Montana. They told me that they were travel agents, returning from a business junket to Seattle, where they had attended an Amtrak seminar to learn how to sell ski tours. They were giddy, like schoolgirls out of town, and they took turns flirting with me before dinner, each one giggling at the other's remarks. They each had a beer and, twittering, dared each other to have another. When they saw me typing, they began to tease me. "You must be a famous writer," one said.

"No," the other giggled, "he's a spy, writing secret dispatches."

"Let us see! We want to see what you're writing! We want to help!"

"I'm just about finished, actually," I replied.

"Then let's write a mystery story! We can all write it together. You start and we'll add part and then we'll each take a turn. Like *Murder on the Orient Express!*"

I put them off as gently as I could. "I'm on my way to dinner in just a minute, but if you'll watch my compartment for me, I'll leave the typewriter out and you all pass it around and see what you come up with."

For dinner I enjoyed baked salmon, basted in butter and herbs and garnished with an orange slice, the best dining car meal of my entire trip. I lingered at my table and forgot entirely about the two women from Cut Bank, and when I returned I found their compartment door closed. Still curled around the platen of my typewriter was a page-long story they had composed, a fanciful tale about two beautiful and clever women and a man who was half goat, a creature inspired more, I assumed, by the mascot of the Great Northern railroad than by Greek mythology.

Later that night I could hear the two of them, lying in their bunks and gossiping about friends and acquaintances back home—unruly children, marital infidelities, social gaucheries. The usual grist. "Did you know that Sally showed up at Nancy's door," one said, "waving all of Dave's letters at her. She read all his letters, all his complaints about Nancy—her nose was too big, her boobs were too small. Can you believe that? She'd been drinking, of course. Nancy called Dave at the office, told him he'd better come home. They went to counseling, but it took a long time to get over that. You can imagine!"

Late that evening, the car attendant came around to my compartment again. Everyone else in the coach had turned in for the night and he had no duties until twelve-thirty in the morning, when he had to board a passenger at Spokane. My compartment was cluttered with books and bags and papers and for a while we talked standing up in my compartment, then we moved out in the aisle, and finally we found an empty sleeper compartment down the hall where we sat and talked for more than an hour. He had a blunt, pleasant face, and he had a soft deep voice with a steady murmur to it, like a cat's purr.

He used to play the drums. "I got a kit in my basement now," he told me. "When I was a kid, I had an uncle, man, he played the bass fiddle and the clarinet. Didn't mess with the saxophone. He knew all them cats. He was in the army with Cannonball and Junior Mance and all them cats. Whenever Cannonball would come to town, he'd come by in a great big limousine and take us kids out for a ride. Everybody loved Cannonball. So much life in him. Loved to talk. Jolly as he could be. He was a hell of a person. I think that's why it bummed everybody when he died. Only thing my dad didn't like about him, every time he came to town, he'd come to the house, eat up all the food. The last time I saw him he came by, came with, who's that guy used to play the piano—'Mercy, Mercy' Joe?"

"Joe Zawinul. Guy that wrote 'Mercy, Mercy,' Cannonball's big hit? Played for Betty Carter? Weather Report?"

"That right? Sure. He's too much, man. Too much. The last time I saw Cannonball, he came by, they had that 'Mercy, Mercy, Mercy' out, and he came to the city to do something for Jesse Jackson, you know, that preacher? Something for Operation Push. It was on a Thurs-day, and he came by, he was staying at the Mansfield Hotel in Chi-cago. That was the last time we saw him. Those were some days."

He nodded to himself, remembering. "He would come to town with Miles, when he had Cannonball, John Coltrane, he had Red Garland."

"My favorite piano player."

"And Philly Joe Jones, Paul Chambers."

"My favorite rhythm section was that section he had in the late fifties of Red Garland, Paul Chambers, and Art Taylor."

"OK. I hear ya. Whatever happened to Art Taylor?"

"I wish I knew. If I remember, he split for Europe in the sixties, France or someplace. After that, I don't know. I heard he was teach-ing somewhere. Paul Chambers died young."

"Yeah, yeah he did. And Trane, they were both young when they died. So many of 'em. But you know, I was lucky. I got a chance to see all the cats, all the great cats who played jazz, such as the Duke and Bird. I even got to see Pres. Duke, and Bird, and Pres, all gone now, and who's the trumpet player that got killed in that car accident?"

"Clifford Brown."

"He died so young. Just those few years. Something about his playing, sort of like Cannonball to me, sounded like a man you'd like to know. Sounded so warm."

It was a few minutes before midnight. A traveler in a compart-ment on the lower level of the car came looking for Julius to make up his bed. "You ready, now?" Julius asked him. "I'll be right there."

A few minutes later, Julius came back and settled in again to con-tinue reminiscing. "New York was something in those days, man. Those were some days. I used to get in there on the Broadway Lim-ited round about four-thirty, I'd go out, get a bite to eat, go back and take a shower, and I'd wait till round about twelve o'clock at night, and then I'd go round the clubs, even just on the street, I'd hear music you just wouldn't believe. I know there's as much talent out there now as ever was, but it just doesn't seem the same. The clubs aren't there, not like they used to be, not even in New York. I know the big clubs, but the scene, the scene just ain't the same. And in Chicago, you've got nothin' but the blues. And I mean you can hear some blues, cats that can get down. But as far as jazz, you only got, let's see, that club where those brothers—what's their name?—Freeman?"

"Von Freeman? Has a son, Chico, who's a saxophonist?"

"Yeah, Von Freeman. There were three of 'em all together. Von plays the piano. They played out there at the Matador. You don't have that many, like I say, jazz clubs. You only got maybe four in Chicago. That doesn't seem right, does it? I don't know why. I think the people just don't understand the music, maybe that's the problem."

"Maybe so. It took me a while. I came to it from simpler music, the blues mostly. Then somebody played an Ellington record for me and that was it, but at first I could only hear earlier jazz. The first time I heard a Bird record, I didn't know what was happening. I was in way over my head. By the third bar I was lost."

"I hear ya."

"All his stuff is close enough to the blues so you get that right off and that feels good, but to really hear what's happening, it took me a long time, and I still work at it."

"What about Miles, man?"

"He had that tone. So much of Miles was that tone."

"But, man . . . I got a new record of his, about a year ago. He always was kind of way out, but . . ." Julius shook his head, raised his eyebrows and laughed. "He came to Chicago a couple of years ago for the big blues and jazz festival and they must have had a hundred thousand people out there. Man, he was playing somethin' crazy. Four or five different types of music, all at the same time. And loud. Woke up the next morning, I could still hear it. He's got to be a weird individual. But he's still putting us all through the changes." He reached in his shirt pocket, beneath his red Amtrak vest, and pulled out a pack of Pall Malls. He shook one up and extended it toward me. "Cigarette?"

"No, but you go ahead," I said.

He laughed. "Very seldom somebody asks me for a cigarette. Very rare."

Finally, he looked at his watch and shook his head and said, "Spokane coming up. I guess I got to go to work. I got some passengers coming on at Spokane. Maybe then I can get some sleep."

"Not too much, I'm afraid. You got to get me off this thing at six-thirty."

"You getting off at Whitefish?"

I nodded.

"You're gonna have some weather over there, from what I hear."

"So I'm told," I said. "If I'm all you got at Whitefish, why don't you sleep through? I can get myself off."

"No. We'll change crews there, take a few minutes if we get in on time. We usually take on a few there, anyway. I'll see that you get off. You best get some sleep if you can."

"I guess I'll give it a try, then," I said. We both got up and stretched. By then we were approaching Spokane, so I set my watch ahead to Mountain time and at 1:14 A.M. I stood in the open door of the car, watching as the Portland-to-Spokane cars were coupled to the Empire Builder for the remainder of the trip to Chicago. Back and forth, the train maneuvered in the yard, past hopper cars in the dark and the lights of the Spokane station. Then I retreated to my compartment, packed for my early morning disembarkation, and fell quickly into sleep.

At six thirty-five that morning, I watched my warm bed pull away from Whitefish in the dark. I had to find a car to rent before I could go anywhere, and the town was still asleep, so I waited in the depot for the day to begin. For twenty-five minutes I sat by myself in the tiny waiting room, which seemed to be of an earlier time, with board walls, paneled wainscoting, and ornamental iron bars in the agent's ticket windows that gave a proper Old West sense that some desperado might try to steal the gold shipment. In Seattle, a day before and five hundred miles west, I had heard that a blizzard was due in western Montana, and all along the line I had been warned that winter was coming, but the waiting room in the depot was warm and snug.

18

Storm Warning along the Great Northern

Come, Ahab's compliments to ye; come and see if you can swerve me. Swerve me? ye cannot swerve me, else swerve yourselves! man has ye there. Swerve me? The path to my fixed purpose is laid with iron rails, whereon my soul is grooved to run. Over unsounded gorges, through the rifled hearts of mountains, under torrents' beds, unerringly I rush! Naught's an obstacle, naught's an angle to the iron way!

—Herman Melville, *Moby Dick*

I n the Whitefish depot, I considered my next few days. It was Friday morning, the twenty-sixth of October. I had planned to spend two days and two nights in the Glacier area of Montana, then reboard the Empire Builder at six-thirty Sunday morning at Whitefish, ride all day Sunday across Montana and across North Dakota most of the night, and arrive at Staples, Minnesota, where Janice had promised to meet me, at four Monday morning. After leaving Montana, I would be catching ten trains in eleven days, with stops in Minnesota, Chicago, Albany, Montreal, Springfield, Boston, Providence, and New York, and a day or two mired in the Montana snows would tumble my complicated reservations for those trains like a row of dominoes. There was nowhere left to make up the time. I was running out of days.

At seven, it was still pitch dark outside. From the pay telephone in the waiting room, I called Bemidji, Minnesota, where it was eight o'clock. Janice sounded sleepy when she answered.

"It's George. I know I probably awakened you. I'm sorry, but I wanted to catch you before you got out for the day."

"I'm not teaching today. Where are you?" Her voice was soft and confused.

"I'm in Montana, near Glacier. And you thought you could sleep in today. . . . Sorry. I'll get to the point and maybe then you can go back to sleep. The weather here looks pretty bad. The morning line has this part of the state under a few feet of snow by tonight. If I go up to Polebridge, there's a good chance I won't be able to get back here to Whitefish to catch the train Sunday morning. I could stick close to Whitefish, just put up in a motel here for two nights, but I don't see much charm in that. I'd rather be in Minnesota. Can I push my invitation up a day? It would mean picking me up in Staples on Sunday morning and being stuck with me for an extra day, but I'm easily amused."

"Are you sure?" she asked. She still sounded a little as though she was trying to place my name.

"Just get me out of the weather. You can do whatever you need to do and I'll just catch up on my notes for a day."

"No, no, about the train. Which morning?"

"Sunday morning, but it's still going to be four A.M., so it might as well be Saturday night. Saturday night, Sunday morning. Oh-four-hundred Sunday morning. At Staples."

"That's tomorrow night," she said, a little surprised.

"I know you didn't ask for all this. I'll owe you one. I'll buy you dinner. And yes, that's tomorrow night." I couldn't believe I was asking a woman I didn't know to drive three hours in the middle of the night to meet a train.

"I'll be there. Staples. Four, Sunday morning. Are you sure you'll be able to catch the train? You won't get caught in the snow?"

"That I can make. I'll get off at Staples. You get there when you can."

"I'll be there."

I asked the agent to make the change in my ticket. When she keyed my ticket number into the Amtrak computer, she was perplexed to see dozens of different connections scroll across her terminal screen. "I need to make one simple change," I told her, "and you can do it. Just change my reservation from the twenty-eighth to the twenty-seventh. The same train, the same trip—Whitefish to Staples, Minnesota. Everything else stays the same."

The second agent, a man who was handling bags and baggage, told me, "This is going to be a blizzard. If you want to make that train, you'd better be back here in Whitefish by two this afternoon, before it closes the highways."

I went back to the pay phone and thumbed through the Whitefish yellow pages and didn't find any prospects for a rental car. On a hunch, I called the local Ford dealer and spoke to a woman named Judy who agreed to rent me an Escort if I could walk to their lot two miles outside of town. I made one more stop before leaving Whitefish. At the Ben Franklin five and dime I bought a cheap plastic raincoat, one of those slickers that comes folded in a plastic pouch into which it will never again fit. I bought the only size they had, knowing it would be too small. For $1.50 it gave me some small sense of security going out into the weather. By the time I reached the outskirts of Whitefish it began to rain gently, but my Panama hat kept the raindrops off of my glasses and I kept walking. When I started the car, the radio came on with the motor and the first thing I heard, before I had even fastened the seat belt, was an urgent weather advisory.

The National Weather Service has issued a winter storm warning for the mountains west of the Divide and southwest Montana for today and much of tonight. In addition, a winter storm warning has been moved ahead to this afternoon in the northwest portion east of the Divide, a warning for tonight in the central and south portions of the state, and a winter storm watch is in effect for northeast Montana. Snowfall associated with this developing winter storm is expected to be heavy and will be accompanied by rapidly falling temperatures and high winds. So, if you are planning on heading over the Continental Divide, either way, be advised the weather is going to be extremely nasty.

On the way to West Glacier, the rain began to turn to snow. Big soft snowflakes smacked the windshield like wet kisses. Slush piled up quickly on the road, and the Escort demonstrated very skittish handling on the uncertain footing. I considered turning back, but pressed on, driving carefully. Entering the park, I drove through an underpass beneath the very Burlington Northern tracks traveled by the Empire Builder, and I passed motels and trading posts boarded up for winter—a "Closed for the Season" sign hung in a front window of the West Glacier Cafe. The park rangers who had discouraged me had been right: winter was sealing off the park. I peered at the roadway, trying to see if other tires had preceded mine, but the snow was falling too fast to tell.

I was beginning to realize that the storm would drastically restrict my horizon. The Going to the Sun highway over the Continental Divide would be impassable and the two roads to Polebridge, Route 486 west of the park and the North Fork Road through the park, were both gravel roads that would be a treacherous stew of mud, ice, and snow by nightfall. I was determined, however, to reach McDonald Creek.

Each autumn since the late 1930s, hundreds of bald eagles have congregated at lower McDonald Creek, near Apgar in Glacier National Park, to feed on kokanee salmon as they spawn. From summering grounds in the Mackenzie River system of Canada, in northern Alberta, northwestern Saskatchewan, and the Northwest Territories as far north as the Beaufort Sea, the eagles migrate south to winter in the western and northwestern United States. (Few eagles remain in Glacier through the harsh winter; almost all move on farther south to Utah, Colorado, Nevada, and other parts of Montana.) As the eagles are on the move in late September, October, and early November, kokanee salmon—a landlocked variation of the anadromous Pacific sockeye salmon—are swimming out of Flathead Lake upstream into its tributaries to spawn.

I drove across the Middle Fork of the Flathead River on a low bridge and stopped for a few minutes to stand on the bridge and watch the snow fall over the shallow, gently curving river. I saw no sign of other visitors nor park personnel. Just beyond the river, the road entered a forest of tall pines and passed the park entrance station. The station was closed and shuttered, but no gate barred my way, so I drove on. I reached Apgar about eleven. Snow was falling thickly, in fat heavy flakes that fluttered in the still air.

I parked near a small visitor center and met a young woman, a seasonal park ranger, as she came out. Her hat, the traditional Smokey the Bear hat of the park service, was covered with plastic, like a shrink-wrapped toy. I asked her about the eagles.

"Oh yes, they're in. Just up the road there a few dozen yards is a trail you can follow over to the creek. It's too cold to stay out there for long, though. I'll be giving a talk to a group of high schoolers in the little red Apgar schoolhouse just up near the trail. Why don't you come back there when you want to get out of the snow and get warm."

The snow was falling in clumpy flakes as I walked the narrow path through the woods to McDonald Creek, which flows out of Lake McDonald and through the forest for a little more than a mile before joining the Middle Fork of the Flathead River. Visitors are restricted to a bridge over the creek. Since 1970, the park service has closed the area around the creek during spawning season to protect the eagles from disruption and harassment. From the bridge the streambed appeared to be paved with red bricks. Kokanee salmon, a foot to a foot and a half long, were jammed together like bricks in a sidewalk, filling the stream from bank to bank and as far downstream as I could see. Occasional, feeble, wriggling motions rippled through the packed salmon, but otherwise they seemed not to move.

I peered through the falling snow and in the trees along the creek I saw the eagles, perhaps a dozen, the white of their heads and tail feathers standing out even amid the swirling snow. The larches along the stream banks had turned yellow in the autumn but, for the most part, had not yet shed their needles, so the eagles congregated in the dead trees where they could find open perches on the bare limbs. Four eagles perched up and down the mast of a single dead pine, clinging to the close-cropped limbs like telephone linemen. Every few minutes an eagle would take flight, swinging out over the creek, swooping down to pluck a salmon from the water, and then carrying the fish back to a perch to tear it apart with its beak. A few juvenile eagles wandered along gravel beds at the edge of the creek and waded out into the shallows to grab a salmon. A couple of magpies loitered down the stream, ready to scavenge salmon carcasses left by the eagles. The ranger had told me that mink, otter, coyotes, and occasionally grizzlies are also drawn by the abundant salmon to McDonald Creek. The eagles come to the creek in the early morning from their night roosts and stay most of the day, feeding intermittently on the salmon. An adult eagle will take perhaps a half-dozen salmon before returning to roost for the night.

For a few minutes I was alone on the bridge, until a young man arrived with a camera and binoculars and quietly took up a post at one end of the bridge. He was an engineer for an oil company, working in the oil fields around Havre, Montana, a town on the Milk River in north central Montana, east of Glacier.

"It's a two-hundred-mile drive," he told me, "but I like to come over whenever I can get away. I stay at the Izaak Walton Inn up on Route 2. It's a wonderful place, up in the mountains, very rustic, and the food is great. I get a room and just rest and relax, come down and watch the eagles. It's good to get away."

Through the middle of the day the snow continued to fall. After two hours, freezing water bathed my toes, melted snow dripped down my nose, and my beard was encrusted with ice. My glasses were streaked and fogged and my hands were numb to the knuckles. So my friend from Havre and I walked back through the woods to the small wooden building where the young ranger was speaking to a class of schoolchildren. "I don't think they'll want to stay out very long," she told us as she led them out to see the eagles. "Why don't you stay and thaw out. I showed them a film on grizzlies and some slides of the eagles. You can rewind the film and watch it if you want. You might be interested in the slides, too. Some of them are pretty good."

We were glad to peel off our wet outerclothes. I rewound the film and rethreaded the old sixteen-millimeter projector and we watched the film, a Marty Stouffer film with splendid footage of bears in the wild and a maddening singsong narration. The slides, photographs of eagles taken at Glacier, were more interesting, being more particular and specific, and giving us an impression of just how many eagles convened at McDonald Creek. Biologists estimate that as many as one thousand eagles typically pass through McDonald Creek to feed while migrating, although only several hundred of those are present simultaneously. Park biologists have been concerned about a decline in those numbers since 1981, since bald eagle populations have been particularly susceptible to pesticides. Photographs from earlier years showed the trees along McDonald Creek crowded with bald eagles, as common for the moment as crows.

We were still watching slides of the eagles when the ranger came back. "There aren't many eagles out today. I think it's the weather. They've probably gone back to the roosts early," she told us. "It's turning into quite a storm out there. We sent the kids home before it gets any worse. I hope you guys don't have far to go tonight."

The three of us sat in the little schoolhouse awhile and talked about the park. Her round face, straight dark hair, and round eyeglasses gave her a bookish, even an owlish look. I asked her if they received much pressure about the occasional grizzly maulings.

"Some," she said. "There are the people who say, 'If you would get rid of those damned bears I'd come to the park.' But our mandate is to protect the wildlife of the park as well as the people, and, frankly, I want the bears to stay. This is the last stand for the grizzly. Glacier is considered the most threatened national park. We are under pressure at our borders. They are looking for oil up in the North Fork now. That's our most abundant wildlife habitat. Some days, all over the park, you can hear the seismic crews setting off detonations."

In midafternoon, the engineer from Havre and I ventured out for a last look at the eagles. We were all alone. Fresh snow had fallen into the childrens' tracks. Even most of the eagles had retreated from the storm. A half-dozen or so still kept to their perches at the bend of the creek, but the snow was too thick to see them clearly. As we stood on the bridge, a single eagle flew overhead, sweeping down the creek from McDonald Lake, over the few remaining eagles in the trees and out of sight in the mist and falling snow. As it passed overhead, I was surprised by its size. Its wings spread at least six feet and their dark leading edge cut an ominous shadow. It flew without crying, but I thought I could hear its wings beat and when it swiveled its head around, showing the sharp hook of its beak, I flinched instinctively. I could clearly see the primary feathers at the tip of its wings, outstretched and separated like five fingers silhouetted against the whitened sky. I was glimpsing one of the supreme predators from the helpless position of its prey and, at that moment, the last vestige of warmth seemed to pass out of me and the cold flooded in.

We walked through the snowy woods to our cars. As far as I could tell, we were the last visitors in that part of Glacier. "Why don't you come up to the inn and have dinner with me?" my friend suggested. "I can recommend the food and I'd like to hear about your travels. Havre seems a long way from anywhere, and the only people I get to talk to there are townspeople who never go anywhere or people in the business."

"I'm tempted," I told him, "but I'm afraid it would be foolhardy, given the weather. I've got to catch a train at six-thirty tomorrow morning, and if I miss it I'll have to answer for it down the line."

We each started our cars. He was driving a big American sedan with the name of his oil company emblazoned on the door, a company car. I started my little Escort and let the motor idle as I scrounged around inside the car for something with which to scrape the windows. The snow was layered so heavily on the windows that light barely penetrated. Suddenly something swept across my windshield and light burst through. I opened the door and stepped out, but he was already scraping the snow off my rear and side windows. It flew off in bursts and plopped softly to the ground.

"If you need a friend in Havre, call me," he said, smiling.

"Thanks," I answered. "Drive carefully."

I stopped at the park office to say good-bye to Jean, the young park ranger. She was on the radio, relaying reports on road and weather conditions as rangers worked to batten down the park for a siege of severe weather. "I'll be heading south soon," she told me. "I wish I could stay. But they can't use me in the winter. I'm not permanent staff. Someday I hope I'll be here year round."

"Even with all the problems the park faces?"

"It's all I want to do," she said.

We were interrupted by a report relayed in on her radio: "We've got an update on road conditions. Snow continues to fall and is expected to remain heavy into tonight. Blowing snow, deep drifts, near-zero visibility, and declining temperatures are creating treacherous driving conditions. Highway 2 is closed from West to East Glacier and also west of Kalispell."

My friend from Havre was at that moment driving east on Highway 2. I wondered if he would make it through before the road shut down. When I could delay no longer, I said good-bye and drove out of Glacier. The snow on the park roads was four or five inches deep, and my inadequate little Ford skated down the road. I stopped for a minute where the Going to the Sun highway turned northeast, up toward Logan Pass through the face called the Garden Wall on the Continental Divide. Then I drove on, past the boarded-up entrance gate, over the Middle Fork of the Flathead again, where now even the stones in the river were capped with snow, past the trading post shuttered for the season, and beneath the Burlington Northern tracks.

Just outside the park I passed the Belton stop, the train stop at West Glacier where I had originally planned to disembark. I counted my blessings: it was nothing but a long curve in the tracks, a couple of signal lights, and a long walk uphill through the snow and the pine trees to the Vista Motel, which was closed for the season. One signal light glowed red, a single speck of color in the monochrome landscape, gleaming through the falling snow like a hand-painted eye in a black-and-white photograph.

I drove slowly, very slowly. I hunched over the wheel and strained to hear the whoosh of the tires in the snow, listening for the change of pitch that would tell me I was losing traction. The defroster hummed like a turbine. Snow blew across the road, white devils spinning across the highway. Between Belton and Hungry Horse, I passed three or four cars belly up where they had slid off the road and rolled down embankments. While vehicles far better than mine fell by the wayside, I inched my way down Highway 2 to Columbia Falls and on across Route 40 to Whitefish. The Escort was a sorry snow vehicle, but I had going for me my shameless willingness to drive slower than anything else on the road. Cowardice brought me through, and I made it back to Whitefish about five in the afternoon. I drove up Spokane Avenue to the center of Whitefish and looked for somewhere to eat and take shelter.

I passed up the Great Northern Bar and the Palace Saloon (Poker Every Night) and chose Mr. P's Family Restaurant. It was the tail end of the dinner hour and couples and families were finishing their meals. I overheard cowboys at a couple of tables talking about their plans for a rowdy Friday night. The chili was better than I expected, with discernible chunks of tomato and strips of sirloin instead of hamburger. Pausing for long stretches to scribble in my notebook, I stretched my meal out for three hours, finishing with a slice of Rocky Road chocolate pie, which was full of nuts and had a homemade crust. The waitress, a young woman in jeans, earned my gratitude by returning every ten or fifteen minutes to refill my coffee mug—and otherwise ignoring me completely. "Faithful customer," she called me every time she came around with the coffeepot. Once, when I thanked her for tolerating me for so long, she looked at me carefully and said, "I wish they were all like you." When the two waitresses began to vacuum the dining room and scrape the grill, I closed my notebook and paid my check. As I was leaving, the waitress called out, "Come back for breakfast."

The snow was still piling up and the rain that had fallen early in the day had frozen into an underlayer of ice. I was afraid to venture far from the railroad station. My attention had come to be focused solely on catching the Empire Builder at six-thirty in the morning. Nothing else mattered. I was through taking chances for the day. I had promised Judy that I would leave the Ford at the railroad station in the morning. "Just refill the gas tank and leave the key in it," she had said. "We'll send someone around later in the day to pick it up." I had visions of starting out at six in the morning from some motel on the outskirts of town and bogging down in the snow and ice. The one certain way, I thought, to make that train would be to be there waiting for it. I drove back down Spokane, turned on Second Street to Central, and drove the last two blocks to the station.

I could spend the few remaining overnight hours in the waiting room, where it would be warm and snug and comfortable enough. I would read, write notes, cards, and letters, and doze in a chair until early morning. No worse, I thought, than a night in a coach seat. I walked to the door. It was locked tight.

I parked the Ford in the gravel lot alongside the tracks and decided to just outlast the night. I reclined the seat and wrapped myself in everything I had, which was not much more than I was wearing, and tried not to think about the cold. I would doze off for twenty or thirty minutes and then the cold would wake me. Finally, I fell into a pattern: when the cold became unbearable, I would start the car and run it for five or ten minutes, long enough for the motor to warm up and the heater to burn the chill out of the car, and then I would shut off the motor and shroud myself in the plastic raincoat and try to sleep. In the cold the plastic raincoat congealed into a stiff brittle cocoon, but it helped to form a vapor barrier around me. As soon as I turned off the motor, the cold would begin to seep in within seconds. I was tempted, sorely tempted as the night wore on, to leave the motor running so I could sleep for more than a few minutes, but I anticipated the headline that would appear in the Whitefish newspaper: "Stranger Asphyxiated in Railroad Parking Lot." Eventually, I entered into a kind of delirium, a state of reduced metabolic activity that itself probably precluded any sensible appraisal of just what a foolish thing I was doing. Sometime in the early morning hours the snow stopped falling and the temperature fell decisively, bottoming out, I later learned, somewhere in the mid-teens.

Progressively—as my blood withdrew from my fingers, my toes, my brain—I quit thinking critically and commenced simply to count the minutes. I concentrated doggedly to remember to turn off the motor before falling asleep again. The warmth from the heater was a dangerous drug, a seductive, hypnotic elixir that I longed for and feared. My choice was either sleep or warmth; I could not risk both. My dreams grew more intense and began to spill over into the twilight of my waking moments. I was awakened for the last time by a long Burlington Northern freight pulling slowly into the yard, four locomotives at its head and the Rocky Mountain goat insignia of the Great Northern Railroad emblazoned on its boxcars.

At five-thirty, I pulled gingerly out of the parking lot and drove with difficulty the two blocks back to Mr. P's Family Restaurant for another cup of coffee and breakfast. The waitress was counting the Friday night take. "We didn't do much last night. Only one twenty in the till," she said to the cook. "I thought we did better than that." Along the counter, all the stools were turned expectantly toward the street, waiting for morning customers. "It's going to be a slow Saturday morning," she said, looking out the front window. "That storm'll keep 'em out of town."

I left the Ford in the station lot with the key under the mat, just as we had arranged. The eastbound Empire Builder pulled out in the dark just after seven in the morning. I was very, very grateful to be aboard it.

When we passed West Glacier, twenty-three miles east, the predawn light was just revealing the long curve and signal lights I had noticed the afternoon before, and in the scant blue light and deep snow it was a lonely spot. From West Glacier, the Burlington Northern tracks turn southeast and follow the Middle Fork of the Flathead River along the northwestern shoulder of the Flathead Mountain Range. As we climbed into the mountains, snow was still falling, blowing along the tracks and drifting in the cuts, and clouds hung low in the passes. For fifty-seven miles, the tracks skirt the southern tip of the park, climbing over the Continental Divide and emerging on the plains of western Montana. Just as the sun rose high enough to wash the mountains with white light, we passed the Izaak Walton Inn, a beautiful timber lodge on the Flathead River. The porch light was still burning, shining warm and yellow and inviting, and a few early risers stood on the front steps waving as we passed. I looked in vain for my friend from Havre, wondering whether he had made it through in the storm.

Marias Pass, where the Burlington Northern tracks cross the Continental Divide, is the lowest summit along the divide between Canada and New Mexico, but that morning it looked like the roof of the world—white, windswept, and lonely. A statue stands on the side of the mountain. It is a statue of John Paul Stevens, the railroad engineer who scouted Marias Pass for James J. Hill of the Great Northern Railroad, pushing through temperatures of forty degrees below zero to survey the route. In these days, a surveyor may seem a prosaic figure, but the men who broke the trails for the first great transcontinental railroads were adventurers and visionaries, and on their choice of a route often turned the eventual fate of an entire railroad. A poor path, a route with too many steep grades or needless detours, crippled a railroad for life like a congenital malformation. The man who found Marias Pass granted his railroad, and all the trains that have followed, safe and sure passage. High up in the Montana Rockies, the bronze statue of him stands like a shrine to a forgotten saint.

From the summit of Marias Pass on the Continental Divide, the route of the Empire Builder describes a 1,500-mile descent to Chicago, steep at first, dropping down more than half a mile in the first 200 miles across western Montana, and then easing into an elongated, shallow decline, flattening out with every mile across eastern Montana, North Dakota, Minnesota, and Wisconsin—over the last 660 miles, from Fargo to Chicago, the tracks descend only a little more than 300 feet. The only irregularity in this arc is a rise of a couple of hundred feet as the tracks climb through the hills of the Missouri Coteau between Williston and Minot, North Dakota.

We descended from the pass suddenly, spilling out among low, rolling, mostly treeless foothills that, covered with sparkling snow, looked like piles of sugar. At high speed, we traveled across sunny rangeland, where the hoof trails of cattle wandered crazily through the snow, like scars in wormy wood. For hour after hour, the jagged tectonic wreckage of the Glacier Rockies jutted into the sky behind us, diminishing in scale almost imperceptibly mile after mile. East of Browning, the foothills smoothed out and I watched a hawk circling in the sky. About ten in the morning, the thrill of the mountain crossing receded and fatigue overwhelmed me. I closed the door of my compartment and slept into the early afternoon as the Empire Builder crossed western Montana, cutting across the tributaries of the Missouri River—Willow Creek, Eagle Creek, and other streams that flowed south into the Marias River, which itself flowed into the Missouri farther south.

I awoke in the oil country of central Montana, near Havre, where the route of the Empire Builder joined the Milk River, which it would follow for another 150 miles to the Missouri River at Nashua, Montana. The rampart of the Rockies had finally vanished from sight, and the land had flattened out into long rolling swells of cultivated sections. I now saw white boxes scattered in fields, hives for bees to pollinate the alfalfa crop. A few minutes after two in the afternoon we were still behind schedule. The conductor announced that we would soon be stopping at Malta, Montana, where Billy the Kid once held up a Great Northern train, the Oriental Limited.

We passed over a small creek that was frozen solid. I had been told that the temperatures were colder here on the eastern side of the divide. We were traveling through wheat country, where dryland farming is practiced—in more years than not, less than fifteen inches of rain will fall on this part of the upper plains. In his *History of the Westward Movement*, Frederick Merk wrote, "The settlement of the Great Plains, at the north and center, may almost be said to have been a railroad colonization." The railroads lured settlers to a land of marginal rainfall, where years of sufficient precipitation often proved to be only bait in a trap of cyclical rain and drought. To encourage settlement, which would bring freight business and revenue, the railroads sometimes painted a fraudulently rosy picture of the western territories. They promulgated specious theories that downplayed the aridity of the Plains, suggesting that changing weather patterns would bring more rain, even suggesting that the stringing of telegraph wires or the roar of locomotives would precipitate rain. Jay Cooke, financier of the Northern Pacific, arranged for the publication of weather maps suggesting that warm winters followed his railroad. Newspapers occasionally mocked the Northern Pacific as Jay Cooke's Banana Belt.

Since morning the ride had been rough, with the cars rocking violently from side to side. I was feeling a bit queasy, in part no doubt from my night of fitful sleep and the accumulated tension and fatigue, but also from the rough ride. The insistent rocking takes its toll, first on the weak and halt, and eventually on anyone trying to manage a task, like writing or typing or reading, or even playing cards. The frustration builds. Nothing will stay where you put it. The upper bunk rattled constantly; the compartment door thumped in its socket. Everything I tried to read danced before my eyes. My typewriter banged and rattled on the desktop, my fingers slipped from its keys. Like the wind on the plains, the vibration was ceaseless. The Empire Builder had been running at the track limit, seventy-nine miles per hour, most of the day, and at that speed the upper level dipped and swayed like an old Cadillac on soft springs.

By three in the afternoon, the Empire Builder was east of Glasgow, Montana, still paralleling the Milk River. In late afternoon leaden clouds settled in and snow began again to fall, blotting out the sun and blurring the horizon. A freight passed on an adjoining track, its headlight shining through the gloom. The day ended prematurely under a veiled sky.

At Williston, we boarded two women on my sleeping car, and as we stood waiting for them on the platform, my car attendant stood on the platform stamping her feet and complaining good-naturedly about the cold, muttering, "I'm going to get my longhandles." She was a stout young black woman named Phyllis, red-haired and freckled, and something of a ham. When I stepped off to photograph a group of grain elevators and a Burlington Northern locomotive on a rail siding she scolded me, "Take your pictures and get back on 'cause I'm closing this door." When I kidded her about not being able to stand some cool air, she said, "If you lived in Chicago you'd hate it too." She reminded me that the Amtrak-issue navy blue overcoat she wore looked much warmer, with a plush collar and heavy padding, than it was. She looked left and right, up and down the quay, shook her head, and told me, "I'll never forget this place. Last Christmas it was fifty below coming through here."

The Empire Builder departs from the Missouri River east of Williston and crosses the Missouri Coteau to Tioga, where I noted a time-and-temperature sign on a local bank that read fourteen degrees at 7:20 P.M., and on to Stanley, where I watched a young woman with an infant in her arms climb down from our car into an oblivion of blowing snow. She stepped down with her bundled child in one arm and a suitcase in the other and disappeared within twenty steps into the swirling snow. I could imagine her, her child, the station, and the entire town swallowed by a blizzard, a whiteout on the plains. Phyllis swung the door closed, peered through the window after her, and muttered, "I hope her man came for her."

Baked silver salmon on the dinner menu enticed me to the dining car. The occasional appearance of a regional delicacy on the Amtrak menu is a vestige of grand dining service, of the vanished time when crack extra-fare passenger trains would make a special stop in the Colorado mountains to take on freshly caught trout for the evening meal. As I ate, I tried to sort out the riddle of time. When the Empire Builder crossed the state line into North Dakota in the late afternoon, we changed from Mountain time to Central time, losing an hour. That I understood, but since it was Saturday, the twenty-seventh of October, we would also be coming, at two in the morning, to the expiration of daylight savings time, when the state of North Dakota would gain an hour. For the butchers and candlestick makers, sound asleep, there would be no problem; even the bakers at work in the wee hours would simply set their clocks back from 2:00 A.M. to 1:00 A.M. and capitalize on the extra hour of labor. For a train, which has to keep a continuous schedule as it travels through space as well as time, the trick is more complicated.

There was a time, surprisingly recently, when every train beyond the local commuter faced that quandary every day. Every town felt free to function on its own clock, suggested by the mean sun time at its particular longitude but often left to local authorities or even local jewelers to specify and keep. The *Chicago Tribune* once claimed to find twenty-seven different local times in Illinois. The result was anarchy. For the railroads it was a nightmare. Schedules rigged to local times confounded logic: a train might leave one city at 9:30 and arrive at another ten minutes down the line at 9:25. As early as 1870, the *Railroad Gazette* advocated a single national time, and in 1883 William F. Allen, editor of the *Official Guide of the Railways*, persuaded the railroads to adopt a system of four distinct time zones. On Sunday, November 18, 1883, the railroads commenced a system of national schedules based on the four time zones, and most of the country conceded the practical advantages of railroad time and adopted the system. There were, however, prominent dissenters, including the Attorney General of the United States, who advised government departments that they need not follow the new system until Congress adopted it, which the recalcitrant Congress did not see fit to do until 1918.

I went to the lounge car where I asked the Amtrak chief, a young man, about the change from daylight savings to standard time. When October 27 came to an end at midnight, a new Amtrak schedule would take effect, a schedule based on standard time. Once the change was made, the schedule would be straightforward, but this one night a unique conundrum arose: if the Empire Builder kept to its normal schedule, it would be leaving Fargo not only before its scheduled departure time, which it clearly should not do, but also before its arrival, which simply would not do. He explained it to me this way: "We get to Fargo precisely at 2:00 A.M., at which time North Dakota changes from Central Daylight Time to Central Standard Time and we have to set the clock back to 1:00 A.M. Since we stop at Fargo for only four minutes, if we made our usual stop, we would be leaving the station at 1:04 A.M., an hour before we are supposed to. Since a train just can't leave early, we have to sit at Fargo for an hour."

"So we just sit on the tracks and wait for time to catch up to us?"

"That's about it. Too bad we don't get in a little earlier, we could go play blackjack, but I think they shut down just at one."

Before midnight, we stopped at Devils Lake, which is known as a mecca for waterfowl gunning: lots of potholes, lots of grainfields, on the flyway. The brakeman on the division was a hunter. "The antelope season is over," he told me. "It's deer season now. Over in Montana they need to trim the herd. You can kill four or five each season with a fifty-cent license." We were talking in the vestibule of the sleeping car when he took out his wallet and showed me a small color print. In the photograph, he was crouched in his driveway, still in his camouflage hunting clothes, lifting the heads of two dead antelope by their horns, turning their muzzles toward the camera. "Pretty nice bucks, don't you think?" He leaned toward me and touched their images with his finger. "They're waiting for me in the freezer."

I retired to my compartment, where I laid out just what I would need in the morning, then took my bags downstairs and stowed them in the luggage rack near the vestibule, so they would be ready to go at 4:00 A.M. I lay in my bunk for a few minutes, rocking from side to side with the constant succussion. I wondered how the debut performance of Susan's company had gone back in Kansas City. She had been quite worried. I wondered what I would find in Minnesota, but only for a moment.

About three-thirty, I was awakened by a knock on my door. I reached out and pulled the curtain open a few inches and saw the brakeman, smiling sympathetically. "Staples in thirty minutes," he said gently when I cracked open the door. Just as I finished dressing, Phyllis came to my door, wearing her heavy winter coat and looking very sleepy.

"Sorry you have to get up," I told her. "The brakeman woke me up and he could let me off. It doesn't make much of a night."

"You get off my car, I'm gonna be there to close the door. You don't get off, it's not going to be my fault," she replied, with mock sternness.

The lights in the car were dimmed. Everyone was sleeping. I was the only passenger disembarking at Staples. As we rolled through the last little towns before Staples, Verndale and Aldrich, I waited in the vestibule with my bags at my feet and wondered what I would do if no one was there to meet me. I would, I thought, do what I always did—I would be ready to ride when the train came through again. At 4:03 A.M., dead on time, Phyllis opened the door and I climbed down at Staples, wearing my Panama hat only because I couldn't pack it and I would not throw it away. Minnesota was even colder than Montana.

The platform was as empty as a country crossroads at midnight. I looked up and down and started walking up the tracks, wondering whether I should call Janice or wait until morning. Before I reached the station, she came bursting out of the door, bundled in a heavy coat and scarf, and threw her arms around me. "You made it!"

"It wasn't me I was worried about," I said, with much relief. "I hope you haven't been waiting. I was worried that you might get here on daylight savings time and have to wait around an hour. I guess I should have called, but I figured it out only a few hours ago, myself."

"We've been here for a while. We didn't know what the schedule would be, but that's all right. We didn't want to miss you." I noticed a man standing behind her. He stepped up just as she said, "This is Rob. He came down with me."

"I hope you got time and a half," I said, shaking his hand. "This is a hell of an hour to meet a train. Let's get out of the cold."

"Can't do that," he said, with a wry grin. "This is Minnesota."

19 Something of Minnesota

ove your hat," Janice said as we climbed into the car.

"It was an impulse."

As he opened the door and got behind the wheel, Rob said, "Don't see too many of those here."

In only a few minutes we were out of Staples, driving down a narrow two-lane highway in the dark. I looked over my shoulder and saw that Janice was sound asleep, bundled in her heavy coat and wrapped in a blanket. The heater poured hot air onto my knees, but even so my feet were cold. Fine flakes of snow danced in the headlights and swept past the windshield as though we were falling. The car smelled like a wet dog.

"You must be a very good friend," I said to Rob, "to make this drive with Janice." I felt like a hitchhiker obliged to make conversation in return for my lift. I was certainly a stranger to Rob. If Janice had told him everything she knew about me, it wouldn't have filled a file card. Now we would be riding through the dark for two hours, knee to knee.

"I don't mind," he said. "It's something different. Tell me about your trip."

I prattled on for a few minutes about what I was doing, where I had been, and trains in general, and he asked a few questions that were pretty astute. I liked his curiosity. In turn, I asked a few questions about Minnesota, and he gave me a quick thumbnail history of the forestry industry in the north woods.

"You seem to know a lot about this stuff," I said, in the form of a question.

"I work for the Forest Service. I destroy forests. Just kidding. I'm an engineer. Mostly I design roads. Lay them out with the survey crews and decide how to build them. The idea is to get the job done while minimizing the environmental impact."

The snow kept falling and I wondered if I was going to get myself snowbound in Minnesota after escaping from Montana. About fifteen minutes outside of Staples, we passed a man walking unsteadily along the right of way. Rob glanced quickly at me, I shrugged, and he braked hard. Janice, startled, called out from the backseat, "Rob?"

"I think we better give this guy a ride, Jan," he answered. "It's too cold for him to be out walking in this weather. Looks like he might have had a few too many." He threw the car into reverse and started to back up slowly. To me, he said, "Hope you don't mind. I just want to make sure he's all right. Guys get into town and have a few beers with their buddies and decide to walk home, full of that warm glow, and end up frozen to death."

That turned out to be precisely the case. He was a man in his late thirties or early forties carrying a railroad lantern and a snootfull. When he got into the car his breath reeked and he was unsteady, but grateful for the ride. We carried him up the road a few miles to a mobile home at the edge of a field, where we let him out and waited while he stumbled across the yard and fumbled his way through the front door. "I guess it's a lucky thing for me," I said to Rob as we waited, "that you don't mind picking up strangers in the middle of the night."

Janice was asleep again almost as soon as we were back on the highway, and for the next two hours Rob and I talked, about my trip and about his job and about Minnesota. I remarked that his accent did not suggest that he was a native.

"No," he said, "I'm from Pennsylvania. The Forest Service is like the army, you go where they send you, but I wanted to come to Minnesota. I came out here once while I was in college and always wanted to come back. I fell in love with the country and I've come to appreciate the people. They're not like easterners. I'll say more in a few minutes than they'll say in a day. But you learn to interpret."

"The reputation of the taciturn Minnesotan is true?"

"More than you would believe. We'll go out on a surveying job. Start out in the morning when it's too cold to move. The first thing we do is build a fire and stand around it to warm up. The loggers will stand around for thirty, forty minutes, an hour without saying a thing, just looking at each other and nodding every now and then and saying, 'Uh huh.' Finally, one of them will rub his hands together, look around at the others and say, 'Well, I s'pose.' And that's it. It's time to work. They're satisfied. They've had a conversation. If you want to live here, you've got to get comfortable with silence."

I found myself liking Rob. He had a sense of humor, an open mind, and some convictions of his own. The first hour passed quickly. In the second hour, as we talked, he caught me yawning and closing my eyes a few times. "You must be tired," he asked.

"I've had a few short nights."

"Well, we'll stop at my house and you can sleep until you feel like getting up. I've got to go in and do some work later on today and then you and Janice can go on to Bemidji. If we have time today, I'd like to show you around the national forest where I work. We can drive around Pike Lake and you can see what Minnesota looks like."

We turned off the highway, still in the dark of the night, and drove down a long sequence of dirt roads and emerged just as the sun was coming up at Rob's cabin on the shore of Lake Benedict. It was an odd, jerry-built structure, with a concrete-block garage and wood-shed that gave it a raw look, but it was snug on the inside with a large front room overlooking the lake. As soon as we opened the door, two big dogs came bounding toward us, jumping and pawing and circling, and when they had greeted Rob and Janice they sniffed me over carefully. These were Raven, Rob's black Lab, and Brook, Janice's golden retriever. When I said that I wanted to walk down to the lake to watch the sun come up, Janice said, "Do you mind if the dogs go with you? They need a run and I'm too sleepy." I went out the backdoor and climbed down a steep path to the lakeshore. The dogs had been cooped up in the house all night waiting for us, and by the time I got to the bottom of the path, they were already frolicking in the shallows, splashing gleefully through the frigid water. I walked through the woods along the edge of the lake for a few dozen yards and sat on a downed tree and watched the sun come up. Orange light spilled over the trees at the eastern end of the lake. As the sun lifted over the treetops and burned through brightly, the light cooled from red to orange to blue, unmasking the nighttime clouds as benevolent white billows in a chilly blue sky. It was an exhilarating scene, but suddenly I was exhausted. I hollered to the dogs and climbed back up the path to the house. Halfway up, they bounded past and were waiting for me at the door.

In the afternoon, after we'd slept and had a Sunday breakfast of wild rice pancakes, we took both cars, Janice and I in hers and Rob in his, and drove north on US 371 to the town of Cass Lake, where Rob worked in the headquarters of the Chippewa National Forest. On the way, we drove through a marsh where Janice pointed out beds of wild rice. "Harvesting wild rice is just like hunting or fishing up here," she explained. "It's regulated by the state. If you want to harvest it, you have to use native methods, harvest it just like the Indians always have. You have to pole or paddle your own canoe or boat and collect the rice by bending the stalks over the boat with one stick and thrashing it with another to shake the grains of rice into the boat. It's a lot of work, but the rice is wonderful, not like the highly polished wild rice you buy commercially. Most of that is grown in private paddies and it's not the same."

We spent the balance of the afternoon driving the back roads of the national forest, bouncing happily down rutted, potholed, primitive forest roads as Rob pointed out the many varieties of trees, and aspects of the woods as familiar to him as if they were the houses in his neighborhood. All went well until Rob and Janice got into an argument trying to decide whether a particular conifer was a balsam or a spruce. We were in a stand of younger trees and it was hard to tell from the immature shape, so they snapped off a twig and examined the needles and still could not agree. When a Minnesota wildlife officer on patrol drove up, Rob roped him into the debate. He took one look at the tree and said, with all the authority of the law, "Balsam." But Janice waved the sprig at him and he took it in his hand, ran his fingertips over the needles for a moment and said, sheepishly, "Well, then. I believe that's spruce." By then we were all convulsed with laughter, no longer much concerned with the facts of the matter.

We drove on and Rob pointed out an eagle nest. "I thought we'd see an osprey nest along here. I know I've seen one recently, but ospreys are much more fragile here than eagles. Eagles and ospreys both build substantial, massive nests, but eagles will choose a sturdy white or red pine, tall and strong, for their nest. Ospreys, on the other hand, will build anywhere and their nests are often blown down."

We came to the end of the forest road just as the setting sun was touching the tops of the trees on the far shore of the lake. We walked the last few feet between the pines and emerged on the open shoreline. As the sun went down and the air turned suddenly cold, solitude descended like a night chill. A single loon floated far out in the lake. As we watched from the water's edge, it dived, disappearing from sight for minutes it seemed, and reappeared even farther away.

"You should come back for the Eelpout Festival," Janice said.

"What's an eelpout?"

"The only true game fish," Rob said, laughing. "Actually, it's a rough fish that gets treated like a game fish for a few days every year. It looks something like a cross between a catfish and an eel, sort of slack-bodied, with big fleshy lips."

"They're horrid-looking creatures," Janice said. "The festival is mostly just an excuse for everyone to get out of their house and drink a lot and go crazy. Cabin fever is a big problem here in January and February."

Later Rob showed me the special souvenir edition of the local newspaper, the *Pilot-Independent*. The opening piece, "WELCOME TO THE INTERNATIONAL EELPOUT FESTIVAL," began:

Welcome to the Sixth International Eelpout Festival, a world-class sporting event of mammouth [sic] proportions drawing novice and professional anglers alike to the windswept ice of Leech Lake in search of the elusive eelpout, the world's only true game fish.

It promised a special team endurance award to the fishing team able to pass a rigorous physical and mental examination at the conclusion of the festival:

All members must be able to stand—or sit—erect (no time limit); ricite [sic] somebody's name; and at least three members must be able to identify the location of their vehicle or the keys to same.

The Walker Fire Department had swept this special competition three years running.

The evening had come to a flat calm. The air was still; the lake was unruffled. The surface of the water was a perfect reflection of the twilight sky. The loon's pointed reptilian head reflected clearly in the mirrored surface and two long, curving arcs curled in its wake, like sure brush strokes on rice paper. The three of us watched transfixed on the lakeshore as the sky changed colors, darkening overhead to a deep vermilion and ripening to a line of blazing orange along the western horizon.

We dropped Rob at forest headquarters and Janice and I collected her golden retriever and drove the last twenty miles to Bemidji, where she did indeed live, just as she had told me in New Mexico, in a tiny two-story cabin isolated on many acres of farm and forest land. We bought a few groceries and a gallon of Prestone at a little store along the way. "I think I've got a leak in my radiator. I might have to get you to help me find it tomorrow," she told me. We stopped at her mailbox long enough for her to collect her mail and then turned down a long rutted drive between a fenced field and a woodlot. The temperature was well below freezing and the cabin, which had been empty and unheated all weekend, was only a few degrees warmer than the outside air, but she had an ample woodpile and soon we had the wood stove roaring.

The cabin was no more than twelve by fifteen feet, with a small double-hung window in each wall. There was no bathroom. Janice had pointed out the outhouse in the headlights when we drove up. The floors of the cabin were bare wood planking, covered here and there with worn throw rugs. Along one wall sat a tattered sofa and beyond it in the corner, the old wood stove. A kitchen counter, a propane stove, and a refrigerator were lined up along the far wall. There was no running water, only a sink with a drain in the countertop. Across from the sofa, on the other wall, open stair treads climbed through an opening in the ceiling to the second-floor sleeping loft. As a dwelling, this cabin would have fallen short of code in the meanest town, but there, set amidst miles of grainfields and forests, it was warm and habitable.

We stir-fried some vegetables and cooked a pot of wild rice and I made guacamole from a couple of ripe avocados I had found at the store. We ate sitting on the floor next to the wood stove. Before turning in, I went outside to the woodpile by the front door to collect some wood in case the stove burned out overnight. Janice stepped out with me, and while I carried in several armloads of wood, she disappeared into the darkness. As I was stacking the last of the wood by the stove, she came in. "I'm worried about the horses," she said. "They got out while I was gone and I thought they'd be back by now. Maybe they'll come back tonight."

"You want to go out and look? I'll go with you," I said, trying not to betray my lack of enthusiasm for a task that would take us back out into the cold. I had seen the thermometer next to the woodpile: it was already in single digits.

"No, thanks. We'd never find them at night and if we did, we'd never catch them. When they want to come in, they'll come. If they're not back in the morning, though, we'll have to go round them up."

Several times in the night I trekked to the outhouse. The sky was cloudless and clear and the air was so cold it stung my lungs and condensed my breath in my mustache where it froze in moments. The stars looked like table salt sprinkled on black velvet, brilliant crystalline gems. The astronomers tell us that with the naked eye we can see perhaps 3,500 stars on a clear night; with binoculars, perhaps 50,000 stars; with a small telescope 300,000; with a large research telescope, billions. The heavens looked that night as endless as we know them to be. It was a night to remind us that to think of our sky only as the atmosphere that envelops our little planet is to be a parakeet that sees only the blanket draping its cage.

There was no moon when I first went out, and, walking across the yard to the outhouse, I had to feel my way through the dark, shuffling my feet through the frosty grass. Several times I thought I heard the pawing and snorting of horses and I had the sense that they were following me across the field, watching and exhaling clouds of warm vapor.

In the morning we both washed our faces in a basin of water fetched the day before from the well. When we had finished, Janice asked me to pour it on her hair. "Go ahead, pour it on my head. Don't make me stand here in the cold!"

I gritted my teeth and poured the kettle of frigid water over her. It cascaded forward through her hair and splashed into the sink as I shivered sympathetically. She squeezed her hair between her fingers, wringing out the water, and stood upright, tossing her damp hair backward. She swept wet strands back from her forehead with her hands, shook her head, and brushed her light brown hair vigorously.

"You've made me late. I've got to hurry to register at the college or I won't get the courses I need. I was going to be there an hour ago. Would you feed the horses? Just pitch them some hay. I'll only be an hour or two." She tossed her hairbrush aside, pulled on her sweater and boots, and dashed outside. The starter of her old Subaru ground reluctantly in the cold, and I heard her swing the car around in the field and start down the long drive to the highway.

I watched her drive away and then started thinking about coffee. I had poured the last of the kettle of water on her head and down the sink, so I let Brook, her golden retriever, out, hoping he would lead me to the well, but he galloped off in four directions at once, full of morning playfulness. I followed along as best I could and we enjoyed a brisk constitutional, across the fields and through the woods, but I never found the well.

I fetched a bale of hay from the barn and tossed it over the fence next to the salt block for the horses, which had indeed come home during the night. The sky was pale blue and cloudless and the sun felt warm, but the temperature was still below freezing. Back in the cabin I rummaged more carefully and found just enough water in another pot to make a short cup of coffee that sustained me while I wrote some notes and waited for Janice.

We ate breakfast at a diner out on the highway. The breakfast special, two eggs, potatoes, toast, and coffee, was $1.04. By the time we sat down at the counter, the cook, a barrel-bodied young man in an apron, was chalking the lunch special on a blackboard, and I had a bowl of clam chowder along with my eggs. We spent the early afternoon riding through the farmland and the edge of the national forest on her two horses, a part-Arabian named Nicky and a quarter horse gelding named Sham that she rode bareback. The sun had warmed the clear air to just above freezing, and by the time we had walked out to the highway and trotted a mile or two down the roadside past grainfields and cornfields, I was warm in just a sweater. I have never been able to sit a western trot well, so every time Nicky changed gaits I missed the first beat and hammered my spine. We turned onto a path through oak and birch woods, with stands here and there of popple, the local name for aspen, and as soon as we entered the woods Janice let her horse ease into a canter. My horse was familiar with the path and the routine and he too rocked into a canter, which was a relief to both of us. Her golden retriever raced along with us, swerving between the horses, darting ahead and turning out into the woods to chase a squirrel or a shadow, and then tearing back onto the trail behind us and dashing among the flying hooves into the lead again. The first few times Brook raced in front of me, I tried to rein in my horse and almost sent myself flying into the treetops, and after that I just let the horse run, having come to the realization that of all the runners in the race I was the only one who didn't know what he was doing.

Near the end of our ride, we walked the horses slowly, cooling them down, through a forest of conifers. The horses padded softly on the pine needles beneath the arbor of overarching boughs and Brook bounded ahead, dashing in and out of our view. Up ahead, a buck walked slowly out into the alley between the trees and stopped, looking at us with deliberation, and then walked stiff-legged into the woods again.

We groomed the horses and put them up and drove to Lake Itasca. Janice wanted to show me the headwaters of the Mississippi River on the way to Rob's cabin at Benedict, where we would eat dinner before they drove me back down to Staples for the 4:00 A.M. train. By the time we got to Itasca, it was late afternoon and the sun was low and orange. We snapped a leash on Brook and walked down a trail through the woods to the edge of the lake. A rustic signboard gave the historic details of the search for the source of the Mississippi and its discovery at Lake Itasca by Henry Schoolcraft in 1832. I took a photograph of Janice and Brook standing on the stones where water flowed out of Lake Itasca between their legs into a tiny brook that is said to be the source of the Mississippi.

Rob was in the kitchen of his cabin washing mushrooms when we came in. The radio was tuned to the Bemidji station of the Minnesota Public Radio network and the evening symphony concert was in progress. Janice gave him a quick kiss, told him that she had registered for the courses she needed and told him about our day, the ride and the visit to Lake Itasca, and fell naturally into step in the kitchen, helping Rob chop vegetables and rolling out a pie crust, and I leaned against the wall and basked in the domesticity. We were joined for dinner by Dave, one of Rob's friends in the Forest Service, and a new Forest Service employee who had just moved to Minnesota. The newcomer wore freshly laundered and pressed blue jeans and smiled nervously without saying much. Dave, on the other hand, would have been garrulous in any society and in taciturn northern Minnesota must have stood out like a stand-up comic in an abbey. We set the table in the front room and ate and talked and drank New Ulm beer.

Rob nodded his head toward me and said to Dave, "Jan and George went up to Lake Itasca today." Looking then at me he explained, "Dave is a wildlife biologist for the Forest Service."

I said, "I just came from Montana, up at Glacier where the eagles are in."

"Guess they're up there like blue jays now. I had a woman up on the lake who swore, swore up and down, that a bald eagle swooped right in and carried off her dog," Dave said, grinning and shaking his head in disbelief. "Now it was a small dog, but the chances of that happening . . . not likely."

I was relishing the company. In only a few hours this interlude would be over and I would be back on the train. The next eleven days would be the hectic home stretch of my trip. I tried to put it out of my mind. We all needed to get some sleep. Rob was due to assume a new post at Deer Lake the next day, and he would not get back from ferrying me to Staples until nearly seven in the morning. But we did not want to let go of the day. We talked about Minnesota, about the national forest, told fish stories and animal stories. Dave didn't drink, but the rest of us had another beer, and then we made a pot of coffee and talked on. We cleared away the dishes and pushed our chairs back and crossed our legs and each told a final story. Rob told us about his first trip to Minnesota, a disastrous foray during his college days when he had come out with a friend to go snowshoeing and had gotten hopelessly bogged down in the snow and hopelessly enamored of Minnesota. Dave reprised a favorite yarn about a fishing trip he had once taken with his father in the Ontario backcountry. I strung together a few vignettes from the past weeks into a sketchy travelogue. With snow falling outside and a subfreezing wind whistling at the windows I conjured up images of steamy, semitropical torpor in New Orleans.

The evening stretched on toward midnight. Finally, Dave and his friend said good night and went out into the cold. Rob saw them out and was still laughing when he came back. "Dave loves telling stories. I've heard that one two or three times."

Rob and Janice and I piled the coffee mugs in the sink and the beer cans in the trash, doused the candle and dimmed the lights, and set an alarm for a little after one. They retired to his bedroom to sleep for an hour or so, and I stretched out on the sofa in front of the wood stove. The Bemidji radio station was playing a program of opera excerpts, and I dozed in the radiant heat, listening to arias. I dreamt of unrequited love.

It snowed most of the way down to Staples. We arrived at 3:55 A.M. for the 4:03 train and hustled through the empty little station and out to the platform just as the train rolled hissing to a stop. The conductor directed me to the rear car, and we trudged back along the track in the cold, the wind threatening to peel off my ridiculous Panama hat and carry it away. The porter was ready to roll, impatient to get under way. Rob handed me a bag of wild rice. "We harvested this ourselves. You should take something of Minnesota with you." I took off the blue down jacket I had been wearing since that first night and handed it to Rob. He tried to give it back. "It's an old coat," he said, holding it out. "You're going to need it where you're going. You can always mail it back if that bothers you. I've got another."

"No, Rob. It's done its job. For two days I've been warm." Up the track the conductor was watching us, waiting for the signal. I tossed my bags on board, turned to Rob and shook his hand, "Thank you." I hugged Jan, said only "I'll be in touch," and climbed aboard.

The Empire Builder, the Lake Shore Limited, the Adirondack, and on to Boston: In Next Week Tomorrow

"Glorious, stirring sight!" murmured Toad. . . . "The poetry of motion! The real way to travel! The only way to travel! Here today—in next week tomorrow! Villages skipped, towns and cities jumped—always somebody else's horizons! O bliss! O poop-poop! O my! O my!"

—Kenneth Grahame, *The Wind in the Willows* (Mr. Toad expounds on the joys of mechanized travel.)

For two hours I watched at my window as the Empire Builder, the familiar train No. 8, made through the predawn darkness toward Minneapolis and St. Paul. By the time I settled in my compartment, another economy sleeper, we were passing through Little Falls, where the Burlington tracks begin a flirtation with the Mississippi River that continues for the one hundred remaining miles into The Cities. In the dark, I could only feel the railroad bridges and sense the water below as we crossed the river again and again, the same river I had stepped across twelve hours before where it was a tiny brook spilling out of Lake Itasca.

We made one stop, at St. Cloud, shortly after five in the morning, and just before six-thirty we crept through a vast freight yard just west of Minneapolis. Sneaking through these freight yards, where the real business of railroading is done, a passenger train seems frivolous, like a sloop among trawlers or a sports car easing past the diesel pumps at the interstate truck stop. We were running on schedule and due into St. Paul's Midway Station just before seven. Long before we got there, I fell asleep. The Empire Builder traveled on for more than three hundred miles: through The Cities, Minneapolis and St. Paul, through Red Wing, Minnesota, down the Milwaukee Road tracks along the Mississippi for almost a hundred miles to La Crosse, Wisconsin, and then east through the Dells and across Wisconsin.

As I slept, I was tossed about in my bunk like dice in a cup. The Milwaukee Road track was the roughest ride I had encountered. Even at reduced speeds the undercarriage of the coach was jerked about so violently that for the first time I feared derailment. Yet the very trackage over which we clattered had once been the course for the fastest regular running trains of the steam era, the Hiawatha trains on the Milwaukee Road, which reached speeds of more than 100 miles an hour between Chicago, Milwaukee, and St. Paul.

In the late 1930s, railroad passengers were growing enamored of the new diesel streamliners in service on the Burlington, Rock Island, and Union Pacific lines. Many eastern railroads, such as the New York Central, the Norfolk and Western, and the Pennsylvania, with ready access to coal, were reluctant to make the capital investment in diesel power, and so endeavored to make their steam-powered service competitive by running longer, heavier trains at less spectacular speeds. The Milwaukee Road, which competed with the diesel streamliners of the Burlington Railroad between Chicago, Milwaukee, and St. Paul, chose instead to challenge their speed with steam. The Milwaukee's high-speed steam-hauled Hiawatha express covered the approximately four hundred miles between Chicago and St. Paul in six and a half hours; the Amtrak Empire Builder takes nearly eight hours. Within four years, larger 4-6-4 locomotives were put in service to meet the demand for the fast steam trains. Outfitted with special streamlined bodies in the Art Moderne style that came to influence all manner of industrial and architectural design, these new locomotives were capable of attaining comfortably 120 miles an hour on level track.

I awoke that afternoon as we passed a field south of Milwaukee stippled with rows of green and red cabbage. Minnesota, particularly during my last night at Staples, had been in the grip of winter, but in southeastern Wisconsin a benevolent autumn lingered. Pumpkins lay orange and ripe on withering vines, and stands of field corn were baked golden by the sun. The pines and spruces of Minnesota were gone, and the oaks of Wisconsin were mottled in warm glowing tones. Along the tracks hedgerows were brown and dry, and I imagined I could hear crickets, stirred by the afternoon sun, rustling in the brittle grass.

At ten minutes to three, only twenty minutes behind schedule, we approached Glenview, the last stop north of Chicago, past the backyards of contented suburbs, with houses, almost uniformly white, that looked like their first owners had paid off the mortgage and stayed on. Leaves that would certainly soon be raked lay like brightly colored swarf in rings around backyard trees.

I spent something less than three hours in Chicago, just time enough to store my bags in a locker at Union Station, walk across the river to the Sears Tower, and ride the "world's fastest elevator" to the 103d-floor Skydeck observation level. I watched the afternoon light dim over the lakefront and the city lights come on as the commuters headed home. I scribbled a few cards to friends and family, seeking to express in a few square inches how I felt as I entered the last days of my trip. Truthfully, I wrote that I was not weary of traveling nor of being alone, having reached that equipoise where it seemed more natural than not. Even so, I was tired of all the good-byes, the recurring partings, whether from old friends or from new friends. The sudden swings from intimacy to solitude had begun to wear me down. Too many times I had gotten back on the train and felt suddenly bereft.

From the concourse of Union Station I called back to Bemidji to satisfy myself that Janice and Rob had made it home safely from Staples. I bought some salami, some cheese, a hard roll, and two Heilemans Special Export beers at a deli in the station, fetched my bags, and hustled down to track 19 where the Lake Shore Limited was waiting, due to depart at 6:20 P.M. A train ready to roll seems to exude a restlessness that is palpable.

I was hurrying forward to my car when I saw a familiar face hurrying toward me, a young woman laden with bags, rushing to make the train. It was Carol, the Amtrak employee I had befriended on the train from Galesburg. Several times since leaving her in Salt Lake City I had wondered what had become of her. I helped with her bags as she boarded a car several behind mine, and in the moment before the train pulled out we had only enough time for a smile of recognition and for me to say, "I'm up here a few cars in a sleeper. Let's talk." I didn't even have time to ask her if she was working that trip or just riding.

The Lake Shore Limited pulled out almost as soon as I put my foot on the step. No more two-story Superliner coaches, no more spacious lounge cars with floor-to-ceiling windows. East of Chicago, everything—the country and the rail cars—seemed confining by comparison. I had booked an economy slumbercoach berth, a compartment more like a diving bell than a private room.

I made myself a sandwich, opened a beer, and took out my typewriter and started a letter. In part to relieve the claustrophobia, I left the door open into the hallway. I was on the second or third page when Carol walked by, stopped in the aisle, and said, "Boo." She told me that she was trying to decide whether to eat in the diner or the lounge. I said that I had made my dinner and was content with it, but that I would join her for a beer. "I'll be in the lounge, then," she said.

I wrote another page or two, jotted down some notes, then went forward to the lounge where I found her sitting alone at a corner table next to the concession stand. A plastic sandwich wrapper littered her table and she was finishing a package of cheese crackers and a soft drink. We laughed again to see each other, at the improbability and the inevitability of it.

She told me about the rest of her trip on the Pioneer from Salt Lake City to Seattle. "I bought a voucher in Salt Lake City for the run on into Portland and Seattle. That took care of that, although I still didn't know if I would lose my job. Coming back, out of Seattle, I said to myself, 'No way I'm going to get in that mess again,' but the train attendant told me, 'Don't worry about it. You don't need a ticket. I'll work it out with the conductor and you won't have any problem.' So, foolishly, I got on in Seattle without a ticket again. The conductor came around and asked for my ticket and I panicked. I told him that I had a ticket but had lost it, and he said OK, fine. But then he went back and checked his receipts. He didn't find any record of my ticket and went to talk to the train attendant about me. The attendant, who was a man, satisfied the conductor by apparently telling the conductor that I was 'traveling with' him. The conductor came back to me and said, 'That's OK, but I wish you had just told me the truth.' At that point, I broke down in tears and said, 'Let's talk.' We found a compartment and I told him the whole story, from Chicago on, and he thought it was funny. He was very kind and sympathetic and told me not to worry about it, and we talked for some time and became friends. But later the crews changed, at Williston, I think, and suddenly I realized that I had a new conductor and I went into the ladies lounge and stayed there for four hours. I came out finally and laid low for the rest of the trip back to Chicago."

I told her the story of my day in Montana and my days in Minnesota. Then I asked her if she was working this trip and where she was going. "I'm just riding, not working," she said. "And I'm going home, sort of."

I didn't reply. Maybe I raised my eyebrows a little.

"That's a long story," she replied to the unspoken question. She opened a package of cheese crackers, offered me one, and went on. "For the past nine years, I've been married and living in Bowling Green, Ohio. I do like my husband, but I haven't been very happy. I just don't think I know how to be married. When I married him, my friends all said, 'You know, it'll never work.' I guess they were right. I'm an adventurous person. My husband is not. I want all the experience I can get; he's content with what he has. He always says to me, 'You are so brave to do what you do.' I try to make him understand that it isn't brave at all. I have to do these things. So we are estranged. I applied for this job with Amtrak, and I enjoy it. I don't know what will happen. When we would go to marriage counselors, they would always suggest that there was something wrong with me because I was dissatisfied with our marriage. My husband thinks it's fine the way it is and doesn't see any need to change. Then I found out that most of these counselors were divorced. And I'm the problem?"

She looked at her watch. It was almost eleven-thirty. "Toledo is my stop. I'd better go get ready. Are you sure you don't want to stop over a day or two in Ohio? My husband wouldn't mind. It would be no problem. He really is a very nice person."

"I have to meet someone in Albany tomorrow."

"Well, then." She stood up and extended her hand. "Good-bye."

I stood up and shook her hand. "Whatever it is you want . . . I hope you find it." I didn't know what else to say.

I followed her through the lounge car, through the vestibule, and through the coach, walking a few steps behind her. Halfway through my sleeping car, she stopped in the narrow aisle. The train was swaying. In two steps I had caught up with her. She turned back toward me, smiled ruefully, and said, "What the heck, how 'bout a cheezy kiss?"

I slept fitfully as the Lake Shore Limited traced the south shore of Lake Erie from Toledo through Sandusky, Cleveland, and Erie, Pennsylvania, to Buffalo and then followed the Erie Canal and the Mohawk Valley across New York State to Schenectady. The Lake Shore Limited is the Amtrak successor to the New York Central's famed Twentieth Century Limited. I awoke to a gray day somewhere east of Utica. Small towns of steep-roofed frame houses and old brick mill buildings crouched down among autumn-colored hills. Broken windows and faded block letters stenciled on crumbling brick walls confessed the names of manufacturers in decline or already stolen away: "LITTLE FALLS FELT SHOE COMPANY," "MOHAWK CARPET MILLS."

The Albany Amtrak station is actually located across the Hudson River in Rensselaer. Ken, an old friend who lived in Troy, New York, just a few miles up the east bank of the Hudson from Rensselaer, was meeting me at the station. While I waited for him, I called Susan in Kansas City. The debut performance of her company had gone well, "wonderfully" she said, but yet she sounded discouraged about the company's future. When I reached her she was in the act of firing one, perhaps two, of her dancers who had been unable to keep the frustrations of their unhappy romance from souring their work with the company, and that unpleasant task depressed her. Later in the week she would be going to New York City to meet with a consulting firm that specialized in the arts, and to, as she said with a note of sarcasm, "see what's happening in the big city."

A few years had passed since I had last seen Ken. I had known him since college, when he was a bright, slightly surly kid from Maine with a theory for everything and a mordant sense of humor. In those years, we had in common several good friends and the confusion of our times. His brief career as a musician was aborted when the anxiety of a gig before an indifferent crowd in a rowdy beer joint brought on full-fledged nausea. Since those days, he had settled in Troy and established himself in art restoration and as a successful artist in his own right. In my mind he was still the bearded lad in a denim jacket, and I was surprised for a moment when he walked into the train station with thinning hair and a tweed suit coat. Whatever surprise he felt at my appearance he kept to himself.

Ken and I went first for a cup of coffee to an Albany donut shop, where the waitress was dressed for Halloween as a witch, with a black cape, whiteface, eyebrows painted stark black, and ruby lips. I sat down, ordered my cup of coffee with cream on the side, and hardly noticed. I just didn't care. Something had burned out in me.

Ken led me on a walking tour of Albany, and then we ate lunch in a diner not far from the state house. We talked through the afternoon, mostly about our lives—Ken had recently been forced by illness to change his career from art and art restoration to writing about art and architecture and theatre—until, as the crowd of happy-hour drinkers flooded in after work, it was time again for me to catch a train.

The Adirondack left Rensselaer at five, first crossing the river to Albany in the dusk. The Adirondack follows one of the most scenic routes on the Amtrak system, north between the Green Mountains of Vermont and the Adirondack Mountains of New York and along the rocky shore of Lake Champlain for seventy-five miles. North of Platts-burgh, the Adirondack crosses over into Canada on Delaware and Hudson tracks and continues up through the Richelieu River valley to Montreal. But because the Adirondack travels north at night, all of that was hidden to me.

After the great cruise trains of the West—which by their size, com-fort, and the vast distances they traveled had reminded me of ocean liners—the eastern trains felt like river ferries or packet boats. In other seasons, perhaps, the Adirondack carried vacationers to Lake George and Lake Placid, but the night I rode it was a commuter train, with no dining car, no car attendants, no pillows, no leg rests, and only the overhead racks for baggage. I told myself that I should go up to the dinette car, the bastard half-lounge, half-coach car up ahead, and try to strike up a conversation, but I didn't have the heart for it. I was quickly losing what enthusiasm I had for this jog to Montreal. Instead of inspiration, I was traveling on resolve, a dim-witted resolve at that. Only six other travelers shared my coach, all as lifeless as I.

The cars seemed deafeningly loud, the people cold and lonely.

At 9:08 P.M. the conductor came back through my coach and asked me if he could "knock down" the lights so the other coach passengers could sleep. "Can you get along with just the reading lights?" he asked.

"Go ahead. Let 'em sleep. I wish I could." It was Halloween night. Ken had told me that he had to get home so he and his wife, Gayle, could take the kids trick-or-treating. I thought about children, all over the country, facing the goblins and gremlins of their imagination and the real monsters of today who savage them in horrendous ways. That morning the copy of the *Pioneer Press* that had been shoved under my door on the Lake Shore Limited carried on its front page news of a dozen or more adults indicted for abusing and perhaps murdering children. Authorities, said the article, were dragging the river for bodies. We had become a species that devours its young.

The handful of commuters sharing my coach were snoozing in the near dark. The rattling of the train car, which, if introduced suddenly, would have been almost deafening, had subsided by virtue of its constancy and regularity first to a norm and then a null and, finally, a peacefulness more soothing than quiet. In the din I heard tiny scratching sounds as clearly as rustlings in a quiet wood, and, just as I looked, a mouse darted across the threadbare carpet.

I spent Halloween night in the Montreal YMCA on Drummond Street. Windsor Station had been almost deserted when the Adirondack pulled in a few minutes before eleven. From a telephone in the empty waiting room I called a few small, reasonable hotels that had been recommended to me, only to find that none had a vacancy. I couldn't find a cab; the streets around the station were empty. I hoisted my bags and lugged them the few blocks to the Y, which offered two salient virtues—it was close and affordable. I was too tired to care about anything else. The single room was small, clean, and, except for a color television, spartan. It reminded me of a college dormitory: a secure room on a long hallway sharing a common bathroom. As much as a bed I wanted a shower, but I discovered that I would have to schedule my shower around the series of trysts taking place through the evening in the shower room. Fortunately, the schedule, specific to the half-hour, was scrawled on the walls of the toilet stalls, so I waited in my room, watching a Marlene Dietrich movie dubbed into French, until the evening's amorous activity subsided, and then took a long and welcome shower.

I slept late and spent the day walking through Montreal, a city I had passed through only once before, many years earlier. The wind was brisk, sometimes fierce. In Dominion Square, leaves, discarded newspapers, and food wrappers soared over the treetops with the pigeons and swifts. In a basement bookstore and cafe on Mansfield Street near McGill University, I ate shepherd's pie and sat for an hour drinking coffee and reading the October 28 *New York Times Book Review*.

It was almost four o'clock when I emerged from the subterranean bookstore onto the street. I walked through stone gates onto the campus of McGill, where two teams of girls were playing flag football on the leaf-littered green, surrounded by seven sooty gray stone buildings of the college. On the sideline, an animated crowd of men lined the playing field, husbanding the belongings, gym bags, and bookbags of the players, and cheering their play. As I watched, a professorial type in a heavy overcoat and hat, carrying a bookbag and reading a newspaper, strolled oblivious across the green along a well-worn path that took him through the playing field. Coincidentally, the progress of the game had placed the line of scrimmage directly in his path as he crossed the field, and he had to dodge the players as they broke the huddle and trotted up to the line of scrimmage. Never looking up from his newspaper, he sidestepped the players like a commuter negotiating familiar traffic. The referee blew his whistle and stopped play, and the players stood patiently and watched him pass through their midst with the same tolerance they would show a lost dog.

As the afternoon light began to fade, the yellow lights in the college buildings around the green glowed brighter, as if someone had turned up the wick on an oil lamp. I saw students at their carrels in the library. Fallen leaves, caught up by little whirlwinds, were swept across the field by the breeze. As students emerged from the library, they stopped, resting their bookbags on the stone wall, and watched the game for a few minutes before moving on. When the last whistle blew, the winning team huddled at midfield and cheered the losers in unison. Within moments the field was taken over by soccer players and boys tossing footballs, running imaginary pass patterns in the twilight.

I left the library steps and started down an alley into the city, where office workers who had missed the warm moments of the after-noon were beginning to flow into the day's-end streets. Low clouds, dingy as soiled laundry, were packed in wads across the sky. My hands began to burn in the chill wind. Then I turned and came back to the campus green, where Indian summer lingered. Not the sweet, gen-tle, basking-in-the-sun, making-love-in-the-grass Indian summer. This was the death rattle of warm days, late autumn in a cold clime where winter, soon to arrive, changes your life.

Again, I turned away from the campus, back into the commercial quarter. In Place Ville Square the night wind, funneled among the office buildings, buffeted stylishly dressed office workers and whipped up tiny whitecaps on the pool of the fountain. Walking on through the going-home streets of the city in the early evening, I heard caril-lon bells and organ music, but I couldn't fix the direction in the narrow streets, and when I stopped a few people as they hurried past, they couldn't tell me where it might be coming from and were amused that I would care.

I had checked my bags at Central Station in the morning, so I had nothing left to do but wait for my train, the Montrealer, listed in the Amtrak timetable as train No. 61 but on the VIA Rail Canada board at Central Station under its Canadian number. When I checked my bags, I had to ask if they were the same train. Windsor Station, where I had arrived the night before on the Adirondack, is a Victorian relic, ornate and shopworn. Central Station, only a block or so away, could not be more different. From the street I descended a long steep flight of steps—the escalator was being repaired—to a subterranean mall with food shops, newsstands, film and camera shops, record shops, bars, and hairdressers surrounding a gigantic waiting room. Frequent commuter trains (*banlieu*) arrive at Central Station in the morning and depart from it in the evening, and the station was bustling with activity while I waited for the Montrealer, which was listed as depart-ing at 19:10—another reminder of Montreal's bicultural nature. In what seemed a whim at the time but which I later took to be a subconscious expression of my faltering state of mind, I bought a paperback copy of Conrad's *Heart of Darkness* to read on the train. The Penguin paperback edition cost me $2.50 Canadian, and with the last of my Canadian currency I bought a can of O'Keefe Bière and tucked it in my bag.

When I boarded, the coach was moderately crowded, but I found an empty seat and claimed it for myself. The coach was another of the old refitted cars, different in design from the one on the Adirondack, somewhat more spacious, with more legroom, but perhaps a little more shopworn. Many of the other passengers were speaking French, and I felt like a foreigner. Rolling through the Montreal suburbs, I watched the familiar constellation of porch lights, distant streetlights, and automobile headlights on the bridges and highways pass by in my window. Over the weeks of travel, I had made a discipline and then a habit of always knowing, or doing what I could to discover, the route I was traveling and what I was seeing in my window. I knew I should consult my schedule and my books and maps to see what was out there hidden in the dark, but that night, for me, the world was inside—inside the coach, inside my mind, and, maybe, inside my heart. Still more than a thousand miles from home, I could nevertheless sense it. Like a runner nearing the end of a long, hard workout, I had quit pressing and was slowing my stride, concentrating on my rhythm, trying not to lose what I had gained in the effort.

When I boarded in Montreal, a trainman had handed me a United States customs form, asking me to declare what I was bringing into the country, asking me to confess if I was bringing in more than five thousand dollars in currency (no danger there) or any fruit or natural living thing that might contaminate United States agriculture or wildlife, and asking me to declare and itemize all merchandise I was bringing back into the United States. Residents are generally allowed to bring with them four hundred dollars of merchandise duty free. I did not anticipate a problem. I was returning with two beers, which were unlikely to make it to the border, my newly acquired copy of *Heart of Darkness*, valued at two dollars American, and an apple. I contemplated what insidious pest might lurk beneath the apple's waxed skin, and did the only honorable and patriotic thing. I ate it.

We were halted for almost an hour at the border while customs officials checked each passenger. They dealt with me in cursory fashion, dismissing me so quickly that I was almost insulted for being taken to be so innocuous. While I waited for them to finish with the other passengers, I went to stand on the vestibule landing to smoke my pipe, my first in a few days. The shadow of a tree, cast by a nearby streetlight, danced wildly on a wall as the wind lashed its branches. Rummaging in my pockets for matches, I found only a Blue Diamond kitchen match left from lighting Janice's wood stove in Bemidji. Odd, what memories reside in the commonplace.

Under way again, I went to the lounge car and ordered a hot dog and a Molson. Against the rules I smoked another bowl of tobacco in the lounge, and by eleven-thirty it was burning sweetly in the fat part of the bowl. I was still wearing the pair of cords that I had worn riding with Janice in Minnesota, and the faint aroma of saddle leather and horse sweat was not unpleasant. I had lost enough weight so that, even with my belt snugged up to the last notch, they hung loosely. When I thought about it, my back and rump were sore.

At 4:00 A.M., I stumbled off the train at Springfield, Massachusetts, into an empty, tawdry, dirty little station. The Lake Shore Limited would not be coming through until early afternoon. I looked around: a few sculpted plastic chairs, some lockers, three phones, and a coffee vending machine. Ceiling tiles had fallen out and not been replaced. Cigarette butts lay on the floor, swept up against the wall where they stayed. I sat there dumbly with my bags. The stationmaster and his helper got coffee in a styrofoam cup from the machine and the stationmaster said to me, "Somebody picking you up?"

"No. I'm waiting for the Boston train."

"You got nine hours to wait."

"I know. Are you closing up?"

The two of them conferred quietly. The stationmaster turned back to me and said, "Nine hours is a long time. You want to go up to the track and sleep in one of the coaches? He comes in to clean at eight, but you'd be more comfortable—and safe—there until then. We get all kinds of people in and out during the night."

I thanked him, put my suitcase and camera bag in a locker, and followed the station helper, a lean man in his thirties with a beard, wearing ragged jeans, work boots, a flannel shirt with the tails ballooning out above his belt, and a baseball cap, up to the tracks in a service elevator. We walked down to an empty coach on a siding.

"You want the lights on? I can turn the lights on if you want."

"Just a reading light is all I need." I picked out four facing seats, found an old *New York Times*, flicked on the reading light, and made myself at ease. I read old news for twenty or thirty minutes and then, soothed by the world's problems, grew sleepy. I pulled the seat cushions off, placed them in the aisle, and laid down to sleep.

At 8:01 A.M. the service crew came aboard and one said, "You the guy waiting for 448? You can come back in a half-hour or so." I put the cushion back, picked up my bookbag, and climbed down into a cold, windy, wet, gray New England milltown morning. I walked a few blocks to Rick's Country Kitchen for breakfast.

At the counter, I hesitated, recalling New England custom, when the counter man asked if I wanted my coffee "regular?"

"No, just black'll be fine."

My train, No. 448, the Boston section of the Lake Shore Limited, departed at 1:10 in the afternoon, so I spent the few hours in the late morning hopping city buses across town and visiting the National Basketball Hall of Fame, which has since been relocated to new, more elaborate quarters, but was then housed in an unprepossessing building on the campus of Springfield College. By the time I got there, I had only forty-five minutes or so remaining, but I never regretted having taken the time. With little or none of the sacred air that enshrouds the Baseball Hall of Fame at Cooperstown, the Basketball Hall of Fame had the musty, impoverished atmosphere of a local museum devoted to county history or to a local agriculture, like rice-growing in eastern Arkansas, or to a vanished industry, like whaling on the New England coast.

I was the only visitor on that Friday midday, and I wandered down into the musty basement to look at old black-and-white photographs and read yellowed clippings from newspaper stories of forgotten games. I was struck by the game shoes Walt Bellamy wore as professional basketball's rookie of the year in 1961–62, a pair of canvas and rubber Beacon Falls Top Notch shoes he had worn playing for the Chicago Packers. For some of us in my generation, a generation that grew up wearing Keds and P.F. Flyers and playing basketball in Chuck Taylors, our innocent confidence in the superiority of all things American vanished forever the day we first saw a pair of Adidas shoes on a basketball court.

Train routes are revealing. No one goes to any trouble to tidy up the landscape for train travelers. Railroads run through our collective backyards. The Lake Shore Limited moved very slowly out of Springfield, past piles of old tires and heaps of rusted cars in the cattails, and I found myself thinking of the first owners of each of those junked automobiles, polishing out the least tarnish in the finish, fitting seat covers to shield the fabric from wear, dangling ridiculous tokens from the mirror, and fretting over the oil consumption—investing life in it with family outings, sibling squabbles, daily commutes, teenage fondlings, awkward conversations.

Glenn Paquin in Santa Fe had tried to make me understand how his people perceived life in all of nature. We try so hard to put life into our own creations, but it will not stay when we no longer honor it. When Paquin's grandfather gave someone a ring, he gave the week of his life it took to forge it, and the recipient assumed that trust. No such trust accompanies a new Ford. The train to Boston moved on, out of Springfield, past the red brick and ornate yellow stone building of "W. F. YOUNG, INC. HOME OF ABSORBINE JR."

I lost track of the handsome, curried little towns, each with a mill along a creek or river. We passed through frequent bogs, where matted golden grass, glinting in the sunlight like a lion's mane, fringed dark water. Farther east more pines appeared, mostly small and scrappy, and we broke more often into open fields where the weak winter sun splashed on the hedgerows. Deep in the woods, old stone walls, demarcating fields no longer cultivated nor even discernible, lay in broken lengths. Oak leaves, stirred by the motion of the train, flew by my window like coal cinders from a steam locomotive.

At 2:28 I looked out on a panorama of Worcester rooftops, gothic cathedral towers, and Protestant steeples. A few minutes after three we stopped at a Framingham station that looked like it had been recently firebombed. The pace, from Framingham into Boston, was that of a commuter train, barreling through Wellesley and being outrun by the Friday afternoon traffic along the Massachusetts Turnpike through Newton and into Boston's South Station on time at 3:40.

South Station was undergoing overdue refurbishing and was in chaos. I planned to stay with a friend, a woman who worked for Delta Airlines as a flight attendant and was returning on a flight later that afternoon. I took a series of city buses through the northern suburbs—Chelsea, Revere, Lynn, and Swampscott, the contiguous but autonomous towns along the North Shore—to Marblehead, where I got off just past the movie theater and walked up the hill in the dark to her house.

The next night I took the bus back into Boston and out to Brookline to meet an old friend who was finishing her graduate work in Boston. We had known each other since childhood, but had seen each other only occasionally since college. I remembered her as one of the most intelligent of my schoolmates—she was, in fact, completing her doctorate in philosophy when I came through Boston—and it was in consideration of my respect for her and our old, if interrupted, friendship, that I allowed her to take me that night to a meeting of Boston Buddhists.

The Buddhism I encountered that night, the Nichiren Shoshu Sokagakkai of America, was nothing like the Buddhism I had read about, nor was it quite like anything I had encountered before. I heard scant mention of the "noble truths" I remembered from my admittedly superficial reading of traditional Buddhism—existence as suffering and desire as the root of suffering. The last thing these believers seemed to have in mind was the renunciation of desire. On the contrary, several of them encouraged me to chant for what I desired most, whether it be money, success, or boundless virility unleashed. One young woman insisted on telling me in detail how her recent conversion and her diligent chanting had brought her the boyfriend she had long desired. It was a sort of evangelical Buddhism, whipped up and carried aloft on a level of enthusiasm and fervor that an Amway acolyte would envy.

An enthusiastic young man welcomed us all, particularly the visitors, and asked us all to join in the communal chant. "'Nam-Myo-Ho-Ren-Ge-Kyo,'" he explained, "literally means devotion to the mystic law of cause and effect through sound. And when an individual begins to chant 'Nam-Myo-Ho-Ren-Ge-Kyo' their life starts to change, in other words, when you chant 'Nam-Myo-Ho-Ren-Ge-Kyo' you are harmonizing your life with this universal law that permeates everything and then you are able to bring out a very high life condition and gain benefit and good fortune into your life."

After a thumbnail history of Buddhism, he introduced the meat of the program. "Next, from all over Connecticut, the Young Mens'

Division members got together and they put together a martial arts presentation that they would like to present to you. So at this time, we'd like to show the fighting spirit we have to overcome our own difficulties and own problems when we chant 'Nam-Myo-Ho-Ren-Ge-Kyo.' So, I'd like to introduce Connecticut headquarters Young Mens' Division!" A half dozen teenagers trotted to the front of the room to applause and cheers and gave a ritualized demonstration of martial arts that involved much clashing of sticks.

"The Young Mens' Division fighting our own cynicism, our own negativity, our own lack of hope and apathy. Now another fighter is going to fight for you on the violin!"

A young man bounded to the stage brandishing a violin and called out, "How do you feel, everybody?"

"Great!" came the response.

"Great! OK! I'd like to play a short piece, a presto by J. S. Bach, and, uh, here goes, ready or not! I hope you like it!" A serviceable and enthusiastic violin solo followed, a brief contribution to Buddhist spirit by the cantor of Leipzig. Again, fervent applause.

As the last strains faded, someone on the dais shouted out, "The Young Womens' Division Chorus!" and a host of girls and young women filed onto the stage. An electric organ rippled out the bouncy melody to "One," the theme song from the musical A Chorus Line, and the chorus began to sing topical lyrics about world peace and unity through Buddhism.

Then followed a series of personal testimonies, as men and women from the audience came forward and told their private stories of conversion and triumph. Each volunteer was greeted with enthusiastic applause and his story of triumph over personal, family, and professional obstacles was cheered. Someone read a poem about world peace. A guitar choir performed. A jazz ensemble, consisting of musicians from Boston's Berklee School of Music, played.

As the applause swelled, another enthusiastic young man leapt to the stage and shouted out his appreciation for all of the performers in expansive terms. "Thank you for coming tonight, thank you! I really think this is the best show in town tonight!"

When the applause subsided, he launched with no diminution of passion into what turned out to be the night's lesson. "There are over eighty thousand volumes of Buddhist teachings that are written. It's such a profound philosophy of life, that there's no way we can even begin to scratch the surface of that philosophy, but there's one concept that forms the cornerstone of Buddhist philosophy, which is the idea that each human being has within them the potential for ten conditions of life. Hell is the lowest. Many early teachings said that heaven or hell existed outside of ourselves, but we know from our own daily life that heaven and hell exist within our own life." Beginning with hell—suffering, depression, and negativity—he described the Six Lower Paths: hell; hunger; animality; anger; tranquillity; and rapture.

"But with a tremendous effort on our part we can enter into a higher life condition." He went on, exhorting us upward, toward loftier rungs of truth and compassion on this ladder. With each advance, the excitement grew as he carried us still higher. "And Buddhism teaches that there is one last life condition that humankind has not yet experienced, lying dormant within their life, which is a condition of absolute happiness, where you can overcome every obstacle in your life and create tremendous joy every single day of your life. Buddhism teaches that by chanting 'Nam-Myo-Ho-Ren-Ge-Kyo' and really challenging ourselves to practice hard we can find this golden nugget, this jewel within our own lives of our own happiness and bring it out of our life and really enhance all the conditions of our life and help other people. So when you leave here today, how can you bring out the wonderful joy of that Buddha life condition in your own life? That is by chanting "'Nam-Myo-Ho-Ren-Ge-Kyo.'" He gave the impression that he could barely contain the rampant happiness within, that it might at any moment burst his fittings and flood the room, and the exalted laughter, cheers, and beaming faces of the people sitting around me suggested that they were, each and every one, well-nigh enraptured by what of it leaked out around his seals.

The day's lesson included other elaborations of theology that eluded me, distracted as I was by my grumbling stomach. A few apparent inconsistencies troubled me, but, in fairness, I would concede that they arose from insufficient understanding. And certainly from insufficient faith. I looked around the hall as the unison chanting gained fervor and was impressed by the wide range of people—young, old, white, black, Asian, prosperous and not so, well-educated and barely literate—all apparently joined in mutual affection and commitment. World peace, should it ever arise out of religious faith, would be far more likely to take root and blossom in that group than in the insular and class-bound churches on Main Street.

I left my friend at a midtown bus plaza, where I boarded the last bus back north to Marblehead. It was a long bus ride, forty-five minutes or more, and by now a little bit familiar, through the centuries-old towns along the North Shore, towns with names I first heard as mileposts on the marches of Revolutionary War armies. Ten or fifteen other riders boarded the bus with me in Boston, but as it meandered in turn through the streets of each of the North Shore towns we left the other riders in the dark, at the edge of church greens and on quiet street corners in front of pharmacies, until by the time the bus reached Lynn I was alone. I took out the small white card I had been given when we left the meeting. On it was a phonetic spelling of the chant that would bring my world into harmony "NAM-MYO-HO-REN-GE-KYO" and beneath it the legend "Individual happiness = World peace."

21 The Merchants Limited, the Shoreliner, and the Crescent Again: Closing the Circle

> They piled on more coals, and the train shot into the tunnel, and the
> engine rushed and roared and rattled, till at last they shot out at the
> other end into fresh air and the peaceful moonlight, and saw the wood
> lying dark and helpful upon either side of the line.
>
> —Kenneth Grahame, *The Wind in the Willows* (Mr. Toad, sentenced for
> motoring offenses, makes his escape from prison by train.)

Like Phileas Fogg steaming toward home, I was determined to
finish my trip on deadline, but unlike Mr. Fogg I found myself
ahead of schedule near the end. Rather than arrive in New
York in the middle of Saturday night on the Amtrak Night
Owl, I postponed my departure until Sunday. I spent a leisurely Saturday walking around Marblehead, watching the
yachting crowd at play in the harbor and meandering up and
down through the narrow, cobbled streets. For an hour or more in
the afternoon, I talked trains with the proprietor of the local tobacco
store. I had strolled in off the street intending only to pick up enough
tobacco to get me home. In the course of the transaction, as I sniffed
his tobacco jars and bought a couple of ounces of one of his English
blends, we exchanged a few casual remarks about tobacco and from
there went on to talk about Marblehead and, finally, when I revealed
that I was traveling by train, he told me that he had spent his career
working for the Interstate Commerce Commission on safety standards for railroads.

He obviously retained a keen interest in trains, especially freight
trains, and, particularly, the hauling of hazardous materials. Over

the course of thirty minutes more, he gave me a primary course on the whole laundry list of noxious, explosive, toxic, and flammable substances rolling day and night through the countryside. As I stood at the window, looking out on the sunny street, he said, "Day like today, it'd be a good day for a leak. On an overcast day, it hangs right around. Most of that stuff, ammonia, chlorine, LP gas, heavier than air, you know."

Down along Front Street, I stood by the dock and watched yachts worth more than the average American house, and only a shade smaller, gleam in the sun. A man dressed in a Santa suit was posing for a photographer at the helm of the largest yacht. A grizzled old man leaning on the rail next to me nodded toward the scene and said, "Some catalog, I guess," and spat between his teeth out over the water. Ring-billed gulls hovered in the air over the masts and rigging of the yachts, holding their position head-on into the wind and flicking their heads from side to side like snakes. I looked straight down into six feet of water below the dock. It was clear, like green tea, and through it I could see tendrils of sea lettuce surging softly on the sandy bottom and a length of mossy chain.

I left Boston aboard the Merchants Limited early on a Sunday afternoon, on one of those Sundays when the morning sun begins to die soon after breakfast and the light continues to fade so gradually that it seems you are left by midafternoon in a still, shadowless, dark room, but you hesitate to turn on a light because the brightness of it will obscure what fragile daylight remains, daylight that seems all the more precious for the long winter to come. Like the end of arctic summer.

"Court Square Press" read the legend on the smokestack of an old brick mill building under a blanket of low clouds. Pale splotches of rose tinted the underside of the puffy gray clouds, like a bloodstain seeping through dingy cotton bandaging. On the ground it was just another chill gray Boston day, when a walk around the block makes one want a bowl of bean soup and a cup of hot chocolate. Heading toward Route 128, we rolled past rows of white and gray and brown three-story frame houses. Already, in early afternoon, light glowed from the windows. The tracks left Route 128 and turned south toward Providence, as a steady parade of other passengers trooped through to the cafe car. The tracks felt corrugated. The cars rattled with the din of jackhammers and shook so that my teeth chattered. I rode with my mouth slack and my jaws parted, careful to keep my tongue out of harm's way, wondering how the cars survived the abuse. Riding in a smoking coach, I was breathing foul air and remembering the sweet smell of Minnesota and the soft sting of flying snow on my face in Montana.

I stopped off for an hour in Providence, just to have a look around. The plaza in front of the train station was being excavated for some major civic project: what I remembered as a pretty wooded park lay open like a grave. Piles of dirt, gray as coal dust, were bulldozed up against the statue of General Burnside, small trees lay uprooted, the old brick walks had been ripped up. I skirted the square and walked over the river and up the hill.

I spent a few minutes retracing familiar sidewalks up Waterman Street past the Rhode Island School of Design and across the Brown University green. There were fewer trees than I remembered. From a pay telephone in Wriston Quad I called a friend back home in Chapel Hill, who also happened to be the music director at the public radio station where I worked. "Will I have a job when I get back?" I asked him.

"We'll be glad to have you back. We've been doing a lot of muddling through. How's the trip been?"

"All my reservations have turned out to be well-founded, but I, too, have muddled through."

"You ready to go back to work? We've penciled you in for Thursday and Friday. I can't wait to hear Duke Ellington again."

"Me, too, Craig. See you soon."

I had only twenty-five minutes more to make the fifteen-minute walk back down the hill, out of the East Side, to the station. On the way I passed the Rockefeller Library, which clings to the edge of the hill overlooking Providence. Many afternoons I had watched the sun set over the city from the tall windows of the second-floor reading room. Curious to see how the vista had changed in a decade, I trotted up the steps and into the library. At a turnstile in the front lobby a guard stopped me. "You can't go in without an ID." He was a young man with a mechanical counter in his hand, clicking off the students as they passed.

"Do you mind if I just have a brief look around? I have only about thirty minutes, but I'd like to see the library before I go."

"It's not open to the public. Not unless you're associated with one of these." He shoved a list in front of me, a full page, double-columned, of allied colleges and universities, libraries, and scholarly research organizations.

"No, I'm not associated with anyone. I'm just someone who'd like to see the library. Just look around for a few minutes." A couple of students flashed ID cards and brushed past me through the turnstile, carrying briefcases. "I'll leave you my driver's license for collateral. I don't want to borrow any books."

"No chance you can borrow books. You can't even go in."

"That's the way it is?"

"You got it. My job is to tell you that you can't come in here. The university says I can't let just anybody in."

"I guess not," I said. "Anyway, I've got to catch a train." I turned and left.

By five o'clock I was back down the hill at the Providence station, where pigeons roamed through the waiting room, strutting about with complete command. From the platform, as I waited for my train, I could see the dark red Biltmore Hotel sign on top of the old hotel. Several young couples were caressing each other, whispering endearments and obscenities, on the platform under pools of yellow light. Other groups of students circled around piles of knapsacks like nomads around a desert fire. At 5:12 P.M. my train, the Shoreliner, rolled up and I boarded in a crush of passengers. My tattered packet of tickets was looking just about as ragged and disreputable as I felt after six weeks of hard use. My collar was soaked with sweat from the exertion of hauling my bags; my hair, shaggy after six weeks, felt lank and dirty; and, moreover, I had a splitting headache.

The Shoreliner to New York was an express that stopped only at New London, New Haven, and sometimes at Stamford, a conditional stop. At a few minutes before six I was sitting in the lounge car with a feeling of acceleration and numbness. Since Minnesota, either the pace had picked up or my curiosity had flagged. The train runs had been shorter and less characteristic. Passengers and train people had become less distinct. I could not remember the name of a single porter or trainman since Phyllis had put me off in Staples. Two young men sat across from one another at a nearby table. In the open brief-case lying on their table I could see copies of *Science Digest* and *Scientific American*, and their attention was fixed on a musical score spread out between them.

At 6:09 P.M. we stopped briefly at New London. Disembarking passengers were called to the cafe car at the middle of the train and asked to exit together. A young woman sat down opposite me and took out a legal pad and a pen. "Do you know the date?" she asked, barely glancing up.

"November the fourth."

In a compact hand, she inscribed the date at the top of the page. Two lines below she wrote simply, "Al," and on the next line she began, "Thanks for the" and there she paused. After a moment's consideration, she continued with, "wonderful weekend in Little Compton." There she stopped, staring down at the paper and rolling her pen between her fingers. A minute later, she began to tumble the pen over and over between her first two fingers and her thumb. She had a dark complexion and curly, upswept hair, and she wore a white sweater, baggy gray pants, and lots of gold costume jewelry.

She crossed out her first line and began again. After New London, the lounge began to do a land-office business, filling with students talking, writing, and drinking. She crossed out her second preamble and put on a pair of Walkman headphones. At New Haven, just after seven, we sat for ten minutes in the dark while the train switched from diesel to electric power. She put away her legal pad and began again, this time on a sheet of Brown University stationery.

I returned to my coach seat and took out my copy of Conrad. South of Stamford the on-board lights dimmed momentarily and I could see down the suburban streets. At eight-thirty, I was looking into apartment windows and onto back porches. The coach lights clicked off and on several more times. It seemed hard to believe that a week had passed since I had left Minnesota.

I was riding on the Amfleet, in an Amcoach, which was nicely carpeted, with red carpet on the floor, dark brown carpet on the walls, and contrasting light brown carpet above the luggage racks. The sidewalls were painted a soft cream and the reading lights above the seats worked. At 8:43 P.M. we crossed the river. High-rises appeared on the right, beehives of light and dark cells. The car rocked rhythmically from side to side and a regular groan ushered through it, a soft deep whooshing sound like the panting of a dog.

Approaching a city at night by train is a dreamlike experience. Views change suddenly and without apparent reason. At 8:48 we were slashing through a tunnel or culvert. We emerged in a transit yard full of city buses and passed quickly through. Streetlights off to the right were merely pinpoints of light. We rolled through dark industrial alleys. Suddenly, at 8:57, the city was revealed: the long, jeweled suspension bridge; the river; the glittering, crawling avenues. City lights reached to the horizon, burning brightly near and dimly farther away, like distant smudge pots or the watch fires of a siege army. Low clouds erased the top stories of the tallest buildings. The lights of the city cast a pale, glowing aurora that ascended up into the dark, dark gray sky like a fire in a peat bog on a moonless night.

I rebuffed a drunk on the Penn Station platform and dragged my heavy bags upstairs. The main waiting room was crowded with people sitting, standing, and milling about. Two cops hustled a panhandler up the long flight of steps and into the street. I spotted Tom about thirty feet away, wearing a wool cap with earmuffs folded up toward the crown and carrying his cane. I called out, "Tommmm!" and he turned and saw me. We caught the first cab we could hail. I sat in front, and Tom and I began to talk, but as soon as the cab driver understood that I was interested in trains, he started to complain about the New York subways.

Tom and Molly had an apartment, modest but comfortable by Manhattan standards, up near Columbia University. It was Sunday night, November fourth. Susan called to say that she was finished in the city, but would stay through part of Monday if we could get together before late afternoon. "I don't want to fly back," she told me, "at least not alone. I'm thinking maybe I'll try the train. What do you think?"

"Take something to read. Maybe something to eat, too. And don't try to do it in coach. You're too old. Take my word for it."

I slept on a futon in Tom and Molly's living room. All night long heavy trucks barreled up and down Amsterdam Avenue below the window, rolling over steel gratings that covered excavations in the street and thundering like God's own kettle drums, but I was so exhausted I heard only sweet music. Tom and Molly left for work early Monday morning and I lingered in the apartment, drinking coffee and making telephone calls. I arranged with an old friend, who lived in Brooklyn but would be working in the city that day, to meet at Penn Station in the late afternoon. Around eleven I caught the M-11 bus and rode down Amsterdam and Columbus with a host of little old ladies to meet Susan at her aunt's apartment on Seventy-ninth Street. Together, we walked down Columbus to Seventy-second where we ate lunch at a small Japanese restaurant and sushi bar. Susan ate something in tempura and I ate something on a skewer. We talked about my trip, what I had seen since she had put me on the Southwest Limited in Kansas City, and about her company's debut performance in Kansas City the previous weekend. She felt good about it, the dancers felt good about it, and the chief critic of the *Kansas City Star* had been impressed. This would mean that she would be able to raise enough money to survive the winter. The course, however, would continue to be rocky.

After lunch, we bought some fruit for her train ride, picked up her things at the apartment, and took a cab downtown. In Penn Station we took the balance of the cab fare and bought emergency rations for her trip: a few bagels, a bottle of white wine, and a big chocolate chip cookie. I helped her find her car on the Broadway Limited, downstairs on track 11. She had booked an economy slumbercoach, more comfortable than a coach seat but perhaps the most claustrophobic accommodation possible. I showed her how the bed reclined, got her settled, said good-bye, and stood on the platform as the train pulled out. It was an odd sensation, putting someone else on a train.

David met me on the platform just as Susan's car rolled past. David had come to New York several years before to find work as an actor and musician, and I had not seen him since. By coincidence it was his birthday, and he had invited me back to Brooklyn for a celebration dinner at the apartment he shared with his companion, Sue. David and I walked up out of the station, down Sixth Avenue past a row of plant shops and the sidewalk fishmongers, their wares, kingfish and bluefish, trimmed down after a brisk day's business almost to fish heads. We walked through Chelsea and took the subway over to Brooklyn. On the way to his apartment we stopped at a fruit market and at his neighborhood butcher, where we picked out a three-and-a-half-pound round roast and David ordered a fresh turkey for Thanksgiving. The butcher asked, "How big?"

David answered, without hesitation, "Twelve pounds, just like last year."

"You got it!" The butcher jotted it down on a greasy piece of paper behind the counter.

"Got any fat for drippings with this roast?"

"No. Afraid not. Sorry." The butcher started to walk toward the rear of the shop where he was trimming some meat.

David called out, "Don't you want to know when we're going to pick up the turkey?"

Without turning around, the butcher hollered back over his shoulder, "You live on Tompkins Place and you want it the day before, right?"

"You remembered."

"Sure. See you then."

This pleased David, to be remembered in his local butcher shop, and he left elated on his birthday. In the kitchen of their apartment, the basement floor of a town house on a shady, one-block street in Brooklyn, we talked as we began preparations for dinner, mixing the batter for Yorkshire pudding. I told a few stories about my trip, and David talked about their lives in New York and about the petty problems they had been having with their landlady, who lived upstairs and was a little crazy. Sue came home, nursing a sore throat. "Every year we've been in New York I get this in November and can't lose it until May," she said. Her face had thinned a bit since I had last seen her, but she looked good, a little ruddy, almost tanned. She made an asparagus and red pepper salad, and the three of us sat at their kitchen table and talked and drank a few of the beers David had brewed, a Scottish ale, a brown ale, and a very good sweet stout, pausing to put a few baking potatoes and the Yorkshire pudding into the oven at the correct moment.

We ate, finishing the meal with a chocolate mocha cake Sue had made for the occasion, and then we adjourned to the small front sitting room and talked some more. Then it was time for me to go and let them sleep. They both had to rise early to make the commute into the city. David walked me to the subway stop, about a twenty-minute walk through Brooklyn, and as we approached the stop, I heard the Seventh Avenue Express rumbling in the tunnel, so I dashed down the steps, shouting back to David, "Happy birthday!" It took only about thirty minutes more to get back to Manhattan via the No. 2 express to 96th Street and the No. 1 local to 116th Street.

Tom and Molly were asleep when I came in, and the apartment was hot and stuffy, so I poured myself a beer and opened the window wide on Amsterdam Avenue. With the window on the other side of the apartment also open, a cool breeze flowed through, falling to the floor and flowing across my feet like a shallow stream. The noise floated up from the Avenue, trucks rumbling downtown and sirens moaning over on Broadway. I wrote a long letter and a few pages of notes. When I was exhausted, I folded out the futon, tossed a pillow from the sofa onto the floor, stripped off my clothes, closed the window halfway, picked from the shelf a book on names for children, and lay down to read. Within two minutes I was sound asleep with the light on.

I awoke Tuesday morning to see Tom in his tie and coat, standing at the door with his cane, ready for work. He apologized for not waiting up for me: "I knew that today would be a rough day." He had told me that he would be spending the day at one of the city hospitals working with terminal AIDS patients. "I get called in for a clinical opinion. I see a young man, abandoned by society, rejected by his family, suffering debilitating pain and facing certain and imminent death, and they want me to deduce why he's depressed. You figure it out. I'll see you for dinner."

I spent most of the day catching up on my notes, trying to reach some conclusion on what would be my last full day on the road, and, failing that, just to get my proverbial ducks in a row before heading home. By late afternoon, the sunlight had faded finally from the streets and the clouds had packed together, showing only their gray soles to the city. As I waited for Tom and Molly, the apartment was invaded by that winter twilight that can play so profoundly on one's emotions, when it is easy to feel lonely, when sad music can sound so rueful. I could remember falling under the spell of such afternoons when I was younger and not recovering from the melancholy for days.

This was Tuesday. Wednesday I would sleep in my own bed. In the dark. I wondered: Am I ready to go home? Will those last miles seem slow, or will they roll easily by? I remembered that first night on the train as well as any other along the way, seeing Celia on the platform, my first friendly face. It was all new to me then, all so curious and unfamiliar. And now it seems so familiar. I have become more comfortable on the train than on the ground. I've been floating, boosted aloft by a gentle wind, immune from the buffeting and grinding currents down below, able to drift on beyond their reach when the winds got too strong, or when they died and becalmed me in the daily routine. It's time to give that up, that special untouchable status of the traveler. I have to admit that I've enjoyed it. It has been years since I've taken a trip like this, since I've taken a journey, and now that the appetite for it has been reawakened, it will be hard to quell and may haunt me. It's something to fear. It can make one restless in daily life.

Wednesday was a bright fall day in the city. Tom took the morning off and we spent four hours talking, hours that flew by. We talked about the child that he and Molly were expecting, about his health, which was made precarious by faulty heart valves, one of which had already been replaced and the rest of which were suspect, about his work, psychology, and about the country's mood, which he saw as a form of character disorder. In the early afternoon, Tom walked with me to the subway stop at 116th Street where we said good-bye and I caught the No. 1, the local, down to Penn Station at 34th Street. I wanted to store my bags until train time, so I asked the Amtrak ticket agent for change for a baggage locker.

"You found a locker?" he asked, as if he knew the answer.

"No, not yet."

"Forget it. People live out of those lockers. Go 'round the corner to the baggage agent."

Instead I toted my bags with me to the Nedick's in the station, where I ate a hot dog, and to the bar, where I had a beer while I waited. At train time I took the escalator down to track 14 where the Crescent waited. Carrying my bags, I passed down the gauntlet of car attendants, each at the open door of his car, to the end of the train. There at the last car was the Amtrak attendant who had boarded me that first night, six weeks before, in Greensboro. Then he had been in shirtsleeves. Now he was bundled in a heavy wool coat and winter gloves. He didn't recognize me. No reason that he should have.

In fifteen minutes we were out of the city. I didn't study the route. I didn't watch the mileposts or calculate the stops. Finally, on this last leg, I relinquished control and let the impressions overwhelm me. Warehouses, manufacturing plants, mills, trucking depots, machine shops, highway overpasses, New Jersey commuter stops. In New Jersey I saw a sign familiar to me for years from the black-and-white photograph on the cover of an early recording by a favorite saxophonist, Richie Cole—"TRENTON MAKES/THE WORLD TAKES." Backyards, stoops, red brick row houses burning in the reddening sun. A few minutes before four, we crossed over the Schuylkill River in Philadelphia. Rowing shells skittered like waterbugs on the river. At 5:08, near Baltimore, a perfect full moon, warm yellow and perfectly defined, rose over the water. At 5:15, as we entered Baltimore, the sky was perfectly bifurcated—tangerine in the west, cobalt blue to the east. Pale streetlights glimmered feebly down long streets, stretching away into the dying red. On the eastern side of the tracks, against the deep night sky, the fading western afterglow was reflected in the third-story windows of crumbling row houses. Into a tunnel, into black, and out again into a midnight blue valley, a railyard in an ugly urban ditch, then under the streets and into a subterranean station, gloomier and more eerie than a subway stop. The paved brick platform reflected the faintest glimmer of light. Overhead wiring above adjacent tracks for electric power. An Amtrak caboose, number 14001, the first I'd seen. Under the streets again, leaving the station. Pickups parked amid the rubble. On through a tunnel or cut, lit by intermittent fluorescent lights, stripes of cold white light falling across the windows of the car with increasing speed, like flashing strobes. Then out into the medium blue night. The moon and the streetlights in perfect balance now. The moon, whiter, the streetlights, yellowish, the sky a dusky blue on the horizon, a deeper blue, a clear pure endless blue higher up. The same sky everywhere, the same sky hangs over Arizona mesas.

Five thirty-seven P.M. and dark. The moon in the east and a thin salmon line on the western horizon. I have watched my last sunset from the train. Now it is the private time, the dinner hour, the time

when the attention of the train turns inward. Five fifty-three P.M.
We change engines in Washington, D.C. Did we come this far out of
New York City with electric power, electrified rail? Amtrak car and
Amcoaches sit on the tracks, dark and idle. When they disconnect
the engine, we'll lose our power for about ten minutes.

After Washington, the ambiance on board the Crescent turned to
night. The sleeping car passengers retreated to their warrens, the
coach passengers curled up to read or to sleep, covering themselves as
best they could, and the night owls and revelers headed for the lounge
car. I snoozed some and remembered. Those long, languid days on the
western Superliners. The heat in West Texas, the cold in North Dakota.
The sheen of Glenn Paquin's silver work spread out on the bricks of
the Palace of Governors portico in Santa Fe. The smooth cradle of
rock where I laid on the edge of the Grand Canyon in the dark.

I remembered sitting in Milton's bar in Kansas City with Susan,
recapturing for an evening that simple innocent pleasure in each
other's company as we bantered with the bartender about sports and
dance and jazz. I remembered looking into the eye of an eagle as it
passed overhead and disappeared into the curtain of falling snow
over McDonald Creek. And the rolling bicycle ride along the levee in
the warm New Orleans night, bumping along the footpath with the
lights of the waterfront and downtown twinkling up the river and
the muddy scent of the Mississippi in my nostrils. I couldn't, at that
moment, imagine more exhilaration. But then, cantering on Nicky
through the Minnesota birch woods with Janice on Sham and Brook,
her retriever, racing ahead, rolling down the hills and powering up
the slopes and leaning into the curves of the path and finally walking slowly through the canopy of spruce trees, with Brook roaming
and ranging ahead, and watching Janice point out the buck pausing
in the path ahead and then lunging away into the spruce trees and
watching Brook catch its scent, but too late. And at the last, walking the horses back down the road to the cabin, through fields of
corn and oats and wheat. "I think they get several cuttings from the
wheat. I don't know," Janice said, and then, "Are you all right?"

"Yes, Jan, I am just all right."

And she smiled that curious, noncommittal smile.

I snoozed some more. I read *Heart of Darkness* awhile. With thirty pages to go I stopped and put it away. I went to the lounge car, remembering what it had looked like six weeks before. The early stages of the same party were under way. I bought a ginger ale and took a seat, keeping myself apart. The tracks were the roughest I remembered. The can danced on the tabletop like a ringing coin. The vibration hammered through the car, not the sea-sway of the Superliner but the teeth-rattling jarring of an airplane in turbulence. No rhythm to it, just an unhinged rattle.

I'm on my way home. In four hours, I'll step down from the Crescent at Greensboro, and it will all seem like a dream, a long dream in the same way that each stop seemed like a dream. By this time tomorrow night, I'll be stoking up the wood stove, clearing the rubble off my desk, sorting the mail, paying overdue bills, getting reacquainted with my cats. I need new tires and I'll have to tune the car for winter. I'll be back on the air by tomorrow night, Friday night at the latest.

I had hoped that riding the train to the exact spot from which I had departed so many weeks ago would complete the circle, and when I boarded the Crescent in Penn Station and found in my car the same porter, an amiable young man, with whom I had joked on the first run from Greensboro to Charlotte, I took it as an omen that the journey was drawing to an end of its own accord.

I brought a second ginger ale back to my coach seat, sweetened it with the last of the bourbon, and finished *Heart of Darkness*. I laid my head back on the pillow and dozed off awhile, intending to sleep for only an hour or so and then to go back and talk to the porter while everyone else slept. I wanted to ask him which trains he had worked over the six weeks since we had first met. There would be time; we would arrive in Greensboro at 12:30 A.M. The next I knew, he was standing over me, saying, "You're for Greensboro, aren't you? Five minutes."

Groggy and barely conscious, I struggled awake, but I was familiar with the routine. I stored my books and papers in my bookbag, which was still riding on the floor in front of my seat, and I pulled my camera bag and suitcase out of the overhead rack and I carried them, one by one, back to the rear of the coach and stacked them in the narrow hallway that led to the vestibule. The Amtrak attendant was helping a pair of frail older women with their bags. When he had them arranged, I tapped him on the shoulder, "Were you on this run about six weeks ago, the last half of September?"

Without looking around, he answered, "Couldn't be . . . I haven't made this run in three months."

I let it drop. We were both tired and sleepy. A moment later he stopped and looked around at me and said, "No, I remember you. You boarded in Greensboro for New Orleans . . . took some pictures. When was that?"

"That was better than six weeks ago. I've been on the trains ever since. But I remember you."

"That's been a while. Where did you go?"

I told him the truth, broadly stated, "Everywhere. Everywhere Amtrak goes. About fourteen thousand miles."

"Did you get to the West Coast?"

"Twice."

"I used to live out there," he said, wistfully, "Oregon, Washington, L.A. I loved it."

"Where do you live now?"

"Manhattan," he said, and shrugged his shoulders.

We were coming into Greensboro by then, the train beginning to slow down, and he was already moving into the vestibule to open the door and put the loading step down on the platform. With his hand on the door handle, he looked back at me. "Six weeks?"

"Six weeks."

The train stopped and he opened the door and stepped down, and as he did he said over his shoulder, "That's some serious traveling, my friend."

After his ladies had clambered down, I hoisted my bags for the last time and stepped down to the asphalt. We stood for a moment or two in the chilly night air and talked about the West Coast, how much he wanted to get back there, and then I looked down the tracks and I realized that the conversation and the journey were over. I put out my hand, he pulled off his winter glove, and we shook hands. I said, "I hope you make it," and I picked up my bags and started walking. When the train pulled out, headed south, I didn't look back. But I thought about New Orleans.

Train Time: A Postscript

Most of us, myself included, must make travel plans to suit practical needs—most of the time we need simply to get from here to there with safety, convenience, and dispatch. In the proper circumstances, trains serve those needs admirably. When I boarded the Crescent that first night, however, I was seeking from train travel something different. My ride was a journey. Not a notably long journey and not a particularly daring one, but nevertheless different than a trip because I traveled simply for the sake of traveling.

Much of what I discovered about journeying across the United States by train is remarkable only because it is not new. Those who remember the trains of the midcentury will be encouraged to learn that much about rail travel is immutable. For instance, it remains true that a railroad sleeping car is simply the best place I know to sleep, rivaled only by a well-appointed sailing ship in gentle seas. A host of factors combine to make it so: the tidy coziness of the berth or compartment; the gentle, insistent rocking motion; the wide window on the dark countryside. Even the level of noise, a constant murmur, is ideal: just loud and steady enough to mask any disturbance, just distant enough to be unobtrusive. And always, buoying the subconscious even in sleep, the sense of effortless motion.

America remains different as seen by train—different than it appears to travelers by other means. I do not take to trains out of a fear of flying. I love to fly. From the air, however, particularly from the flight levels cruised by commercial craft, one sees very little of the country, only an occasional lordly panorama of the continental plates. The view from our highways, on the other hand, can be busy

—and is tending toward a numbing uniformity as commercial appeals crowd in along every mile. Train tracks, slashed through populated and unpopulated quarters alike, are left alone. No one bids for the attention of the train traveler because there is no profit in it. To ride by train is to feel invisible. Ironically, given their monstrous size, trains pass along most of their way almost unnoticed. Whether through city, suburb, or farmland, the train passenger travels through the backyard of the country, free to glimpse his fellows and their works as they are. And when the tracks veer into the mountains or across the prairies, no one follows.

The peculiarity of train travel is its simultaneous intimacy with and detachment from the country. Because the railroad right of way barely disturbs the land and is itself left undisturbed by gas stations and billboards, the train traveler sees the country in very close to its pure form, passing by just beyond his window hour after hour. At the same time, the constant motion, day and night, the inability to slow, stop, or turn aside, eventually induces a trance, a passivity, even a sort of meditation.

This effect produces a peculiarly gracious sense of time. The steady movement through space at an even, measured pace becomes a pedal point against which the spontaneous activity among the community of passengers provides ever-changing harmonies. If one is given to reflection, a long train trip becomes a circle within a circle within a circle, each moving at its own charmed speed.

There is a saying that God does not subtract from a man's alloted hours his time spent fishing. Perhaps not. It seems equally likely that time aboard trains is granted exemption. A few hours or a few days on train time are enough to make one believe he has them to spare. Whether granted by God or man, train time is to the dearly purchased hours of life as a bit of lagniappe.

All this I found to be true of train time—and it would, I believe, be true for any traveler. Other things I discovered were more personal. Travel, given time enough, particularly solitary travel, can render one unfit for routine living. It is not simply the leisure of it, because it is sometimes far from leisurely. In some ways, it is the vigor of it. I embarked on my journey at a particularly sharp cusp in my own life, and I came home feeling alien to the self I had been and uncomfortable in the life I had led. Eventually the undeniable satisfactions of that life reclaimed me, but, even as I enjoy its pleasures, to this day I feel a little like an imposter. Travel will do that.

When I made the trip about which you have been reading, I thought I might be writing a requiem for Amtrak and for passenger rail travel in the United States. As it has turned out, I was longer than I ever imagined getting into print, and, more surprisingly, in the interim Amtrak has grown stronger rather than weaker. Problems—some of its own making, some unavoidable products of its structure and funding, and some purely circumstantial—still exist, but Amtrak seems now to be more popular among travelers, more sound fiscally, and more secure politically than at any previous time.

In May 1990 a new Amtrak train, the Carolinian, entered service here in North Carolina as a cooperative venture between Amtrak and the state. I was aboard for the inaugural run, curious to see the reactions of citizens regaining train service along its route and curious to question Amtrak officials and travel professionals aboard for the gala occasion. I would board at Burlington, North Carolina. One thing remained unchanged: no one in Burlington could tell me where the train would stop. The Burlington residents I spoke to knew vaguely where the old station was but were unaware that Amtrak had ever served Burlington or was to again. That may change.

As I drove down Webb Avenue on the appointed spring day, the Amtrak stop was easy to spot: a crowd of people had gathered for the inaugural run. A small band belted out brassy arrangements that blew away on the stiff breeze. Balloons bearing the legend "All Aboard Amtrak" bobbed vigorously in the wind. Onlookers milled about, wearing "I love Burlington" buttons and paper railroaders' hats. The Carolinian arrived very nearly on time, announcing itself with a whistle and pausing fifty yards up the track for a banner ("Burlington Welcomes the Carolinian") to be unfurled across the tracks, and then creeping forward. The banner, intended to break ceremoniously, instead tore loose from its keepers in the wind and wrapped itself around the nose of the locomotive, but no one seemed to mind. An American flag flew from the right cab window, a North Carolina flag from the left. The governor dismounted and gave a hearty stump speech from a small platform ("This train has been a dream of mine . . ."), which he would repeat at whistle stops down the line.

En route, I spoke to Clifford Black, a publicist for Amtrak, about its recent years and present state of affairs. Recognizing that his job is to trumpet the success of Amtrak and minimize its shortcomings, I nevertheless found his appraisal encouraging. The Reagan administration tried to kill Amtrak, he told me, and the Bush administration might still want to, but "the survival of Amtrak is no longer an issue." Congress has heard the arguments and has decided that Amtrak should survive.

For the time being, it would appear that Amtrak has weathered its most difficult years. In the early and mid-eighties, Amtrak was in a very competitive market. The gasoline shortages and price spikes of the 1970s, which encouraged riders and politicians alike to support Amtrak, were becoming a dim memory. The early years of vigorous deregulation in the airline industry had spawned a virtual price war, with loss-leader airfares proliferating on many of the major routes served by Amtrak. Thus, for many travelers, automobiles and airlines seemed to obviate the need for Amtrak. By the end of the decade, however, environmental concerns, unfashionable for most of the eighties, were once again under serious discussion. At the same time, bus service to many cities had ceased, isolating many of the smaller communities that have no commercial air service. And after a shake-out of the airline industry, airfares were once again reflecting the real cost of service, with fewer giveaway fares available. Consequently, as we begin this decade, Amtrak seems more valuable than it did when I was aboard—both to the public policy planner and to the individual who simply wants to get from here to there.

Financially, Amtrak is also stronger now. A basic yardstick by which Amtrak publicly measures its financial performance is the percentage of its operating costs that it recoups in revenue. That percentage rose steadily throughout the eighties, from 48 percent in 1981 to 60 percent in 1985 to 72 percent in 1989. The goal for 1990, which Mr. Black considered within reach, was 75 percent. Longer range, the expectation is for the figure to reach 100 percent in the year 2000. This, we must remember, will not mean that Amtrak will then be financially independent of government subsidy—it will still require $200 million for capital expenditures.

Regardless of the bookkeeping, reports from aboard the Amtrak trains confirm that ridership has increased. Coaches are nearer capacity, and sleeping compartments are in demand. Travel agents encourage travelers to book sleeping accommodations well in advance. Ridership at peak seasons is still limited by available rolling stock, but ridership at slower periods has increased to more nearly approach that at busier times, evening out the dramatic peaks and valleys in the demand curve and boosting the ratio of revenue to operating costs.

Amtrak has always considered passenger miles—the sum of all the miles ridden by all the passengers—to be a more important measure than simple ridership and has tried to increase not only the number of passengers but the distance of their travel. In 1989, for the first time in Amtrak's history, the system logged more passenger miles (5.9 billion) than did the private railroads in 1970, their last year of operation prior to Amtrak. This, Clifford Black pointed out, with far fewer trains.

Major capital improvements are on the horizon as well. The Superliners that I so enjoyed in 1984 have logged many miles, and Amtrak is now expecting the first new order of Superliner cars, seventy-five of them, since the initial purchase.

And yet, as I sat amid the press and invited guests on the Carolinian, I wondered how many of these people would ever travel by train on their own initiative. These were the very people who were noticeably absent from the trains I rode—the businesspeople, the regular and frequent travelers, the travelers with the personal wealth or the company expense account to travel well and often. Amtrak should exist if only to serve the rest of us, but I wonder if it can ever acquire the constituency to make its future truly secure without these frequent travelers.

I have been in the habit of urging friends to take their children on an Amtrak train to experience train travel just in case it should come to a sudden end. There seems less urgency now, but it is still a pretty good idea. When I am asked, "Should I take a train?" my answer has usually been some variation of this rule: if you love trains, ride any train you can. There is still nothing like a train. If, however, you have no particular fondness for trains nor interest in their history, fly to Chicago or St. Louis or San Antonio and continue by train west of the Mississippi. A few days aboard one of the western overland trains remain one of the supreme travel experiences of the world. If you can afford a Superliner bedroom, count your blessings and seize the opportunity. The trip can be done faster, it can certainly be done cheaper, but I doubt it can be done better. I still think now and then of the young couple I met on the Eagle, honeymooning by train. Perhaps they are since divorced, life being what it is. I prefer to believe that they are now a happy family with a couple of children. I would not be surprised if their first was conceived somewhere west of Phoenix.

Chapel Hill, North Carolina
June 1990